Arctic Frontiers

UNITED STATES EXPLORATIONS

IN THE FAR NORTH

John Edwards Caswell

NORMAN: UNIVERSITY OF OKLAHOMA PRESS

Library of Congress Catalog Card Number 56–11235

Copyright 1956 by the University of Oklahoma Press,
Publishing Division of the University.

Composed and printed at Norman, Oklahoma, U.S.A.,
by the University of Oklahoma Press.

First edition.

To my Father

ALBERT EDWARD CASWELL

1884–1954

Christian, Scholar, Teacher

Preface

IIIIIIIIIIIIIIIIIIIIIIIIIIIIIIIIIIIIIIIIIIIIIIIII

OF ALL the expeditions that sailed from the shores of the United States between 1850 and 1909, those that went to the Arctic seem to have gripped American imaginations the most. Surprisingly, there has been heretofore no effort to present a systematic account of those expeditions.

This is the narrative, not of isolated adventures, but of a movement. The common aspirations of these men, their personal relationships, the inspiration and instruction that one gave to another, are here commemorated. The obscure explorations that lacked a skilled narrator here find a chronicle along with the more colorful and better-known expeditions.

From the enormously popular volumes of Kane to the electrifying telegrams of Peary, Arctic adventures furnished spice for the intellectual fare of a generation. It was a seasoning of ships and minerals, fossil series suggesting tremendous climatic changes, the haunts of the whale, the breeding grounds of wild fowl, and high adventure.

These expeditions widened the intellectual horizons of the American mind. Most had definite scientific programs. And in the perspective of a half-century, the lasting significance of these expeditions has been in their scientific contributions.[1] Do not wonder, then, at the frequent reference made to the scientific phases of the expeditions.

JOHN EDWARDS CASWELL

Sacramento, California
July 15, 1956

[1] Detailed analyses of the scientific contributions are contained in the author's "Utilization of the Scientific Reports of United States Arctic Expeditions," 1850–1909.

Acknowledgments

|||||||||||||||||||||||||||||||||||||||||||||

PARTICULAR GRATITUDE is due Professor Edgar Eugene Robinson of Stanford University for his faith, encouragement, and criticism while this volume was being prepared. My wife, Alberta Baxter Caswell, deserves like acknowledgment for faith and encouragement, and full thanks for endless hours at the typewriter.

Librarians and archivists of Stanford University, the University of California, the Library of Congress, the National Archives, and the National Geographic Society merit special mention. Miss Veronica Sexton of the California Academy of Sciences, Mr. W. L. G. Joerg and Mr. Herman Friis of the National Archives, Mr. Lloyd A. Brown of the Peabody Library, Mr. Richard Fleming of the United States Hydrographic Office, Lieutenant Commander Robert M. Lunny of the Office of Naval History, and Mrs. Leila (Austin H.) Clark of the Smithsonian Institution were especially helpful.

Among those who have aided me through correspondence are Mr. Vilhjalmur Stefansson, Mrs. Marie Peary Stafford, the late Professor William Herbert Hobbs, and Mr. Alvin Seale.

The Huntington Library has kindly given permission to quote from documents in the Rhees Manuscripts, specific references to which are made in the footnotes.

This volume grew out of a study of "The Utilization of the Scientific Reports of United States Arctic Expedition, 1850–1909," which was reported under that title. The first year of the study was financed by the Office of Naval Research, whose assistance I acknowledge. I appreciate particularly the interest of Dr. Gerald F. W. Mulders and Mr. Albert J. Morris.

To all who gave aid, advice, and criticism on this and the related manuscript concerning the utilization of the scientific reports of these same expeditions, I give my hearty thanks.

JOHN EDWARDS CASWELL

Table of Contents

IIIIIIIIIIIIIIIIIIIIIIIIIIIIIIIIIIIIIIIIIIII

Illustrations

||||||||||||||||||||||||||||||||||||||||||||||||

Maps

IIIIIIIIIIIIIIIIIIIIIIIIIIIIIIIIIIIIIIIII

Arctic Frontiers

UNITED STATES EXPLORATIONS
IN THE FAR NORTH

I

What Is the Arctic?

ЛIIIIIIIIIIIIIIIIIIIIIIIIIIIIIIIIIIIIIIIIIIIIIIII

WHAT IS THE ARCTIC? To some it conjures up schoolbook pictures of snowy igloos against a midnight sky, of caribou and musk oxen scraping through the layers of wind-swept snow to gain their scanty forage of mosses and lichens, of parka-clad dog drivers whipping their snarling packs or wrestling their sleds over ridges of broken ice, of Eskimos sitting hours on end by a seal hole, and of huge glaciers towering above the sea.

To the astronomer, the Arctic is the area north of the Arctic Circle, 66° 32′ north latitude. To the botanist, it is the area north of the tree line, or loosely, the geologist's tundra area bordering the Arctic Ocean. The meteorologist bounds the Arctic by the line (isotherm) representing a mean temperature of 50 degrees Fahrenheit for the warmest month. Or the navigator may think of the Arctic as the area where sea ice normally forms in winter.

The expeditions here considered went to areas that meet most, if not all, of these requirements. Obviously, many a whaler sailed these seas, of whom there is no record but his sailing and returning to port. With him we cannot deal. We shall, however, pay some attention to relief expeditions, even if they were not especially intended or equipped for Arctic exploration.

Our main difficulty will be in knowing when to stop in considering scientific explorations of Alaska and south Greenland.

We shall have to limit ourselves primarily to government expeditions north of the Brooks Range. By 1890, summer voyages to south Greenland and to the Bering Sea presented no novel problems of organization or equipment, nor did they explore unknown areas. Many summer "expeditions" of some scientific merit must perforce yield space to the more significant undertakings.

For perspective on these American expeditions, let us consider both their predecessors and the notions that were held about the Arctic previously and during this period.

General Adolphus Washington Greely has referred to three distinct epochs of Arctic exploration: first, exploration for the purpose of commerce with the Indies; second, exploration for advancement of geographical knowledge; and third, exploration for scientific investigations, primarily geophysical.[1]

Vilhjalmur Stefansson has written of a period of optimism, in which the hope of "a new and better seaway, a resource of land or of ocean" led the explorers to report every bright and fair prospect. This period ended about 1850, when it was realized that Sir John Franklin's expedition to discover the Northwest Passage had indeed perished. After that, "the explorers tended to become pioneers of science if not martyrs of science . . . . There crept in, too, the spirit of the marathon runner and the scaler of mountains." This emphasis on heroics may perhaps have been stimulated by a desire for book sales. Finally, the optimistic side was again set forth by explorers with the temperament of William Healey Dall and by Republican proponents of the Alaska Purchase.[2]

At another time Stefansson classified the explorers according to their attitudes toward the habitability of the Arctic. The first stage was illustrated by Davis and Hudson, who considered the Arctic winter unendurable, and "only made furtive incursions into it by ship in summer . . . ." Edward Parry exempli-

1 Adolphus Washington Greely, *Handbook of Polar Discoveries*, 3rd ed. 6.
2 Vilhjalmur Stefansson, *Ultima Thule*, 292, 296–98.

fied the second group: men who had the courage to face an Arctic winter, but who endured rather than exploited it. Robert E. Peary advanced into the third stage, for he made winter his ally, finding it the best time for travel. While Peary was able to use the entire year, he was limited in his movements by carrying much of his food with him. Stefansson himself broke through this last barrier by learning to live off the country.

The first exploration of the Arctic by an educated European is attributed to Pytheas of Massilia (Marseilles) about 330 B. C. In a ship that may well have been several times larger than Columbus' *Santa María*, Pytheas visited Britain. Reaching the northernmost Shetlands, he learned of an island lying to the north about six days' sail. Following directions, he reached Iceland and continued past it for another day's sail, where he was evidently stopped by floe ice. Greek scientists ridiculed his discoveries, but his descriptions fit the geographical facts.

The way to Iceland may well have been remembered in Scotland and Ireland from the time of Pytheas on, but the unlettered dwellers in those northern climes have left us no logbooks. In the sixth century of the Christian era, according to legend, Saint Brendan led an expedition to Iceland, perhaps sighting Greenland and Jan Mayen Island as well. His contemporary, King Arthur, was credited by one chronicler with having conquered Iceland, along with many of the provinces of northern Europe.

Three centuries later, in 825, an Irish monk, Dicuil, recorded conversations he had had with men who had been to Iceland. Dicuil treated it as no unusual occurrence. All this was before the first-known Norse voyages, which date from about the year 860. The first permanent Scandinavian colony in Iceland was established between A. D. 870 and 874.

The first Norse report of Greenland was from about A. D. 900, although its coast comes within 180 miles of Iceland. Not until 982 did Erik the Red take family, friends, and servants

5

to establish a settlement there. In 986, fourteen vessels, bearing perhaps five hundred people, joined Erik in his colony. The Greenland colony survived four centuries, perhaps five.

Mention of pioneering voyages alone creates a false impression. Regular trade followed colonization. It is a reasonable speculation that until around A. D. 1300, there were several voyages a year from Norway to Iceland and somewhat fewer to Greenland. In return for European products, Greenland exported furs, thongs of walrus and whale rawhide, unsurpassed in quality, and hunting falcons and white bears that became the gifts of kings. After 1412, however, there is no clear record of any voyage to Greenland by the Bergen monopolists of the trade.

To the northeast of Europe, the first voyage of exploration was recorded by King Alfred himself late in the ninth century. Othere, a Norwegian whose exact standing at Alfred's court is unknown, had circumnavigated Europe, probably going as far as the site of Archangel, where the Dvina empties into the White Sea.

For the route that became known as the Northeast Passage, however, there is no continuous record of travel during medieval times comparable to that of travel between Norway and Iceland. Not until 1553 is Othere's voyage known to have been duplicated. In that year the Company of Merchants Adventurers of London sent out three ships, the largest of 160 tons, under Sir Hugh Willoughby. The redoubtable old Sebastian Cabot, governor of the company, wrote detailed instructions for the conduct of the voyage.

The intent of the Willoughby expedition was to open a passage to the Orient, the open letter which it carried from Edward VI being addressed to "the Kings, Princes, and other Potentates inhabiting the northeast parts of the world, toward the mighty Empire of Cathay."

Two of Willoughby's ships became separated from the third. Forced to winter on the Arctic shore of the Kola Penin-

6

sula, the crews of the two ships with Willoughby all perished. The third ship, under Richard Chancellor, entered the White Sea and reached the mouth of the Dvina, where the crew was received at an Orthodox monastery. Word was sent to Tsar Ivan IV of Chancellor's arrival, and he and his men were haled to Moscow, where they spent the winter and following summer at the court. This visit resulted in a commercial treaty, an exchange of ambassadors, and the establishment of trade between Muscovy and England.

Three years after Richard Chancellor reached Moscow, Stephen Burrough was sent out to renew the quest for a route to China and India. He sailed in company with Chancellor until near the mouth of the White Sea, Burrough continuing to the east, while Chancellor turned south to the Dvina.

Burrough met Russian walrus hunters near the present site of Murmansk and sailed with them for the Pechora River. He was the first of Western Europeans known to have visited Novaya Zemlya (New Land, sister islands separated by the narrow Matochkin Strait, which together form the western boundary of the Kara Sea). Burrough turned back at about 60° east longitude, off Vaigach Island. From his account it is plain that these coasts were neither uninhabited nor unexplored—simply Western Europe knew them not. Burrough had extended Western European knowledge of these coasts by some 18° of longitude.

At this point, English attention was diverted to the west by Martin Frobisher's explorations, and later English voyages in search of the Northeast Passage availed little.

The Dutch nation, like the English a rising maritime power, shared the English desire for a route to the Orient that was not dominated by the Spanish or the Portuguese. The first Dutch expedition to the Northeast Passage was fitted out in 1594, four vessels, one no larger than a fishing smack, being sent. The outstanding Dutch explorer was Willem Barents. On this expedition he failed to pass Novaya Zemlya, although two of the expedition's ships penetrated as far as the Kara River, mistaking it for the mighty Ob River.

Returning to the Netherlands, those who had reached the Kara were confident that they had all but rounded the north tip of Siberia and sailed into the warm seas of Tatary. A flotilla of seven vessels was readied for the summer of 1595. Checked by ice at Vaigach Island, the Dutch learned from the Samoyed tribesmen that Russians traded regularly to the Ob, the Yenisei, and even to rivers farther east. Floe ice, however, deterred the expedition from making the attempt.

On the third voyage, in 1596, the pilot of one of the Dutch vessels persisted in setting a course not sufficiently easterly to reach the Kara Sea. Barents' vessel was forced to follow the other pilot's course or to risk separation. The result was the discovery, first of Bear Island, and, farther on, of the Spitsbergen Islands (Svalbard).

Turning east, Barents rounded the north tip of Novaya Zemlya, but ice barred his efforts to cross the Kara Sea. Finally, his retreat was cut off. The sixteen men of Barents' crew wintered on the island, demonstrating that it was possible for Europeans to survive a winter at such a high latitude. Scurvy attacked the party, Barents and three others perishing. Three centuries later his wintering place was found, and many souvenirs, including books and manuscripts, were carried to the Netherlands.

These voyages did not open the wealth of the Indies and Cathay to the Dutch: rather, they disclosed an enormously rich whaling ground around Spitsbergen which the Dutch and English exploited over the succeeding centuries.

The seventeenth century saw a number of efforts to penetrate the farthest recesses of the Polar Sea north of Europe. Three Dutch whalers were reported to have come to within two degrees of the Pole in August of 1655. Fragmentary information concerning the Arctic coast of Siberia began to accumulate as the Russians brought more and more of the country under tribute. Simon Dezhnev rounded the northeastern corner of Siberia in 1648, but his work did not become generally known until Gerhard P. Müller in 1736 found his report in the Siberian archives at Yakutsk.

Meanwhile, Peter the Great seems to have seen the possibility of linking the many river basins of his new eastern empire and establishing a route to China by charting a course along the north coast of Siberia. Surveys were begun in 1725, the year of his death, and, through the perseverance of Vitus Bering, were continued for seventeen years. Called the "Great Northern Expeditions," most of the work was done between 1733 and 1742. The voyagers built boats on the upper reaches of the Siberian rivers, bringing from Europe the materials not available locally. Sailing down the rivers, the explorers made surveys along the coast, until all the surveys were linked. "Land measurers" were sent along so that a professional job could be done. Surveys of the New Siberian Islands and explorations in the vicinity of Wrangel Island were carried out during the succeeding century by Russian explorers, but the problem of what lay in the heart of the polar sea remained unsolved.

The lure of the Orient's wealth beckoned from the West, as from the East. John Cabot possibly had recognized as early as 1497 that Columbus had not discovered the Indies, and on his voyage of 1498 may have been looking for a northwest passage thither. English interest shifted from an eastern to a western route with Martin Frobisher's first expedition in 1576. Queen Elizabeth herself bade him Godspeed. Passing beyond Greenland, Frobisher found a "strait" so wide and long that he believed he had indeed reached his goal. Finding metal ores, Frobisher took samples back to England with him. There some assayer or alchemist was reported to have pronounced the samples to be gold ore. The Northwest Passage was forgotten, and the Queen herself invested in the proposed mining colony. Alas, the gold ore turned out to be iron pyrites. For three centuries explorers failed to investigate Frobisher "Strait," and it remained for an American, Charles Francis Hall, to determine that the "strait" was a huge bay, almost bisecting Baffin Island.

A decade after Frobisher, John Davis penetrated farther north along the Greenland coast than had been done before. Henry Hudson, having made several earlier voyages in the European Arctic, entered Hudson Bay in 1610, thus initiating a series of explorations that are continuing yet.

In 1615 and 1616, Robert Bylot and William Baffin in the *Discovery* investigated the northern shore of Hudson Strait and explored the great bay that bears Baffin's name. Smith Sound, which marks their farthest north, they named after their sponsor, Sir Thomas Smith, first governor of the East India Company.

The Hudson's Bay Company, chartered in 1670, was required to carry on explorations, but made no serious investigation of the northern limits of the continent until 1769–72, when Samuel Hearne reached the mouth of the Coppermine River and explored the coasts near its mouth. Farther west, Alexander Mackenzie followed the river that bears his name to the Arctic Ocean in 1789.

Completion of the survey of the Arctic coast of North America and the acquisition of a fair notion of the structure of the American Arctic Archipelago had to await the end of the Napoleonic Wars.

Ever since 1776, a bounty of five thousand pounds for the first ship to reach 89° north latitude had stood unclaimed. To that was added a bounty of twenty thousand pounds in 1818 for the first ship to make the Northwest Passage.

Under the guidance of Sir John Barrow, two expeditions were fitted out in 1818. The first, under Captain David Buchan and Lieutenant John Franklin, sailed north via Spitsbergen. The second, under Captain John Ross and Lieutenant Edward Parry, sailed for Baffin Bay. Parry was chosen in 1819 to conduct new explorations in the same area. Striking an extraordinarily auspicious season, he crossed the entire archipelago, as it is now known, wintering in the west on Melville Island. He was able to claim a five-thousand-pound reward for having crossed the 110th meridian. Simultaneously an expedition, of which Lieutenant Franklin, Dr. John Richardson, and George Back were members, crossed overland from Hudson Bay to the north coast of the mainland. A long stretch of coast was surveyed.

Meanwhile, Parry set forth again in 1821 and succeeded in exploring Melville Peninsula, at the extreme north of Hudson Bay.

A three-pronged attack on the problem of the Northwest Passage was planned for 1824. Parry was to approach by Lancaster Sound, Franklin was to go by the Mackenzie River, while Captain F. W. Beechey was to take a ship through Bering Strait and approach from the west. Beechey reached Point Barrow, but Franklin was unable to close the gap. Dr. Richardson linked the mouths of the Mackenzie and Coppermine, but Parry failed to record any substantial gains. Linking of the Mackenzie and Point Barrow was left for Thomas Simpson to achieve in 1837. Two years later, Simpson all but completed the survey of the coast eastward, the remainder being accomplished by Dr. John Rae of the Hudson's Bay Company in 1846.

The British Admiralty having determined to renew the search for the Northwest Passage, command was offered to Sir John Franklin, known for his explorations, his interest in science, and his record as an administrator. His second in command, Captain Francis R. M. Crozier, had served with Parry thrice in the Arctic and once with Captain James Clark Ross in the Antarctic. Embarking in the *Erebus* and *Terror*, the expedition set sail for Lancaster Sound on May 19, 1845. The vessels were last seen two months later, near the entrance to Lancaster Sound.

Arctic Frontiers

Nothing was heard of the Franklin Expedition during its second summer, 1846. In 1847, preparations were made to seek it. By 1848, Sir James Ross was sent to Lancaster Sound with two vessels, but returned the following year without finding a trace of Franklin. Meanwhile, Sir John Richardson and Dr. Rae searched by land for the expedition.

An extraordinary series of relief expeditions were organized for the summer of 1850. Two vessels under Captain Richard Collinson were sent through Bering Strait by the Admiralty, while a squadron of four vessels under Captain Horatio Austin were sent by Lancaster Sound. Two merchantmen under Captain William Penny took the latter route, while the Admiralty posted a reward of twenty thousand pounds for the rescue of the expedition.

It was at this point that citizens of the United States became engaged in the exploration of the Arctic, an activity in which one American enterprise or another has been almost constantly afoot for more than a century. British expeditions to locate Franklin continued for several years after this, with the practical result that seven thousand miles of coastline were charted in the North American Arctic.

From the beginning of American exploration in 1850 to the return of Charles Francis Hall from his second expedition in 1869, search for the lost Franklin party was a continuing, although dwindling, motive. Growing in importance was the hope of reaching the North Pole. And throughout, general scientific investigation was present, although frequently secondary to geographical exploration.[3]

[3] Further information on early Arctic exploration may be found in a number of sources. One of those most frequently referred to on the Northeast Passage is Nils Adolph Erik Nordenskjöld, *Voyage of the Vega . . . with a Historical Review of Previous Journeys* (transl. Alexander Leslie). For the Northwest Passage, see Vilhjalmur Stefansson, *Great Adventures and Explorations*. See also "Polar Regions," *Encyclopaedia Britannica* (11th ed.) XXI, 938–72.

II

De Haven, Kane, and Hayes

IIIIIIIIIIIIIIIIIIIIIIIIIIIIIIIIIIIIIIIIIIIIII

THE AMERICAN PUBLIC had been well aware of Sir John Franklin's expedition to find the Northwest Passage, thanks to the newspapers and to the visit Lady Jane Franklin made to the United States. On April 4, 1849, Lady Jane addressed a letter to President Zachary Taylor, requesting the aid of the United States in supplementing the ineffective British efforts to find her husband's party. She called attention to the twenty-thousand-pound reward offered by the Admiralty for the first vessel to aid the party. Unfortunately, said she, the offer had been made too late to notify the British whaling fleet. Secretary of State Clayton replied that "the attention of American navigators, and especially of our whalers, will be immediately invoked." The executive branch of the government would do anything that it felt able to do under the Constitution.[1]

During the summer of 1849, various suggestions were made in the American newspapers or to Lady Franklin directly. Captain W. F. Lynch, United States Navy, went to Washington to volunteer to command an expedition. There he found that Captain Charles Wilkes, who a decade earlier had led the first great American expedition into Antarctic and Pacific waters, was "about to be appointed." The vessels under consideration were small fishing vessels or sloops of war, which Lynch considered entirely inadequate. "After wasting time in

[1] 31 Cong., 1 sess., *House Exec. Doc. 16*, 2-6 (Cong. Ser. 576).

13

fruitless deliberation," Lynch wrote, "the contemplated attempt was abandoned, much, I am told, to the chagrin of General Taylor."[2]

On January 4, 1850, President Taylor sent a message to Congress asking for an appropriation. He said that his former efforts to furnish prompt assistance had failed for lack of suitable vessels, an appropriation for the purpose, and a sufficiently early start.[3]

Henry Grinnell now came forward with the first of three donations that were to win him fame. Having made a fortune dealing in whale oil, he had a wide acquaintance among whalers, and his interest in the Arctic was carried over into geography generally. He was for many years president of the American Geographical Society.

Grinnell offered two vessels, the *Advance* and *Rescue,* for the search. Congress authorized the President to accept them and "to detail from the navy such commissioned and warrant officers and so many seamen as may be necessary for said expedition, and who may be willing to engage therein." Rations and such necessary instruments as could be spared from current stocks might be furnished by the navy.[4]

The *Advance,* flagship of the little expedition, was a hermaphrodite brig, built of white oak in 1847. She had been "intended originally for carrying heavy castings from an iron-foundry . . . . She was a good sailer, and easily managed."[5] The *Rescue,* which seems to have been changed in rigging from a schooner to a brig, was built of hackmatack in 1849, and had made no other voyage than that to New York from her building yard in Maine.

The vessels were converted for Arctic service at Brooklyn

[2] Great Britain, *Parliamentary Papers,* Vol. XXXV, No. 107 (1850), 154.
[3] 31 Cong., 1 sess., *House Exec. Doc. 16,* 1 (Cong. Ser. 576).
[4] 31 Cong., 1 sess., *Public Acts,* No. 4 (approved May 2, 1850).
[5] Elisha Kent Kane, *Arctic Explorations: The Second Grinnell Expedition in Search of Sir John Franklin,* I, 18–19. Henceforth cited as *Arctic Explorations.*

Navy Yard. Their bows were strengthened and shored, while extra beams were put under the decks. As protection against splintering by ice floes, their sides received a full sheathing of one-and-one-half-inch oak plank, with a double sheathing of the same material for four feet above and below the water line. From the bows back a considerable distance, three-inch-wide strips of three-sixteenths-inch iron were placed over the oak. For insulation against the cold and for additional water-proofing, the deck was covered with felt and a second decking of boards placed on top. The length of the *Advance* was eighty-eight feet, while the *Rescue* was but sixty-five feet long.[6]

On May 15, Lieutenant Edwin Jesse De Haven was ordered to command the expedition. He was described by W. Parker Snow, the surgeon of the British search vessel *Prince Albert*, as:

> . . . a young man of about twenty-six years of age [actually thirty-four], [who] had served in the United States exploring expedition, under Commodore Wilkes, in the Antarctic Seas. He seemed as fine a specimen of a seaman, and a rough and ready officer, as I had ever seen. Nor was he at all deficient in the characteristics of a true gentleman . . . . With a sharp, quick eye, a countenance bronzed and apparently inured to all weathers, his voice gave unmistakable signs of energy, promptitude, and decision. There was no mistaking the man. He was undoubtedly well-fitted to lead such an expedition, and I felt charmed to see it.[7]

Although De Haven's orders would probably have been substantially the same in any case, the draft orders written by Henry Grinnell at Secretary Preston's request reflect Grin-

---

[6] Enclosure with letter of De Haven to Preston, New York, May 7, 1850. Navy Unit, War Records Branch, National Archives, Officers Letters, May 1850, No. 84.

Dimensions:	Length	Beam	Depth of hold	Tonnage
Advance	88'00"	21'09"	8'05"	144 47/95
Rescue	65'04"	18'08"	8'06"	90 77/95

[7] W. Parker Snow, "Voyage in Search of Sir John Franklin," *Harper's New Monthly Magazine*, Vol. II (1851), 596.

Map for the De Haven Expedition, 1850–51

The De Haven Expedition barely touched on unknown areas. Lancaster Sound and the passages westward to Melville Island had been penetrated by Lieutenant Edward Parry, Royal Navy, who had wintered on Melville Island in 1819–20. Lieutenant John Franklin, Dr. John Richardson, and others had surveyed much of the continental coast line. Captain John Ross had explored Prince Regent Inlet, the Gulf of Boothia, and under his command his nephew, James Ross, had discovered King William's Land.

North of Lancaster Sound and Barrow Strait, however, relatively little was known. And it was in this region, while drifting up Wellington Channel in an ice field, that Lieutenant De Haven sighted from afar the Grinnell Peninsula.

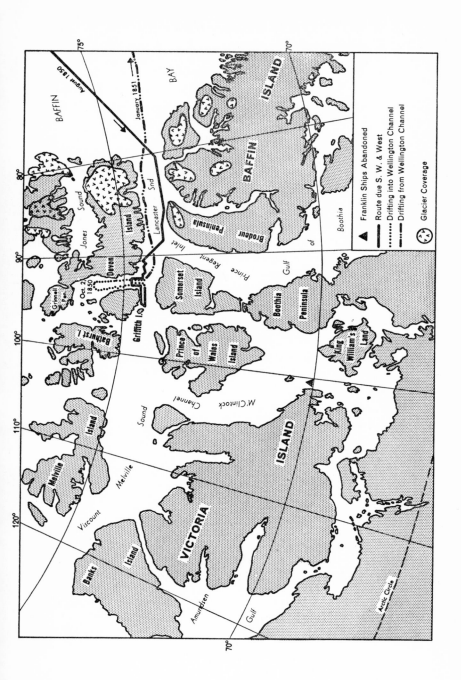

BAFFIN

August 1850

January 1851 →

BAFFIN BAY

BAFFIN ISLAND

Jones Sound

Devon Island

Lancaster Snd

Brodeur Peninsula

Boothia

Gulf of

Prince Regent Inlet

Somerset Island

Grinnell

Griffith I.

● Oct. 2 1850

Bathurst I.

Prince of Wales Island

Boothia Peninsula

King William's Land

M'Clintock Channel

Sound

Melville Island

Melville

Victoria

VICTORIA ISLAND

Banks Island

Viscount

Amundsen Gulf

Arctic Circle

▲ Franklin Ships Abandoned

Route due S. W. & West

Drifting into Wellington Channel

Drifting from Wellington Channel

⊛ Glacier Coverage

nell's own mixed motives: De Haven should seek to enter Lancaster Sound and assign a vessel to search each shore; if no particular difficulty were encountered, he should push on to Banks Land, and if the sea beyond were open, he should head for Bering Strait and San Francisco—thereby completing the Northwest Passage. If he should be unable to penetrate Lancaster Sound, he should try Wellington, Jones, and Smith Sounds in succession. This followed the pattern of the orders given Sir John Franklin. Geographical and scientific information should be acquired so long as it did not interfere with the principal objective. And, "As the Whaleing [*sic*] interest is becoming important in the Arctic Seas, you will obtain all the information in relation to it that you can—."[8]

Matthew Fontaine Maury, the genius of the United States Hydrographic Office, had likewise recommended that De Haven try to find open water through the series of channels running north through the archipelago. The official orders embodied this alternative. As in Grinnell's draft, the orders authorized scientific inquiry, but "only so far as the same may not interfere with the main object of the expedition."[9]

Late August, 1850, found De Haven's vessels in Barrow Straits, some three hundred miles west of Baffin Bay. Camp litter on Beechey Island suggested that the Franklin party might have been there. Turning north up Wellington Channel, the *Advance* soon encountered solid ice that looked as if it had not been broken for three years. The vessels returned south and fell in with the British squadron of Captain Penny.

Seeking a safer shelter, the *Advance* and Penny's vessels retired to Beechey Island, where they were joined by Captain John Ross's *Felix*. A search on August 27 disclosed the graves of three of Franklin's men, dated January and April, 1846. Old rope and canvas, wood shavings, foundations for the anvil, and

[8] Grinnell to Preston, New York, May 10, 1850. Navy Unit, War Records Branch, National Archives, Miscellaneous Letters, May 1850, No. 54.

[9] Great Britain, *Parliamentary Papers*, Vol. XXXIII, No. 97 (1851), 2-4.

other evidence of a winter's camp lay round about. No written records could be found.

Meanwhile, the *Rescue* had been at Point Innes, sending scouting parties northward. The *Advance* joined her there, then both worked their way westward along a lead in the ice south of Cornwallis Island until they joined both Penny's and Austin's British expeditions at Griffith Island.

Captain Austin then put to De Haven the question of joining forces for the next season's search. De Haven discussed the matter with his second in command, Griffin, of the *Rescue*, and decided that their position at that time did not offer such definite advantages as to fall within the meaning of his orders. With the first favorable wind on September 13, the ships began working their way east toward Baffin Bay. The weather had already turned cold. By the nineteenth, De Haven had abandoned hope of returning home that autumn, and tried to reach the shelter of Beechey Island, whence he might send land parties in the spring to explore Wellington Channel.

Caught in the channel by ice, they drifted north and south through October and November. In early December they drifted south until fairly caught in the ice current of Lancaster Sound, where they were borne east at a rate of six miles a day. Before the New Year they were at the entrance to Baffin Bay. Fearing a wreck, they set provisions out on the ice, only to have the ice break up and destroy most of the provisions. During the spring months they were carried south by a huge floe, which broke on June 6. After working forty-eight hours to free the stern of the *Advance*, both vessels set off for the Greenland shore.

At Lievely and Pröven, the crews recovered from scurvy and regained their strength. On June 22, 1851, the expedition headed north for a second season's exploration. Working through the ice pack, they found whalers headed south who reported that ice conditions in Melville Bay were bad. Until August 18, they were scarcely able to move and were threatened with the possibility of again wintering among the icebergs of Baffin Bay. They were now in an unquestionably poor position to proceed with the search, so in compliance with orders, the vessels headed for home.[10]

As one looks on the map today, it is difficult to conceive of a more strategic location from which to have continued De Haven's search than from Griffith Island. The ships had three years' supplies and had been out but three months. Nor does any lack of geographical information explain De Haven's decision. The boundaries of continental North America were known with sufficient accuracy. Prince Regent Inlet and the Gulf of Boothia were known through the work of the Rosses. Parry had sailed as far west as Melville Island, but had not definitely established the limits of the American archipelago. To the north less was known, but as De Haven's orders suggested, a simple solution to the whole problem might lie in that direction. Hence the explanation is probably the fear of wintering in the Arctic, although De Haven was an intrepid ice navigator. In view of the number of vessels that have been crushed by the ice under the most experienced of masters, the danger is not to be underrated.

Much of the expedition's benefit was in the experience it furnished one man, the surgeon of the *Advance*, Elisha Kent Kane. The most famous member of a family prominent in Philadelphia, Kane had already traveled over the world as a naval surgeon. Warned by physicians that a heart ailment might cut his life short at any time, he filled his years with adventure. Kane wrote the only detailed account of the De Haven Expedition. It contains many observations on natural history and an extended discussion of Arctic ice.[11]

To Kane's lively mind, defeat was but a challenge. It is prob-

[10] See report of Lieutenant-Commander Edwin J. De Haven to the Secretary of the Navy, New York, Oct. 4, 1851, 32 Cong., 1 sess., *House Exec. Doc.* 2, *Vol. II* (Cong. Ser. 635), Pt. 1, 26–41, especially 38–40.
[11] Elisha Kent Kane, *The United States Grinnell Expedition in Search of Sir John Franklin*. See Bibliography.

able that he had his schemes well matured before the De Haven Expedition had reached New York. He received a request from Lady Franklin asking him to join an Arctic expedition by way of Novaya Zemlya. Instead, he reached an agreement with Henry Grinnell to search the routes north of Baffin Bay, with the consent and encouragement of the Secretary of the Navy, John Pendleton Kennedy. Presumably, Kennedy became the instrument for obtaining funds from George Peabody, once Kennedy's fellow lodger in Baltimore and later an international financier in London.

Kane entertained no high hopes of finding Franklin, but he believed his route best. He suggested to Kennedy that his orders be styled "at the request of Lady Franklin, for the purpose of taking an Overland Journey from the upper waters of Baffin's Bay to the Shores of the Polar Sea."[12] This worthy motive, if one may read between the lines, was closely joined to the equally worthy but less popular desire to explore new lands in the Arctic and to solve the problem of the existence of an open polar sea. His plan reflects careful thought and investigation of the geographical literature of the day.

Financial support was prompt. The first institutions to furnish aid were the American Geographical Society, the Smithsonian Institution, and the American Philosophical Society.[13] When Kennedy interviewed Kane, he found that "with all the liberality of Mr. Grinnell and Mr. Peabody, the outfit would be very limited." He offered to place Kane and several other naval officers on special duty, thus keeping them on full pay and enabling the expedition to make use of naval facilities. Kennedy, an erstwhile congressman, wrote afterwards that he knew Congress would have no appropriation for the expedition, although "with an appropriation from Con-

[12] Kane to Kennedy, Nov. 15 and 22, 1852. John Pendleton Kennedy MSS (Peabody Library, Baltimore, Md.), Letters to Kennedy, VIII, Nos. 59, 60.

[13] Kane, *Arctic Explorations*, I, 15. Except when noted to the contrary, the following account is based on this volume.

gress the expedition would have been made much more effective and a heavy amount of suffering and privation avoided."[14]

The vessel used was the *Advance*, offered by Grinnell, in which Kane had sailed under De Haven. Ten of the seventeen men were naval personnel assigned to the expedition. Through Kennedy, Kane had sought to get Alexander von Humboldt to recommend an observer.[15] August Sonntag, the man actually appointed, was a native of north Germany, which suggests that he may have been Humboldt's protégé.

Kane's requisition for instruments was drawn up with the help of Lieutenant Matthew Fontaine Maury and sent to Secretary Kennedy.[16] Among the instruments supplied by the United States Naval Observatory were 36 mercury thermometers, 24 alcohol thermometers, 4 maximum and 4 minimum thermometers. Three of the thermometers were 36-inch standards. Some were compared with Tagliabue's 36-inch spirit (alcohol) standard graduated to -70° F. by tenths of a degree.[17] A unifilar magnetometer was furnished by the United States Coast Survey, and a dip needle was supplied by the Smithsonian Institution.[18]

The expedition sailed from New York on May 30, 1853. It made several stops along the Greenland coast, acquiring a stock of reindeer skins and various last-minute necessities. An Eskimo lad, Hans Christian, was taken along as hunter and interpreter. He served later in the expeditions of Hayes, Nares, and Hall, by whom he was called Hans Hendrik.

Four days sufficed for the vessel to pass through the broken pack in Melville Bay and reach the area known, from its usual lack of midsummer floes, as the North Water. Leaving a

[14] Memorandum of Kennedy on letter of Kane to Kennedy, November 14, 1852. Kennedy's phrasing indicates that the memorandum was written after Kane's return in 1855. Letters to Kennedy, VIII, No. 58.

[15] Kennedy to Von Humboldt, February 16, 1853. Kennedy Letters, 417.

[16] Kane to Kennedy, January 29, 1853. Letters to Kennedy, VIII, No. 63.

[17] Charles A. Schott, *Meteorological Observations in the Arctic Seas by Elisha Kent Kane* . . . . Smithsonian *Contributions to Knowledge*, XIII, 1–2.

[18] Kane, *Arctic Explorations*, I, 17–18.

twenty-foot metal boat on Littleton Island, Kane's party sailed on past the Eskimo settlement of Etah and into Smith Sound. After terrific struggles with the ice during mid-August, they were able to tow the little craft by hand lines along the edge of the shore floe.

On finding a fair harbor, Kane left the *Advance* and scouted farther up the channel by whaleboat. Finding no better wintering place, he prepared to secure the vessel for the winter and to make ready for spring sledging expeditions. Autumn expeditions were sent forth, one to make an emergency cache to the south, another under Dr. Isaac Israel Hayes to penetrate the Greenland icecap. Hayes went inland some ninety miles before meeting a four-hundred-foot-high ice barrier.

With the coming of spring, a string of caches was laid out to the north. Then, equipped with such instruments as he could carry, Kane set out northward. He reached a giant glacier, which he named after Alexander von Humboldt. A later party under William Morton passed the glacier, and established a new "far north" record. Stopped by water that had washed away the shore ice from the cliffs ahead of them, Morton scrambled some five hundred feet up the rocks. Looking west and north up Kennedy Channel, Morton viewed a long stretch of precipices and mountains, broken by a major indentation which Kane named Lady Franklin Bay.

To his right, Cape Constitution, two miles away, blocked Morton's view. Ahead, as far as eye could see, was open water. Behind was a channel filled with ice. It seemed, indeed, that the polar sea had been reached—the "open" polar sea of speculation. And so, on Kane's map, the area north and east of Cape Constitution was marked "open sea." Dr. Hayes later conducted an expedition to prove the truth of this conclusion.

Inglefield's survey of the west coast of Smith Sound was extended northward from Cape Sabine by Dr. Hayes in a march fully as difficult as Morton's. Hayes thus achieved the distinction of being the first explorer to reach the coast of

Map for Expeditions of E. K. Kane, 1853–55;
I. I. Hayes, 1860–61

William Baffin had discovered Smith Sound in 1616, but only in 1852 did Captain Edward A. Inglefield substantiate his claims. A year later Elisha Kent Kane found that Smith Sound opened out into a broad basin, only to narrow again into a channel which Kane named after Secretary of the Navy John Pendleton Kennedy.

Kane Basin was filled with ice for two years or more, and Kane was forced to abandon his vessel. Yet Kennedy Channel and the waters to the north were seen to have only occasional floes in midsummer, 1854. This lent additional credibility to the theory that, once one had penetrated a ring of ice, one would find a navigable polar sea.

The explorations of Isaac Israel Hayes on these two expeditions served to outline the eastern shore of Ellesmere Island almost to the Arctic Ocean itself.

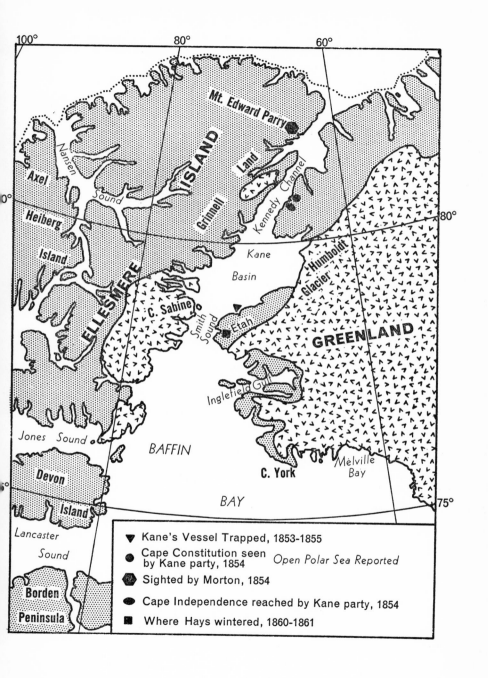

100°　　　　　80°　　　　　60°

Mt. Edward Parry

Axel

Nansen

Sound

GRINNELL ISLAND

Grinnell Land

Kennedy Channel

80°

Heiberg

Island

ELLESMERE

Kane

Basin

Humboldt

Glacier

C. Sabine

Smith Sound

Etah

GREENLAND

Inglefield Gulf

Jones Sound

BAFFIN

Devon

Island

Melville Bay

C. York

Lancaster

Sound

75°

BAY

Borden

Peninsula

▼　Kane's Vessel Trapped, 1853-1855

●　Cape Constitution seen
　by Kane party, 1854　　　*Open Polar Sea Reported*

⬢　Sighted by Morton, 1854

●　Cape Independence reached by Kane party, 1854

■　Where Hays wintered, 1860-1861

Grinnell Land. (Grinnell Land is, in modern nomenclature, the northern half of Ellesmere Island. The deep cleft separating the two halves had been taken for a channel until Peary proved that it was a fjord.)

The late summer of 1854 found the *Advance* as securely in the grasp of the ice as ever. A trip to the south showed how small was the likelihood of the ice breaking up that summer. Frostbite, sickness, and accident had laid up so many of the men that an effort to move boats over the ice to open water would have been perilous. Hence, Kane concluded to spend another winter.

The tales of fortitude and knavery that fill the pages of Kane's journal for the second winter are of the stuff that makes truth stranger than fiction. The vividness of the story made it a best-seller of its generation.[19]

Counsels were divided. Half of the party wanted to try to reach the Danish settlements by boat. Kane, as a naval man, was not disposed to "give up the ship" without trying during a second summer to extricate his vessel; neither was he willing to leave the scientific collections behind. These were carefully packed by Hayes, whose recollection of the event shows how assiduous had been the natural history collectors:

> I was chiefly occupied, during the day, in getting together my collections of natural history, the gatherings of two summers; and in stowing them away in the hold, and in my little room down by the forecastle. The floral specimens, altogether about two thousand individual plants, were wrapped in brown paper packages, labelled with date and locality, and delivered to the commander. The same was done with the small entomological collection, which was in a cigar-box. The bird skins, in all nearly two hundred, were secured in a ratproof chest. The geological and mineralogical specimens; the musk-ox, human and other skulls and bones; the bear and seal skins; the fishes and other

[19] A portion of the original MS journal is in the Rare Book Room at Stanford University. Comparison of the original manuscript with the published version shows that Kane vented his feelings more freely to the journal than to the public.

wet preparations, were in barrels or in the Smithsonian copper-tanks. This work seemed, at the time, very useless; but we knew not what might come, nor how many of these things might in the end be saved.[20]

The party, which included Hayes and Sonntag, set forth on August 28, 1854. The group failed to reach open water with its boats and had to encamp in miserable quarters on the coastal plain, eighteen or nineteen miles south of Cape Parry, near the modern village of Thule. Even there Sonntag was busy studying the geology of the vicinity. After months on the edge of starvation and under constant apprehension of attack by the Eskimos, the party crept back, reaching the ship on December 12.

Even after having experienced the miseries of the "southern boat camp," William Godfrey deserted. In his apologia printed after Kane's journal appeared, Godfrey maintained that Kane's dismissal of the group to go south relieved them of allegiance.[21] Kane, for his part, feared that Godfrey would waylay Hans, steal the dogs and sled, and so cut off their only means of an emergency retreat. When Godfrey appeared at the vessel with the sled loaded with meat, Kane suspected that he sought merely to aid a confederate to escape. Godfrey was placed under arrest, but on his promise to reform he was allowed to go free; he promptly deserted again, and Kane tried to restrain him by firing shots after him. Hans, on his part, confirmed Godfrey's intention, saying that Godfrey had first invited, then tried to force him to surrender the team, sledge, and rifle. Finally, feeling that the morale of the whole party was at stake, Kane made the trip to Etah himself and persuaded Godfrey to return.[22]

[20] Isaac Israel Hayes, *An Arctic Boat Journey*, 35.

[21] William Godfrey, *Godfrey's Narrative*, 156ff.

[22] Kane's account is supported in general by Henry Goodfellow, "The facts relating to the separation of the ship's company of the Brig *Advance* in the fall of 1854. Written out by Henry Goodfellow. By command of Miss Bessie Kane." Greely MSS (Library of the National Geographic Society, Washington, D. C.) No. 330. (Typed copy; location of original not indicated.)

When Kane's expedition had been gone well over a year, his father, Judge J. K. Kane of Philadelphia, set out to raise a relief expedition. From the American Philosophical Society he obtained a memorial to Congress. He also appealed to Kennedy, now out of office, for aid.[23] Kennedy complied promptly, for he had promised Dr. Kane to seek Congressional support for a relief expedition if Kane did not reappear after the second winter. This appeal to Congress "was promptly and honorably met almost without solicitation."[24]

Congress appropriated $150,000 and the Secretary of the Navy appointed a board to select and purchase vessels. The *Release* was a clipper bark of 327 tons, nearly new and fast sailing. The *Arctic* was a light ship, "purchased by the Navy Department and fitted out as a Propeller." Both vessels were strengthened, the bows filled in solid for about seven feet, and their sides sheathed with two-and-one-half-inch oak covered with sheet iron. The lower decks were lined with cork on the ceiling and sides to prevent moisture. Included in the equipment were India-rubber boats and fine whaleboats provided with iron shod runners, four for the *Release* and two for the *Arctic*. The finest of nautical instruments and firearms were provided. Lieutenant Henry J. Hartstene was ordered to the command of the expedition. The personnel were all volunteers, selected from a long list of applicants.

The vessels set out with rations aboard for two years. After twenty-eight days of forcing their way through the ice to the North Water of upper Melville Bay, they examined the coast and islands carefully to within perhaps thirty miles of the *Advance*. On returning, they fell in with the Eskimos of Etah, who had enriched themselves by stripping the abandoned vessel. With the help of an Eskimo vocabulary and drawings, Hartstene's officers learned that Kane and his party had headed south. Knowing that Kane had considered plans to

[23] J. K. Kane to Kennedy, Nov. 20, 1854. Letters to Kennedy, VIII, No. 77.
[24] Kennedy memorandum. Letters to Kennedy, VIII, No. 58.

retreat to Beechey Island, they searched the west side as far as Pond's Bay, then crossed to Upernavik, finally meeting the party at Godhavn.[25]

As if by a miracle, Kane brought his men through the winter and with the advance of spring started to haul his boats south to Baffin Bay. Four of the men were incapacitated and had to be carried by easy stages on a dog sledge. Another man over-strained himself in saving a boat and died a few days later. After the boats were launched, storms delayed the party repeatedly for days at a time; closing leads between the floes made the crew haul their boats up on the ice until all hands were exhausted. At last, however, they reached Upernavik, only to learn that the rescue expedition had passed, heading north. The party was taken south to Godhavn by the yearly Danish trading vessel. They were on the point of departure to Denmark with her when Hartstene's squadron was sighted from a near-by hilltop. The boats were manned for the last time, and the hardy explorers once more trod the decks that to them were native soil.

The Kane Expedition was well equipped to take scientific observations. Kane himself was fairly conversant with natural history. A comparison of his books with Hayes's suggests that the latter was a still better naturalist. August Sonntag, a promising young astronomer, was the expedition's expert in the physical sciences. A transit and theodolite furnished the necessary equipment to make highly accurate determinations of their base and meridian lines. They could make all fundamental magnetic determinations. The meteorological equipment was adequate.

On a rocky shore some little distance from the ship, they had set up their astronomical and magnetic observatories. The astronomical observatory was formed of granite blocks ce-

[25] Orders from the Secretary of the Navy, J. C. Dobbin, to Lieutenant Hartstene, May 25, 1855, and four reports, Hartstene to Dobbin, July 9–October 11, 1855. In Kane, *Arctic Explorations*, II, Appendix IV, 324–30.

mented with moss and ice. Pedestals were made for the transit and theodolite by filling pemmican casks with gravel, pouring in water, and letting the conglomerate freeze. The resulting pedestal was as firm as the rock on which it rested. The magnetic observatory was more spacious, and boasted a floor and copper fire grate. The meteorological instruments were well screened in a shelter near the ship, with lenses so arranged that the observers did not need to come within the screens. At 40° below zero, "the mere approach of an observer caused a perceptible rise of the column." The wind gauge became clogged with moisture too readily to be effective. The tide register was "a simple pulley-gauge, arranged with a wheel and index" aboard ship.[26]

Kane's description of a winter's term-day when magnetic observations were taken continuously is a most graphic account of the difficulties under which scientists labored in the Arctic:

> Our Arctic observatory is cold beyond any of its class, Kesan, Pulkowa, Toronto, or even its shifting predecessors, Bossetop and Melville Island. Imagine it a term-day, a magnetic term-day.
>
> The observer . . . is clad in a pair of seal-skin pants, a dog-skin cap, a reindeer jumper, and walrus boots. He sits upon a box that once held a transit instrument. A stove, glowing with at least a bucketful of anthracite, represents pictorially a heating apparatus, and reduces the thermometer as near as may be to ten degrees below zero. One hand holds a chronometer, and is left bare to warm it: the other luxuriates in a fox-skin mitten. The right hand and the left take it "watch and watch about." As one burns with cold, the chronometer shifts to the other, and the mitten takes its place.
>
> Perched on a pedestal of frozen gravel is a magnetometer; stretching out from it, a telescope: and, bending down to this, an abject human eye. Every six minutes, said eye takes cognizance of a finely-divided arc, and notes the results in a cold memorandum-book. This process continues for twenty-four hours, two

[26] Kane, *Arctic Explorations*, I, 116–18.

sets of eyes taking it by turns; and when twenty-four hours are over, term-day is over too.

We have such frolics every week. I have just been relieved from one, and after a few hours am to be called out of bed in the night to watch and dot again. I have been engaged in this way when the thermometer gave 20° above zero at the instrument, 20° below at two feet above the floor, and 43° below at the floor itself: on my person, facing the little lobster-red fury of a stove, 94° above; on my person, away from the stove, 10° below zero. "A grateful country" will of course appreciate the value of these labors, and, as it cons over hereafter the four hundred and eighty results which go to make up our record for each week, will never think of asking *"Cui bono* all this?"

To the discomforts of the observing were added the dangers of getting back and forth from ship to observatory in the midst of an Arctic night, around new pools of water and over boulders, talus slopes, and ever-crumbling ice.[27]

A generation later, Adolphus W. Greely said that Hayes's exploration of Kane Basin "outlined free-water ways that have been more persistently and safely followed poleward than any other." Greely praised the contributions to natural history. He considered the tidal, meteorological, magnetic, and glacier observations "most valuable, not only by their remoteness from others, but also as forming the basis and stimulus of the existing magnificent series of physical contributions relating to West Greenland."[28]

The appraisal of Kane's work given the American Association for the Advancement of Science by Alexander Dallas Bache, superintendent of the Coast Survey, was couched in superlatives:

[Although] Dr. Kane disclaimed all pretentions of a scientific character for his work, it contained, nevertheless, some of the most important contributions to our knowledge of the natural

27 *Ibid.*, I, 165-69.
28 Greely, *Handbook of Polar Discoveries*, 199.

history and natural phenomena of the interesting regions visited by the hardy explorers. Dr. Kane appreciated highly all the relations direct and indirect which science has to an exploring expedition. He was always careful to surround himself by those who could in their special departments make valuable observations, while his own rare administrative capacity always gave them opportunity for the exercise of their abilities. Himself an admirable observer, and well trained in many subjects, he was always on hand to direct or to assist as the occasion might require. The labors, in physical observation, of Dr. Kane and his associates, had in Prof. Bache's opinion, few parallels, when the difficulties to be surmounted and the results produced are considered.[29]

As Kane's experience with De Haven had inspired him with the desire to lead an expedition, so in turn Dr. Hayes turned to promoting one under his own leadership. While Kane seemed to have experienced no difficulty in raising funds and was able to set forth with a good outfit in little over a year, Hayes was not so fortunate. Five years intervened, the last three filled with intense effort.

Hayes began his campaign with a speech before the American Geographical and Statistical Society in December 1857. In the spring of 1858, he spoke before a number of learned societies, the most important being the Baltimore meeting of the American Association for the Advancement of Science.[30]

Hayes brought to the attention of "this representative body of American science" the opportunity that existed for extending Kane's discovery of "an open sea within the Arctic ocean" and determining "whether the Russians are correct in their belief in the existence of a great continent lying to the northward of Asia." The limits of the American archipelago were

[29] A. D. Bache, "Abstract of the Principal Results of the Magnetic Observations of the Second Grinnell Expedition, in 1853–5 . . . ," American Association for the Advancement of Science (A.A.A.S.), *Proceedings*, Vol. XII (1858), 120.

[30] Isaac Israel Hayes. *The Open Polar Sea*, 4 ff. When not otherwise noted, this account follows Hayes's volume, and specific references will ordinarily be omitted.

Sir John Franklin's expedition wintered on this bleak site, 1846-47. This photograph was taken a century after he broke camp.

Ice off Cape Sabine. Schley took the *Thetis* and the *Bear* across this channel in the teeth of a gale.

Aerial view, looking west in the vicinity of Simpson Strait and showing Richardson Point — the area explored by Charles Francis Hall and Frederick Schwatka.

not known; the northern coasts of Greenland and Grinnell Land had obvious advantages for exploration. He traced the normal southern limits of the ice pack and recounted the attempts by ship and sledge to cross it.

The Russians, like Kane, had reported open water, but only of limited extent. The flight of marine birds northward from the perimeter of all known lands showed that there must be open water where they could feed. Charts of isothermal lines showed two poles of cold, situated near the 78th parallel. Two plants from the little collection brought back by Kane had been found in Russian America and on the same isotherm in Labrador. Various anthropological data suggested that the Eskimos had once lived farther north. Finally, actual measurements of sea temperatures showed conclusively "that the great body of the waters of the Polar Basin has a temperature considerably removed from the freezing point." He concluded with a demonstration of the additions that would be made to climatology, anthropology, and natural history.[31]

The American Association for the Advancement of Science appointed an Arctic committee to counsel with Hayes. The Academy of Natural Sciences of Philadelphia, in voting to endorse him, stressed the importance of the problem of an open polar sea to climatology, geography, and commerce, and the need of research in Arctic natural history, which "would throw light on both problems of physiology and the interrelation of bio-geographical areas."[32] The Boston Society of Natural History voted to offer him their "encouragement and countenance," expressing "confidence that his return will be most valuable to science."[33]

These fair words were not accompanied by equally fine financial support. The subscription lists opened by the societies

---

[31] Isaac Israel Hayes, "Observations upon the Practicability of Reaching the North Pole," A.A.A.S. *Proceedings*, Vol. XII (1858), 234–54.

[32] Academy of Natural Sciences, Philadelphia, *Proceedings* (1858), 164–65.

[33] Boston Society of Natural History, *Proceedings*, Vol. VI (1858), 417.

and the "powerful name" of Alexander Dallas Bache, Hayes's principal scientific backer, had accomplished little. In late July, 1859, Hayes wrote Bache that the American Geographical Society of New York had done nothing, and his lectures in Baltimore and Philadelphia had put him in debt. Would Bache please make sure that the American Association for the Advancement of Science did not discontinue its Committee on Arctic Exploration. Still, Hayes concluded, his hopes were high and he thought he should get off next spring.[34]

His lectures having failed to produce the amounts necessary even for current expenses, Hayes spent the summer of 1859 composing *An Arctic Boat Journey*, the story of his adventures with Kane. He reported to Bache that although he disliked writing a tale of personal adventure, it was now ready for the publishers.[35]

On March 29, 1860, Hayes again addressed the American Geographical Society. Francis Lieber delivered a speech in reply that glowed with colorful rhetoric. Hayes would undertake an Arctic expedition if he could raise but $20,000. A sum of $45,000 would buy him the completest outfit. These speeches were carried by the newspapers and reprinted as a pamphlet in the hope of attracting money.[36]

Hayes's New York friends suggested seeking the aid of Congress. Hayes wrote Bache for his opinion, and Bache responded favorably, advising Hayes that it would be necessary to use personal influence with the senators and representatives. Hayes decided to seek private subscriptions and to turn to Congress as a last resort.

Then Captain Hartstene told Hayes that the British steamer *Arctic* was in condition for service, and Hayes asked

[34] Hayes to Bache, July 28, 1859. Bache Correspondence (Library of Congress).

[35] Hayes to Bache, September 26, 1859. Bache Correspondence.

[36] American Geographical Society, *The Polar Exploring Expedition*, 21–22. See also, "The Proposed Arctic Expedition," *National Intelligencer*, n.d., uncatalogued material in Huntington Library, San Marino, California.

Bache to check into the matter. However, the *Arctic* was not available on any terms.[37]

Finally, on May 3, Hayes wrote in jubilation to Bache,

> I have leisure only to say that the $20,000 was reached last evening, and that the expedition will sail on or about June 20th . . . .
> I know that you will rejoice over the good news and I am impatient to see you and receive your congratulations . . . .[38]

These funds enabled Hayes to buy, not the steamer and sailing vessel he had desired, but a 133-ton schooner, which he rechristened the *United States*. The government sponsorship that had been accorded the De Haven Expedition, the men and equipment that had been furnished Kane, had now dwindled until Hayes received from the government only a portion of the instruments he desired. The Smithsonian Institution, having independent funds at its command, furnished barometers and thermometers, containers and alcohol for zoological specimens, and similar apparatus and equipment. The United States Topographical Bureau supplied two pocket sextants, instruments practically impossible to obtain. The United States Coast Survey supplied "a vertical circle, which contained the double advantage of a transit and theodolite, a well-tested unifilar magnetometer, a reflecting circle, a Wurdemann compass, and several other valuable instruments." A request was made of the United States Naval Observatory for a deep-sea sounding apparatus, which was turned down as "the concession was not provided for by act of Congress."[39]

A leading instrument maker, John Tagliabue, supplied standard spirit thermometers. A four-and-one-half-inch tele-

[37] Hayes to Bache, April 9, 1860; reply, April 10; Hayes to Bache, April 16; reply, April 19. Bache Correspondence.

[38] Hayes to Bache, from New York. Rhees MSS (Huntington Library, San Marino, Calif.), No. 1475. This item is quoted by permission of the Huntington Library.

[39] Hayes, *The Open Polar Sea*, 10–11.

scope and chronometers were provided. Gravity determinations were made possible by a pendulum fabricated for the occasion. Hayes could say with some pride, "Our equipment for scientific observations was reasonably perfect."

The vessel was reinforced with two-and-one-half-inch oak sheathing, and the bow was protected with heavy iron plates. She was strengthened with transverse beams just below the water line, with additional knees and diagonal braces. "For convenience of working among the ice, her rig was changed from a fore-and-aft to a foretopsail schooner."

The scientific personnel included Hayes, August Sonntag, who had hurried home from a scientific survey in Mexico to go with the party, and Henry G. Radcliffe, who served as assistant astronomer. Eight merchant marine officers and men, two boys of eighteen, and two men accepted simply as "volunteers" completed the party as it left the United States.

Hayes assembled his equipment on the docks at Boston, loaded the last-minute gifts of supplies and provisions on the deck, and after anchoring in the harbor to stow the stores, finally left Boston on July 6.

When but well started, careless navigation nearly wrecked the vessel on the rocks of Cape Race, Newfoundland. At Pröven and Upernavik, the last European settlements in Greenland, they sought dogs for sledging. As epidemics had killed many of the dogs, few were available. Hayes recruited three Eskimo hunters and three Danes, one of whom, Jensen, proved invaluable.

In late August, the United States left the last Danish settlement behind. Out of Upernavik she was becalmed and carried by surface currents hither and yon among giant icebergs. To avoid being carried onto a berg and wrecked, the party secured their vessel to one with an ice anchor. Hardly had they done so, when they found it disintegrating. Chunks the size of a building fell off, and the berg rolled and plunged seeking a new equilibrium. A wind sprang up, and they entered Melville

Bay amid snow flurries that so obscured their vision as to bring them repeatedly to the brink of disaster. When they ran out of the storm, they marveled that they had escaped the host of bergs that lay about. Near Cape York they met their first ice field, a belt some fifteen miles wide. There, too, they came across Hans, their Eskimo companion from the Kane Expedition. He joined them, making a home for himself, his wife, and child in a tent on deck.

On entering Smith Sound, Hayes had high hopes of pushing his way northwest to the shores of Grinnell Land. He was soon stopped by a field of extraordinarily thick ice. Then a gale swept down from the north and he was forced to seek shelter. From August 29 for the better part of a week, Hayes struggled against the wind and the pack. Finally, his ship had taken so much damage and the ice was so solid that he decided to go into winter quarters.

The location necessity forced upon them was but four miles from the Eskimo settlement of Etah, which was deserted at the time. Hayes estimated that the Kane Expedition's wintering place was some eighty miles to the northeast. If he had failed to reach the base desired, Hayes took consolation in the fact that the ship would surely be released the next spring. Later, another advantage of the site became apparent. Whereas the Kane Expedition had run desperately short of fresh meat, Hayes was in one of the best hunting grounds known to the Eskimos.

The winter was passed in much greater comfort than many parties had experienced. They could be liberal with food. The quarters were dry. The Eskimo women sewed new fur garments for the crew in exchange for coveted utensils. Until an epidemic swept away over one-half of the dogs, there were plenty to train for sledging. Boredom was exorcised with the customary Arctic newspaper and vaudeville, but even more so by hunting and the innumerable scientific observations.

On October 22, the first exploration was begun. When with

the Kane Expedition, Hayes had traveled overland a considerable distance before reaching the edge of the icecap. Now he led a party over the glacier that descended to the sea near by. They traveled an estimated sixty miles over the icecap before winds and low temperatures, such as they had yet to experience at the ship, forced them back. Although Danish parties had made attempts at the icecap earlier, modern scientific explorations and discussions of the Greenland icecap may fairly be said to date from this trip.

As Hayes needed dogs for the spring sledging parties, he decided to lure the Eskimos to the ship with presents. Just before Christmas he sent out August Sonntag and Hans for that purpose. While running ahead of the sled, Sonntag fell through a crack in the ice and got thoroughly wet. Contrary to Arctic custom, he did not get out of the wet clothing immediately, but with Hans turned back towards a hut. Before they reached it, Sonntag had lost the power of speech, and he died within a day. Thus the party lost its most competent scientist.

A sally was made up the Greenland coast to Kane's winter quarters, thus tying the two expeditions' surveys together. The main sledging expedition started for Grinnell Land on April 4, 1861. Twelve men set out with two dog sledges and a large man-powered sledge, the latter carrying the boat Hayes hoped to use on the "open polar sea." The ice, broken by the surging winter tides, was piled ridge on ridge, "leaving scarcely a foot of level surface." On April 28, Hayes sent back the main party, and he, with three companions, pushed on to Grinnell Land. When with the Kane Expedition, he had crossed the channel in two days; this time thirty-one days were consumed. Hayes and one youthful companion pressed on up the coast of Grinnell Land until May 18, when the crumbling ice turned them back. From a headland, Hayes could look north and see a series of capes, past which he believed he saw his goal: the open polar sea. There is a question about the latitude Hayes reached, although it is agreed that he did not reach the Arctic Ocean. Greely claimed that the position given did not agree with Hayes's description and concluded that he could not have been farther north than Cape Joseph Goode in 80° 11′ north latitude.[40]

Shortly after the return of Hayes to the schooner, the ice broke and released the vessel. On taking his departure, Hayes assured the Eskimos of his intention to return and establish a settlement. Such thoughts were driven from his mind, for on reaching Boston the gloom of the Civil War's first summer showed him how impossible it was to continue his plans for Arctic research.

Hayes's sorry personal plight is revealed in letters to Bache. When April rolled around and Hayes had not returned instruments valued at close to one thousand dollars, Bache wrote him. Hayes replied from Philadelphia in two pitiful letters, telling how he had expected his lectures, photographs, and book to pay the remaining costs of the expedition. When pressed by the sailors for their pay, he had put the instruments up as security for a loan, never dreaming that he would not be able to redeem them promptly.

> The case of the instruments was only one of the many disappointments which I have experienced. Debts to the amount of $1500.00 have harassed me through the winter, and I think that, from the friends of the expedition, I ought to have at least kindly consideration, and that I ought, also, not to be harshly judged for such errors as have resulted from over sensitiveness and excess of hopefulness.

The records and observations that in his first letter he had promised to ship were still waiting because he could not pay the express. A few days later he was able to write that he had received his commission in the army as brevet major, and had

40 Greely, *Handbook of Polar Discoveries*, 201–202.

arranged to have the instruments released, packed, and shipped.[41]

The scientific observations of the Hayes Expedition were broader in scope if shorter in time than the Kane observations. As before, meteorological and magnetic observations were taken, though in less detail. A series of gravitational experiments were made in the fall and repeated in the spring. The telescope was set up with a snow igloo for an observatory.

A survey of the harbor was started in the fall and completed in the spring. In the autumn, Hayes went up the glacier and sighted in a row of stakes. In the spring, he returned and found that the center of the glacier had moved forward 96 feet. He ran a series of levels along the harbor and plotted the twenty-three terraces that rose 110 feet above the high-tide line. The terraces showed evidence of the rising of north Greenland, while south Greenland was reported to have settled during historic times.

Hayes's collection included a set of fossils from Grinnell Land. No fossils had been obtained previously from so high a latitude. They were duly examined, classified, and reported upon in the *American Journal of Science*. Other collections included relics from Eskimo graves for the Smithsonian Institution and a collection of marine invertebrates made by some of the younger men, of which Hayes was proud. Radcliffe made a number of photographs. As Kane had referred to "useless daguerrotype plates," the photographs from the Hayes Expedition must have been the earliest from north Greenland and among the earliest from the Arctic.

We are permitted a glimpse of the business end of the preparation of Hayes's observations for publication in the *Smithsonian Contributions to Knowledge*. The manuscripts were sent by Hayes to Charles A. Schott of the Coast Survey, who had previously prepared Kane's data for publication. They

[41] Hayes to Bache, April 18, 24, and 28, 1862. Rhees MSS. Nos. 1477, 1478, and 1479. Quoted by permission of the Huntington Library.

must have been in Schott's hands for some time when, on November 28, 1864, the secretary of the Smithsonian Institution, Joseph Henry, wrote Schott a letter that probably confirmed oral arrangements, for two weeks later Schott returned the twenty-five volumes of data and four charts to Hayes.[42]

In the letter, Henry asked Schott to discuss and prepare for publication Dr. Hayes's scientific papers. As the Institution's authors were not ordinarily paid otherwise than by reputation received, he could not pay Schott the full value of his services. However, he would gladly pay as much as before—referring, no doubt, to Schott's reduction of Kane's observations—and if the Smithsonian's funds permitted, he would pay more at the time of settlement.[43]

Six months later, Schott billed the Smithsonian for $167.56, charging 75 cents an hour for his work. One-half of this total amount was for reduction of the astronomical observations.[44] In 1867, estimates were obtained for engraving the "Hayes Map." They ran $176.80 for copper plate and $122.50 for lithograph on stone.[45]

A few generalizations may be made about the first three American expeditions. They were begun under the impetus of the Franklin search, but geographical, geological, physical, and biological sciences played an ever increasing role. Government financing, insufficient of itself at any time, played a diminishing part, while popular support, called on to carry almost the entire burden, waned, and with the beginning of the Civil War, disappeared.

[42] Memorandum in Schott MSS (Library of Congress), VII.
[43] Schott MSS, VII.
[44] Copy of bill from Schott to Henry, June 3, 1865. Schott MSS, VI.
[45] Schott to Henry, May 11, 1867. Smithsonian Institution Archives (Smithsonian Institution, Washington, D. C.), Letters Received, 1867, II, 355.

III

The Hall Expeditions

|||||||||||||||||||||||||||||||||||||||||||

LIKE THE FIRST SERIES of expeditions, the impetus for Charles Francis Hall's three voyages to the north came from the search for Sir John Franklin. Again, as the hope of finding Franklin receded, Hall, like Kane and Hayes, was diverted to geographical discovery in the unknown regions toward the Pole, with scientific observations forming an important but secondary goal.

Sensation-seeking writers at times convey the impression that Hall left his blacksmith's forge to explore the wilds north of Hudson Bay. It is true that in his youth Hall had worked as a blacksmith, and that he had had no more than a common schooling. But it is also true that he went on to become a skilled seal engraver, and then made two efforts as a newspaper proprietor in Cincinnati, publishing first the *Occasional* and later the *Daily Penny Post*. Hence a more accurate portrait would be of a physically vigorous man, educated as well as most of his contemporaries, with an abundance of initiative and intellectual interests, and thoroughly steeped in Arctic literature.[1]

In 1854, Dr. John Rae had brought back from an overland expedition to the northern shores of the continent the first clues to the remains and fate of the Franklin Expedition. Captain (later Sir) Leopold McClintock then fitted up a

---

[1] Euphemia (Vale) Blake, *Arctic Experiences: Containing Capt. George E. Tyson's Wonderful Drift on the Ice Floe* . . . . 114–15. Henceforth referred to as *Arctic Experiences*.

private expedition and set forth in 1857 in the yacht *Fox* for the area around North Somerset Island and Boothia Felix.

As early as 1850, Hall had begun to study all the material on the Arctic that he could find.[2] Apparently Hall's first announced plan of campaign was formulated around 1859, when he had a petition printed, addressed to the British authorities, requesting that the *Resolute*, a Franklin search ship that had been abandoned and then had drifted through the Northwest Passage from west to east, be made available to him. Hardly had he obtained the signatures of Governor Salmon P. Chase, Senator George Pugh of Ohio, and the Mayor of Cincinnati, when McClintock returned with further news and relics of the Franklin Expedition. This news proved that 105 men had left the ships alive and had begun the march toward Hudson Bay.

With this evidence that survivors might be along the continental coast, Hall began to plan anew. On February 8, 1860, he issued a circular describing his revised plan, which was endorsed by thirty prominent Cincinnatians. Hall then set forth for Philadelphia, New York, and New London to seek information and gain support. His greatest financial encouragement came from the New London whaling firm of Williams and Haven and from Henry Grinnell of New York. He was given the opportunity to explain his plans before the American Geographical Society.[3]

Although Hall soon saw that he would be unable to have a vessel of his own, Williams and Haven promised him transportation. Henry Grinnell made one donation, and when it appeared that Hall would still be unable to purchase the supplies required, Grinnell came forward again, furnishing a total of $343. Cash donations totaled $980, most of which came in

[2] Joseph Everett Nourse (ed.), *Narrative of the Second Arctic Expedition Made by Charles F. Hall*, xiii. Henceforth referred to as *Narrative*.

[3] Charles Francis Hall, *Arctic Researches and Life among the Esquimaux*, xx–xxi, xxiii.

Map for Expeditions of Charles Francis Hall, 1860–62, 1864–69

Southern Baffin Island was the scene of Charles Francis Hall's first expedition. On two islands in Countess of Warwick Bay, Hall discovered the site where, two and a half centuries earlier, Martin Frobisher's colonists had collected iron pyrites in the belief that they were gold ore. Proceeding up Frobisher "Strait," Hall proved it to be a bay.

The broken lines on the mainland show the principal areas explored and roughly surveyed by Hall during his second expedition. He determined definitely that there were no survivors of Franklin's expedition living among the Eskimos. Although Parry and the Rosses had gone over much of the area a quarter-century earlier, Hall was able to add much detail to the map. Compare the map of Lieutenant Frederick Schwatka's expedition.

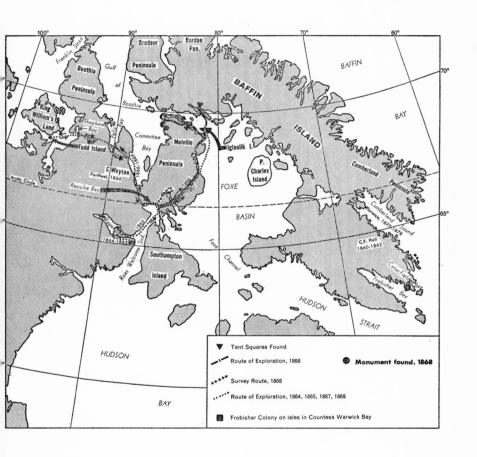

100°   **90°**   **80°**   **70°**   **60°**

Franklin Strait

Brodeur

Bordon Pan.

BAFFIN

70°

Boothia

Gulf

Peninsula

Peninsula

of

BAFFIN

King William's Land

Boothia

ISLAND

BAY

Shepherds Bay

Committee Bay

Melville

Igloolik I.

Todd Island

P. Charles Island

Cumberland

Peninsula

C. Weyton

Peninsula

Farthest, 1866

FOXE

Cumberland Sound

Florence, 1877-1878

Arctic Circle

Repulse Bay

65°

BASIN

C.F. Hall

1860-1862

Grinnell Bay

1864-1865

Foxe Channel

Frobisher Bay

Southampton

Island

HUDSON

Roes Welcome Snd

STRAIT

HUDSON

▼   Tent Squares Found

⊢—⊣   Route of Exploration, 1868

◉ **Monument found, 1868**

BAY

✦✦✦✦   Survey Route, 1868

••••••   Route of Exploration, 1864, 1865, 1867, 1869

▨   Frobisher Colony on isles in Countess Warwick Bay

amounts of $30. A number of individuals and firms contributed supplies and services.

Hall's scientific outfit consisted of two self-registering thermometers, a sextant, a pocket sextant, an artificial horizon, two pocket compasses, an azimuth compass, three ordinary thermometers, a spyglass, and a set of nautical almanacs.[4]

Hall proposed to start from what was then designated Northumberland Inlet, with an Eskimo interpreter and a party of Eskimos, cross the southern portion of Baffin Island, and travel north along the east side of Foxe Basin, uniting the discoveries of Foxe and Parry. Crossing the head of Foxe Basin, he would proceed to the eastern shore of Melville Peninsula and there decide whether to winter at the native village of Igloolik, to return by the same route, to return by following the eastern side of the Peninsula, or to press forward to his goal on Boothia Felix. During all this time, he would learn the Eskimo tongue and customs, the better to pursue his travels and inquiries.[5]

The whaler *George Henry*, carrying Hall, entered Frobisher "Strait," the first major indentation on the southeast coastline of Baffin Island, then continued north to a much smaller bay, which Hall named "Cyrus Field," after the Atlantic Cable promoter. There Hall's fine sailing whaleboat was put in the water. The party had been there but a few days when a storm came up and wrecked the boat and a neighboring vessel. Although Hall's supplies were safe, his movements were handicapped by the accident.

An Eskimo had sailed for Baffin Island on the same vessel with Hall. Through him, Hall expected to win his way with the Eskimos. The Eskimo died and was buried at sea, but Hall was fortunate in finding an Eskimo couple that had spent several years in England. Ebierbing and Tookoolito, called Joe and Hannah by the sailors, served Hall well and faithfully on all his voyages. Ebierbing later served with Frederick Schwatka

[4] *Ibid.* 585–87.
[5] *Ibid.*, xxiii–xxiv.

on his journey to find the Franklin records. Ebierbing exhibited unusual skill as a huntsman, while Tookoolito excelled as a translator.

Hall's first experience with Eskimo life was during a forty-three-day stretch ending February 21, 1861, when he made a trip to Cornelius Grinnell Bay, just to the north.

During the spring and summer, Hall made a number of trips south to Frobisher "Strait," visited with the Eskimos, and through Tookoolito learned the Eskimo legends regarding the Frobisher expeditions of 1576–78. The best accounts were amazingly accurate: " 'First two, then three, then many—very many vessels.' " Five whites had been captured by the Eskimos on the first voyage. All this agreed with English accounts. But rather than being killed, as Frobisher had supposed, the men were held captive for a time, then built a boat and sailed away. Hall later visited several sites where the Frobisher expeditions had left coal, fragments of brick, wood, and a trench which the natives believed had served as ways for a ship, but which Hall thought to be the Frobisher mine that had produced iron pyrites instead of gold. While on these excursions, Hall pushed to the end of Frobisher "Strait," adding to geographical knowledge by proving it a bay.

The *George Henry* too long delayed her departure in 1861, and in reduced circumstances, the crew prepared for a second winter. Hall had further opportunity to collect relics and legends of the Frobisher Expeditions. On August 9, 1862, the vessel raised anchor to sail for home, taking with her not only Hall but his two Eskimo helpers and their child.

If Hall had fallen short of his goal, he had taken the first great step. He knew something of the Eskimo language and had proved himself adaptable to Eskimo life. He had added materially to the information on the Eskimos, had located exactly the Frobisher colony site, and had corrected a false notion regarding the "strait."[6]

[6] The entire preceding narrative is taken from Hall's only detailed report, *Arctic Researches*.

As soon as Hall reached St. John's, Newfoundland, he sent a telegram to his sponsors, "I am bound for the States to *renew voyage* . . . ."[7] The succeeding months were filled with study of the Frobisher reports to clarify and substantiate his own findings, with lectures to support both his own and the Eskimo family, and with plans for a new expedition.

With the nation at war, Hall faced repeated discouragements. His first proposal to Mr. Grinnell and a representative of Williams and Haven was that they furnish $20,000 for the expedition, much if not all of which should be recouped by whaling. Hall should be delivered with three other white men, Ebierbing's family, and other Frobisher Bay Eskimos to the neighborhood of Repulse Bay on the eastern shore of Melville Peninsula. This plan was turned down as involving too much financial outlay. Hall then submitted a half-dozen other plans, all doomed to failure. A schooner was purchased and a yacht donated for the expedition, but they had to be disposed of when the prospects of actually sailing grew dim.[8]

Finally, in May, 1864, a new campaign was touched off by Hall's speech before the Long Island Historical Society. Leading public figures endorsed a drive for funds. Although the donors of supplies and equipment are listed, there is no record of financial contributions which one may compare with those of the first voyage.

Hall's little expedition sailed aboard the whaler *Monticello* on the first of July, 1864. It consisted of Hall and his two Eskimo friends, their child having died. Aboard was a whaleboat which Hall intended to use for exploring the western

---

[7] Nourse, *Narrative*, 4.

[8] *Ibid.*, 28–38. A letter from Hall to Bache, dated May 20, 1863, tells of one minor discouragement. His application to the Secretary of the Navy for a loan of instruments had been rejected. "I was hopeful my country would aid me to the moderate extent asked . . . . Our Government has been, at various times, very ready to give its aid to Englishmen that have come . . . to explore its Arctic borders, but when one of its own subjects solicits its favor for like objects it is refused." Rhees MSS, No. 1422. Quoted by permission of the Huntington Library.

From Kane's *Arctic Explorations:*
First Expedition
Sir John Franklin

U.S. Navy photograph
Lieut. Commander
Edwin De Haven, U.S.N.

U.S. Navy photograph
Elisha Kent Kane, M.D.

The Magnetic
Observatory

Reproduced from Kane's *Arctic Explorations: The Grinnell Expedition, I*
Midnight in September

shores of Foxe Basin. The scientific equipment was of the same nature as Hall had taken before. This time, however, he had a barometer along with him from the first. He seems to have been somewhat more generously supplied, also, with thermometers, compasses, chronometers, and the like. The Coast Survey supplied a dip circle, but this was broken before it could be used.[9]

Landing first at Depot Island, in the northwest corner of Hudson Bay, Hall later was carried by another whaler toward the Wager River, a point believed to be more suitable for beginning the journey to King William's Land. Meanwhile, he had gained one white recruit from a whaler. During the winter, Hall was able to pick up from neighboring Eskimos some positive information regarding the Franklin party. He also met Eskimos who could remember Parry's Expedition of 1821.

In April, Hall moved north toward the Wager, arriving there on the twenty-ninth of the month. He was then where he had originally intended to land the previous autumn. During the summer, Hall and his party moved north to Repulse Bay, which Hall mapped. The winter of 1865–66 was spent in this vicinity. Only on March 31, 1866, was he ready to press forward to King William's Land.

Progress from Repulse Bay was slow. Tookoolito's new baby was sick. Hall's medicines availed nothing. The old Eskimo superstitions swept into the mother's mind, and listening to the *angekok* (medicine man), she gave the child away. This sacrifice availed nothing, for shortly the child died. Although he could not do without them, Hall found the Eskimos a drag. The Eskimos turned aside for hunting or other things important to themselves, but foreign to Hall's purposes. Finally, he reached the vicinity of Committee Bay. Here he obtained some information and relics of the Franklin party. The Eskimos there showed themselves hostile, however, and Hall

[9] Nourse, *Narrative*, 85.

perforce cut his search short, returning by the route over which he had come.

In view of the uneasy peace between the Eskimo tribes, Hall decided that he must have white men when resuming his drive toward King William's Land. As these were not available, he busied himself in other occupations. Much of June and July, 1866, was taken up with surveying the northern side of Repulse Bay, a distance of something like one hundred miles.

During the spring of 1867, Hall was involved in controversies with the captains of the whalers in the neighborhood. He had counted on the use of the Eskimos' dog teams for his spring journey, and by furnishing tobacco and other articles, believed he had made his arrangements. The whalers, however, insisted that they had kept the natives in food during the winter, and must have their services with their dog teams. Thereupon, Hall set off north to the village of Igloolik and was successful in obtaining dogs there. Failing likewise in his hope of obtaining sailors for a summer expedition, he, at the end of the whaling season, hired five men for the space of a year, promising them $500 each.[10] He then busied his party with hunting to lay in supplies for the winter.

Reports of Hall's first journey to Committee Bay had stimulated new interest in the fate of Franklin's men, both in the United States and England.[11] Word of this renewed interest reached Hall by way of whalers newly arrived from the United States, and he was strengthened in his resolve to try once more to reach King William's Land. However, he was diverted from that purpose when word came of two stone buildings, such as might have been built by whites, located on the south side of Fury and Hecla Strait. Eskimos from Igloolik supplied the further information "that within the past three years they had seen near Ig-loo-lik two *white men,* 'one a tall man, the other considerably shorter.'" As the Eskimos' ac-

10 *Ibid.,* 325–26.
11 *Ibid.,* 327.

counts of Dr. Rae's two visits to Pelly Bay and the vicinity were accurate, this story led Hall to believe that two of Franklin's companions might have been alive as late as 1864.

Hall and a seaman, Frank Lailor, set out to investigate the report, taking Ebierbing, Tookoolito, and another Eskimo family. Some distance south of Fury and Hecla Strait, on the shore of Committee Bay, a monument was located near tent stones set in a square, unlike the typical Eskimo stone circle. Although the snow was drifted, the men dug around the monument, trying to locate a message, but in vain. They explored the south side of Fury and Hecla Strait on the return trip without finding any other positive evidence of the presence of whites. Nonetheless, the Eskimos' reports were quite convincing to Hall.

Now it was necessary to lay in provisions for the winter and to prepare for a new endeavor to reach King William's Land. Hall's men were not fired with his own zeal. Their year of service was almost up, and they were worried because no whaler had appeared on which they might leave. Rather than hunting with a will, in view of the possibility that they would need winter's food, they worked badly. When reprimanded, four of the men became surly and the burly leader showed a desire to settle it with fists. As he continued threatening, Hall shot him with a pistol. The man lingered for a fortnight before dying.

Inasmuch as Captain Tyson's account of Hall's third venture, the *Polaris* Expedition, raised a question regarding his capacity for leadership, this earlier incident is worth some attention. Hall's side of the story appears to be the only account preserved, but he made no effort to gloss over the reason for the discontented and uneasy state of mind of the men. It is quite likely that he stung them by ill-concealed scorn. A man in a hurry, he had no use for triflers. According to Hall's own account, he might have proceeded more diplomatically. In his defense, however, it must be said that he was completely at their mercy if he showed himself too weak to use the most drastic means.[12]

When vessels did arrive, the four remaining men left Hall, although his companion of the summer wavered until the last moment. In the autumn of 1868, Hall journeyed to Lyon Inlet, just north of Repulse Bay, and surveyed it. He had a notable list of explorations and surveys to report to the American Geographical Society for that one year alone. He considered his completion of the survey of the northwest side of Melville Peninsula the most important. Hall had also learned from the Eskimos of a rich whaling ground, later named Eclipse Sound, which he rightly considered a valuable piece of information.[13]

On March 23, 1869, Hall set out for King William's Land with "five Eskimo men, three women, and two children." On reaching the point on Committee Bay where they should swing across the isthmus to Pelly Bay, Hall found the Eskimos reluctant to go forward for fear of the Eskimos of that region. When within a day's march of Pelly Bay, the party looked to their arms, expecting trouble. There seems to have been latent hostility, but it failed to break out.

From the first Pelly Bay natives they met, they learned that the Eskimos had taken planking from the side of a Franklin ship, thereby hastening its sinking. They learned more concerning the remains of the white men on King William's Land. Pressing on across Boothia Peninsula, they found a community of Eskimos on Shepherd Bay. Here they gained more information; Hall bartered for some of the Franklin relics, which they had in abundance; and a map was drawn of King William's Land, showing where a number of the bodies might be found.

As the Repulse Bay Eskimos were anxious to return, Hall set out with one of his new friends and two of the Repulse Bay dwellers for an island off the near-by corner of King William's Land, where five bodies were said to rest. Snow made

[12] *Ibid.*, 359–61.
[13] *Ibid.*, 367.

the quest unavailing; on the shore of the large island, however, they found one skeleton, which they interred under a cairn.

Long conversations with the natives during these weeks led Hall to believe that he could account for perhaps seventy-nine of the missing men. Captain Crozier and another appeared to have survived the rest.

As the ice would soon be off the bays between them and Repulse Bay, Hall listened to the urgings of his Innuit companions and set out on the return trail. He still spared the time for another side trip, on which he found boat wreckage. The return home was easy; hunting was good; but Hall was sick for some days. The trip was concluded on June 20, 1869.

Since there were still two months before a whaler could be expected, Hall was soon busy planning his next expedition: one directed toward the North Pole. After that, he said, he might again try to explore King William's Land. Anxieties about the arrival of a vessel were relieved early in August with the appearance of the *Ansel Gibbs*. With Hall, Ebierbing, Tookoolito, and their adopted child aboard, the vessel departed on the twenty-eighth of August, reaching New Bedford on September 26, 1869.

In the face of exasperating delays, Hall had established beyond reasonable doubt that there were no Franklin survivors living among the Eskimos. He had improved the charts of Melville Peninsula, and had made a genuine contribution to geographical knowledge. He turned his Frobisher and Franklin relics and the Eskimo collection over to the Smithsonian Institution for the use of other scientists and explorers.[14]

Hall's luck with his astronomical and magnetic instruments was bad. Subject to extreme cold and the shocks of sledging, the sextants suffered, and in the last year his pocket chronometer stopped. His dip circle was broken the first summer. Nonetheless, he was faithful in his observations, and made a

[14] Smithsonian Institution, *Annual Report, 1871*, 32.

conscientious effort to report scientifically his geographical findings.[15]

Except during the year from April, 1867, to May, 1868, Hall faithfully kept his meteorological notes, making his records three times daily. Unfortunately his barometric record ends on March 31, 1866. He recorded his position, temperature, minimum temperature for the day, wind direction and strength, state of the sky, and snow.[16]

Hall's greatest contribution to Arctic research lay in none of these, nor was it in the extensive ethnological data embodied in his books. It was the demonstration that men might live in the Arctic, adapting themselves to the ways of the Innuit and to the necessities of climate and diet. Thus it was verified that white men, if they would, could live in the Arctic with a minimum of the accoutrements of civilization. That the lesson was learned by only a few was demonstrated by Vilhjalmur Stefansson, who expounded the same principle fifty years later in his classic volume, *The Friendly Arctic.*

As early as 1863, Hall wrote to a friend in St. Louis that his third expedition would be, *Deus volens,* "to the northern axis of the great globe." In the journals of his second trip he referred repeatedly to that goal. Back in the United States in 1869, he was soon in the thick of promoting the expedition.[17]

Writing to Henry Grinnell and J. Carson Brevoort, two of his principal sponsors, he named his objectives as "1st, geographical discovery; 2d, science, 3d, commerce." He might locate the grounds at the south end of Admiralty Inlet, where the Eskimos had caught as many as five whales a day. As other whaling grounds were failing, this should be a significant addition to the industry.[18]

[15] See "Notes on the Observations" on astronomy, developed under the supervision of R. W. D. Bryan, Nourse, *Narrative,* 451–52.

[16] Nourse, *Narrative.* Appendix II, "Hall's Meteorological Journal, 1864–69," 479–550. See also page 320 regarding the lapse in his journals.

[17] Adm. Charles Henry Davis (ed.), *Narrative of the North Polar Expedition. U. S. Ship Polaris,* [17]–21. Henceforth referred to as *North Polar Expedition.*

Supported by memorials from "distinguished sources in various parts of the country," Hall asked $100,000 from Congress to equip his expedition. In the House of Representatives the amount was cut to $50,000. The pay of government personnel assigned, and the use of stock items on hand, appears to have been in addition to the appropriation. The bill was approved by President Grant on July 12, 1870.[19]

The appointment of a leader for the expedition was left in the hands of the President. Hayes had been a rival in seeking an appropriation. Now Henry Grinnell wrote Hall, "When you get the appointment of the command of the Polar Expedition you may yet have some troubles. That Dr. H—— has made the application for the command."[20] In the same group of manuscripts in the National Archives are two on behalf of Hall: one from residents of New York, signed by Grinnell, J. Carson Brevoort, Alexander Hamilton, Jr., and others. The second, from Washington, D. C., was signed by John Sherman, O. P. Morton, James A. Garfield, and lesser dignitaries. Pasted to the second petition is an endorsement signed by many members of Congress. It says, "We most earnestly recommend this—It was undoubtedly the design of Congress in authorizing the appropriation that Capt. Hall should be appointed." And in due time, President Grant did appoint him.[21]

By the terms of the appropriations act, the National Academy of Sciences was to specify the scientific program. As president of the National Academy of Sciences, Joseph Henry was in charge of preparing scientific instructions for the expedition. He entertained no illusions about the role of physical observations if geographical discoveries were to be made. In the letter conveying the "Scientific Instructions" drawn up by the Academy, Henry wrote:

[18] *Ibid.*, 40–41.
[19] *Ibid.*, 26–28.
[20] Dated 11 July, 1870. Miscellaneous Files, Interior Unit, National Archives.
[21] See also O. P. Morton to President Grant, July 11, 1870, in *ibid.*

The appropriation for this Expedition was granted by Congress principally on account of the representations of Captain Hall and his friends as to the possibility of improving our knowledge of the geography of the regions beyond the eightieth degree of north latitude, and more especially of reaching the Pole. [As Captain Hall had selected his personnel on the basis of Arctic rather than scientific experience,] It is evident . . . that the Expedition, except in its relation to geographical discovery, is not of a scientific character [either in the mind of Hall or of Congress].[22]

Despite Henry's skepticism, a full and detailed scheme was drawn up, filled with sage advice. Among the leaders of American science who contributed plans were Simon Newcomb on astronomy, Joseph Henry on meteorology, S. F. Baird on natural history, and Louis Agassiz on glaciers. Accuracy in the observations and in keeping the records was stressed.[23]

The scientific chief and surgeon was Dr. Emil Bessels. He was a graduate of Heidelberg, had made scientific observations aboard the German sealer *Albert* in 1869, and was described by Joseph Henry as an "accomplished physicist and naturalist."[24] The astronomer was a young graduate of Lafayette College, R. W. D. Bryan, who prepared himself by additional study in Washington. "He seems to have enjoyed in an eminent degree the confidence and esteem of all his associates." A meteorological observer, Frederick Meyer, was assigned by the United States Signal Service.[25]

The instrumentation of the expedition was quite complete, thanks to Dr. Bessels' industry. The Navy Department and the Coast Survey supplied the astronomical instruments. Dr. Hayes loaned a pendulum apparatus. A unifilar magnetometer

---

[22] Davis, *North Polar Expedition,* 637.

[23] *Ibid.,* 639–40. These instructions were printed as a pamphlet, but are more readily available in *ibid.,* 637–62, or in Blake, *Arctic Experiences,* 431–52. Or see Smithsonian Institution, *Annual Report,* 1871, 361–87.

[24] Davis, *North Polar Expedition,* 32, 210, 638.

[25] *Ibid.,* 210–11.

and dip needle were taken. Bessels said, "We were richly supplied with meteorological instruments," then proceeded to name a long list, including black-bulb thermometers *in vacuo* for solar radiation and a concave mirror 21.67 inches in diameter for terrestrial radiation, two spectroscopes, and an electrometer.

> We had also a plane table . . . a steel standard yard in case, photographic apparatus, microscope, dragnets, reagents, glassware, copper canisters for the preservation of plants and animals in alcohol, geological instruments, and other things too numerous to list.[26]

Hall chose a veteran of twenty-five years' whaling, S. O. Buddington, for actual command of the vessel. According to George Tyson, Hall first offered him the command, but at the time Tyson was unable to accept. Later, when he was available, Hall secured for him a billet as assistant navigator.

The vessel selected was a seagoing naval tug rated 387 tons before additional equipment was placed aboard. She was thoroughly overhauled, equipped, and protective planking added, at a cost of $90,000. In honor of her new duties, she was renamed the *Polaris,* and was considered well adapted for Arctic duty.[27]

The orders to Hall specified the route to be taken along the west coast of Greenland and instructed him regarding the movements of his escort and supply ships. Upon reaching Cape Dudley Digges, he was to "make all possible progress, with vessels, boats, and sledges, toward the North Pole," using his own judgment as to the route and winter quarters.[28]

The *Polaris* bade farewell to her escort, the *U.S.S. Congress,* at Godhavn. She stopped at Upernavik, and thence found

[26] Emil Bessels, *Die Amerikanische Nordpol-Expedition,* 10–12. Hereafter cited as *Nordpol-Expedition.*

[27] Joseph Everett Nourse, *American Explorations in the Ice Zones,* 3d ed., 270. Hereafter cited as *American Explorations.*

[28] Davis, *North Polar Expedition,* 31; Nourse, *American Explorations,* 271 n.

Map of the Polaris *Expedition, 1871–73; and*
Greely Expedition, 1881–84

Charles Francis Hall's last expedition, in the steamer *Polaris*, carried him much farther than Kane's vessel had been able to penetrate. Hayes, however, had covered almost the same distance afoot. Had Hall not died, from his base at Polaris Bay he might have anticipated the members of the British Nares Expedition in surveying the northern coasts of Greenland and Ellesmere Island. To Hall was given only the privilege of standing on the far side of Newman Bay, and, like Moses, view from afar the land he might not enter.

The Greely Expedition, from its base at Fort Conger, achieved substantially more. Lockwood Island was reached, and Cape Washington seen in the distance. The geography of the interior of northern Ellesmere Island was determined.

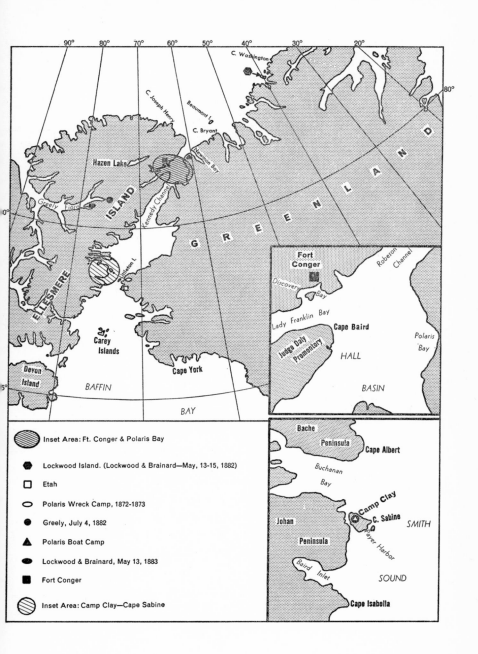

Inset Area: Ft. Conger & Polaris Bay

Lockwood Island. (Lockwood & Brainard—May, 13-15, 1882)

Etah

Polaris Wreck Camp, 1872-1873

Greely, July 4, 1882

Polaris Boat Camp

Lockwood & Brainard, May 13, 1883

Fort Conger

Inset Area: Camp Clay—Cape Sabine

clear sailing until she encountered the first ice field off Hakluyt Island. This was considered a very fortunate run. They were in open water again on August 27, 1871. That evening they passed Kane's winter quarters. At 9:00 A. M., August 29, the ice became thicker, and a fog settled in. They drifted a bit south before the fog cleared, and got noon sights; at 6:00 o'clock next morning, they turned back southward. Their figures, as revised by the United States Hydrographic Office, placed them in 82° north latitude, a new "highest north."[29]

Here occurs a variation in the two principal accounts: Tyson's and the official account drawn up from all the journals by Admiral Davis. All agree that Buddington did not want to press forward, although Tyson and the mate, Mr. Chester, were in favor of it.[30] After making an attempt to cross to the west of the channel, which was named after the Secretary of the Navy Robeson, the ship was berthed in what amounted to an open roadstead, sheltered from the ice drift only by a huge grounded iceberg.

With winter quarters chosen, the scientific staff began to busy itself. Bryan and Meyer made local surveys. On September 30, the tide gauge was set up in the hole kept open beside the ship to fight fires. Meteorological observations were begun hourly on November 4. They included temperature, humidity, pressure, wind velocity, static electricity, ozone, solar and dry [earth?] radiation. An observatory building was constructed of nonmagnetic materials, but the astronomical instruments crowded out the magnetic instruments, which were set up in two snow igloos. Much of the value of the magnetic observations must have been lost, for they were not started until January 26, and were conducted then but for a few months. A pendulum was set up with great care and observations made

29 Davis, *North Polar Expedition,* 75–86.
30 Blake, *Arctic Experiences,* 149–50, 470 for Mr. Chester's testimony; Davis, *North Polar Expedition,* 92-105. Cf. Bessels, *Nordpol-Expedition,* 127–30.

during January, 1872. On February 4, simultaneous observations were made of the magnetometer and of the aurora, Bessels, outside the observatory, pulling a string to warn Bryan to read the magnetometer.[31]

Meanwhile Hall had set out on October 10 with the first mate, Chester, and the two Eskimo stalwarts of the American explorers: Joe Ebierbing and Hans Hendrik. They crossed northeasterly over the neck of Cape Lupton to Newman's Bay, then swinging northwest, they crossed the bay to its northern cape and climbed the nearest high mountain for a look to the north over Robeson Channel. Hall reported, "On our way, grass and various species of flowering plants were seen, and they abounded even up to the mountain's top."[32]

On October 24, Hall returned to the *Polaris;* on November 8, he was dead. Several of the crew knew that Hall thought he had been poisoned. The naval board of inquiry brought out the ill-concealed hostility of Buddington and Bessels toward Hall.[33] The following account is an abstract of Admiral Davis' reconstruction of the circumstances.

Hall returned from the sledge trip and

> . . . had not been in the cabin more than a half-hour when John Herron, the steward, brought him a cup of coffee. He drank it, and was immediately taken very sick . . . . Dr. Bessels, who was at the observatory, was summoned, and after examination expressed grave fears that the sickness might be fatal. At 8 p. m., he announced that Captain Hall's left side was paralyzed, and that he had had an apoplectic attack.

The next day Hall felt better. But that evening he again became sick at his stomach. He grew worse from October 27 to 29, and his mind began to wander. "He refused all medical aid and all nourishment, under the impression that an attempt might be made to poison him." On the first and second of

[31] Davis, *North Polar Expedition,* 120, 136, 218–19, 289, 276–79, 297.
[32] *Ibid.,* 147–70. Quoted, 157.
[33] Blake, *Arctic Experiences,* 469–77.

November, he appeared well, though weak, and would accept food only from Hannah. On the third, he was rational again. On the fourth, "He ate a large quantity of cooked seal-meat, contrary to the doctor's directions." He got up on the sixth and worked on his records, but became ill that night, sank into a coma the next day, and expired early on the eighth of November.[34]

When the first group of *Polaris* survivors was rescued, the board of inquiry, presided over by Secretary of the Navy Robeson, decided, despite Tyson's suspicions, that Hall had died a natural death. Later the surgeons general of the army and navy heard Dr. Bessels and the accounts of other survivors and reported that they were "conclusively of the opinion that Captain Hall died from natural causes—viz., apoplexy—and that treatment of the case by Dr. Bessels was the best practicable under the circumstances."[35]

With Hall's death, Tyson reported, the discipline went to pieces. Various witnesses quoted Buddington and Bessels as expressing relief at Hall's death.[36] Buddington apparently felt that they could now return to civilization without being driven north on a fool's errand.

Bessels loyally sought to carry out the scientific objectives of the expedition. On February 21, 1872, he submitted a plan to Buddington, now the commanding officer, calling for explorations in four directions: one inland, a second to the south to verify the location of Kane's Cape Constitution; following those explorations, a boat trip north; and finally, a sledge trip to resurvey Hayes's work on Grinnell Land. As the ice broke about this time, Bessels suggested that the *Polaris* might sail along the west coast of the channel if an opportunity presented

[34] Davis, *North Polar Expedition*, 173–75. Bessels said that Hall ate too much seal meat, drank too much red wine, and died. The drinking is not in keeping with Hall's efforts to keep liquor off the ship. See Bessels, *Nordpol-Expedition*, 199–201.

[35] Davis, *North Polar Expedition*, 182–83, 602–603.

[36] Blake, *Arctic Experiences*, 469–77.

itself. Buddington approved the immediate trips inland and to Cape Constitution. He said he intended to lead the boat trip north himself.[37]

On March 27, Bessels, Bryan, and Ebierbing set off for Cape Constitution. While Bessels stayed alone for a day geologizing, the others returned to the ship for Hans and another sled, then proceeded south. They failed to reach Cape Constitution, although they identified it in the distance. It turned out by their reckoning to be considerably south of the latitude given by Kane's party. William Morton, the original discoverer (see page 23), agreed on its identity. Kane and Sonntag had shown him how to make observations, but he had been by no means expert when he determined the position of the Cape.[38]

Two sallies were made toward the north. The first party, under Meyer, went by sledge, reaching latitude 82° 09' (Hydrographic Office corrections applied?). They returned to the ship on May 14. On June 7, a party, not under Buddington, but under Chester, set out. Its boat was wrecked; returning, the men got a canvas boat and set out again, but had made little progress when they were ordered back by Buddington.[39]

Late in the season the *Polaris* was freed from the ice and started south. She was leaking, and her coal supplies were low. She was among floes on a snowy and windy night when the engineer came running and said to Tyson that the vessel had a leak aft, and the water was gaining on the pumps. "I then walked over toward my room on the starboard side," said Tyson.

> Behind the galley I saw Sailing-master Buddington and told him what the engineer said. He threw up his arms and yelled out to 'throw every thing on the ice!' Instantly every thing was confusion, the men seizing every thing indiscriminately, and throwing

[37] Davis, *North Polar Expedition*, 305–08, 314.
[38] *Ibid.*, 340–51. For Morton's testimony, see U. S. Navy Department, Secretary, *Report*, 1873, 512. Henceforth referred to as SecNav, *Report*, 1873.
[39] Davis, *North Polar Expedition*, 378, 386–87, 394.

it overboard . . . . I found that the engineer's statement was a false alarm. The vessel was strong, and no additional leak had been made; but as the ice lifted her up, the little water in the hold was thrown over, and it made a rush, and he thought that a new leak had been sprung.

Tyson went out on the ice to restore the provisions to the ship, but at that moment the ice broke apart. Tyson and eighteen others were left on two floes, and the ship slipped out of sight in a moment.[40]

Peter Johnson, a fireman who had been working the pumps, reported, "We heard a crash, and looking out of the window, we saw the ice coming in on us, and told Captain Buddington." As the vessel stayed afloat for some time, it appears that the men thought they were about to be rammed and sunk. Note that they saw the ice through a window. Buddington, probably feeling low, had admittedly been drinking. When word of the leak came, he failed to investigate as Tyson had done; instead, he panicked.[41]

The groups on the ice floes were able to combine next morning and later possessed themselves of two boats. They were fairly well supplied with provisions and ammunition. The drift that followed—from near Littleton Island in Smith Sound, south through Baffin Bay and along the coast of Labrador, until the group was rescued by the sealer *Tigress* on April 30, in 53° 35′ north latitude—was so remarkable as scarce to gain credence at first among captains experienced in that region.

Meanwhile, the party aboard the ship managed to beach her on the mainland about two and one-half miles from Littleton Island, where they built themselves a hut and prepared to spend the winter. Peary wrote of this location:

Nowhere along the coast of Greenland have I seen such a desolate strip of shore as the site of Polaris House and its neighbor-

[40] Blake, *Arctic Experiences,* 197–98.
[41] Davis, *North Polar Expedition,* 429. SecNav, *Report, 1873,* 375.

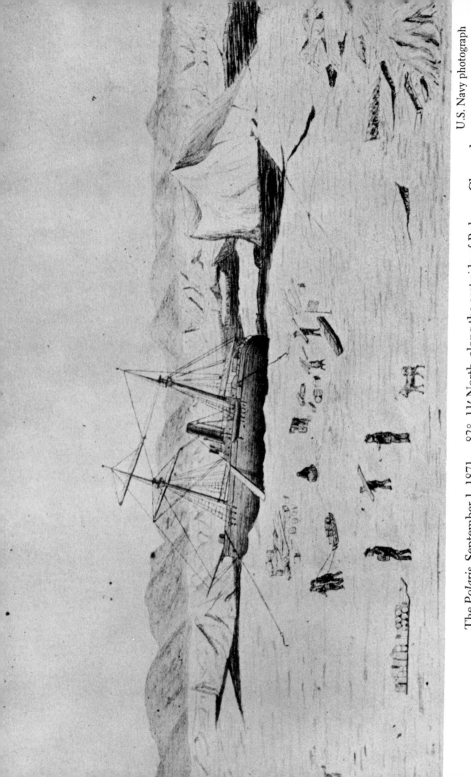

The *Polaris*, September 1, 1871 — 82°, 11' North, along the east side of Robeson Channel.

U.S. Navy photograph

From *Hall's Second Arctic Expedition*
Charles Francis Hall

U.S. Navy photograph
George W. De Long

U.S. Navy photograph
Commander W. S. Schley, U.S.N.

hood, and the first glance shows that the selection of the site was not a matter of choice, but of the direst necessity.[42]

With what instruments they had, a round of observations was begun. Meteorological observations were renewed on November 1. The transit instrument was set up under the hatch cover. The magnetic instruments had been lost, and the earth-radiation mirror damaged. An actinometer was fabricated, however, using white fox pelts in place of swan's down and white lead in place of polished silver. Mauch took the observations from 4:00 P. M. to midnight; Bessels, the remainder.[43]

Twice Bessels set out for the north, nominally to explore Humboldt Glacier. It turned out that his real intention was to go to the *Polaris'* old base, lay in supplies, and go as far north as possible.[44] In May, 1873, Bryan went to Kane's old camp to tie in his surveys with their own.[45]

On June 3, 1873, the party set forth in two small scows that had been built of the ship's timbers. Twenty days later they were sighted by the *Ravenscraig* of Kircaldy, Scotland. From the *Ravenscraig* they were passed along to other vessels, all eventually reaching home in safety. Bessels was taken by way of Pond's Inlet, where he was able to study the Baffin Island Eskimos.

So far as the scientific objectives of the journey were concerned, the loss of most of the observations and collections on the ice floe was a supreme tragedy. Much of the material was placed there by Bryan and Meyer after mutual consultation about the place of greatest safety. The original floe was broken up during the night; Meyer otherwise would probably have salvaged the records. Some records Bessels wrapped up in a blanket, determined to keep them beside him when he aban-

[42] Robert Edwin Peary, *Northward over the Great Ice*, II, 55.
[43] Bessels, *Nordpol-Expedition*, 339–40.
[44] *Ibid.*, 377 ff.
[45] Davis, *North Polar Expedition*, 487–89.

doned ship. These remained aboard and were saved, although a portion of them was lost on Bessels' way back from Great Britain, to which some of the party were carried by a rescue vessel.[46]

Just before leaving Polaris House, Hall's Arctic library the two logbooks of the *Polaris*, and some of the instruments were placed in a trunk and cached about one-fourth of a mile from the house. The *Tigress* rescue party failed to find these, but did find one mutilated logbook and other books in various stages of disrepair. The *Polaris'* men reported that they had copied all records for easier transport.[47]

A particular mystery surrounded the loss of Captain Hall's personal papers. A portable mahogany writing box of his with one sheet inside it was found by the ice-floe party. Meyer, a member of that party, testified on June 6, 1873, that he had been aboard five minutes before the ice broke and saw Hall's tin box with the papers lying beside it in the cabin. Bessels testified that he had seen "a large Japan tin box belonging to Captain Hall, and containing his papers, which was put overboard . . ."—by whom, he did not say. Buddington claimed no knowledge of the matter. Yet Tyson, examining the mutilated logbook picked up by the *Tigress*, noted the memorandum, "*Captain Hall's papers thrown overboard today.*"[48]

Two volumes containing scientific results of the expedition were written by Emil Bessels. *Scientific Results of the United States Arctic Expedition Steamer* Polaris, C. F. Hall Commanding. Vol. I: *Physical Observations*, was published in 1876, but suppressed for errors and apparently never reissued.[49] In 1880, Bessels appealed to the secretary of the Smithsonian In-

---

[46] *Ibid.*, 430–33; SecNav, *Report*, 1873, 476–77, 532–33, 610–11; portions of the testimony printed in the *Report* are also available in Blake, *Arctic Experiences*, 473, 478.

[47] Davis, *North Polar Expedition*, 499, 586; Blake, *Arctic Experiences*, 372–73; SecNav. *Report*, 1873, 476–77.

[48] SecNav, *Report*, 1873, 333, 471–72, 532–33; Blake, *Arctic Experiences*, 372–73.

stitution, Spencer Fullerton Baird, for assistance in obtaining the funds necessary for completing the remainder of the *Report*. Eight thousand dollars was appropriated in the Deficiency Act of June 16, 1880, for completion of the work, and funds were provided to reimburse Bessels for money advanced to engravers, lithographers, etc.[50] The writer has found no evidence that the balance of the work was ever published.

In 1879, Bessels' *Die Amerikanische Nordpol Expedition* appeared in Leipzig. Pages 527–647 consist of an appendix of scientific results. This volume is now rare, but has been more readily available to German students than much of the material produced by American expeditions.

If this expedition fell short of Hall's high goals, it yet contained within it the inspiration for other Arctic explorations. After the rescue of the ice-floe party, the United States Navy dispatched the *U.S.S. Juniata* to seek Buddington's group. Aboard her was Lieutenant George Washington De Long. His imagination was kindled, with the result that the *U.S.S. Jeannette* sailed under his command on her notable voyage along the Siberian Arctic coast.

Representing the United States Signal Corps on the *Polaris* board of inquiry was Captain Henry W. Howgate. He, like De Long, became an ardent advocate of Arctic explorations. And Adolphus Washington Greely became involved in Arctic research through the activities of Howgate, his senior in the Signal Corps. Thus, even in failure, the *Polaris* Expedition prepared the way for future accomplishments.

[49] Adolphus Washington Greely, *Report on the Proceedings of the United States Expedition to Lady Franklin Bay . . . .* 49 Cong., 1 sess., *House Misc. Doc.* 393 (Cong. Ser. 2428), II, 465. A copy of the suppressed volume is available in the library of the National Archives.

[50] William J. Rhees, *The Smithsonian Institution, Documents Relative to its Origin and History, 1835–1899. Smithsonian Misc. Collections*, XLII–XLIII.

IV

The Voyage of the Jeannette

||||||||||||||||||||||||||||||||||||||||||||||||

WHEN THE SURVIVORS of the *Polaris* Expedition's
ice-floe experience reached civilization, the Navy Department
ordered the *U.S.S. Juniata* to search for Buddington and his
party, at the same time engaging the *Tigress* to penetrate the
upper reaches of Melville Bay, where drift ice would imperil
the thin-hulled *Juniata*. As the *Tigress* was some days behind
the *Juniata*, Lieutenant De Long volunteered to take the
Juniata's steam launch and search the coast to Northumberland Island. The *Tigress* might then proceed directly to that
point.

With a crew of eight other volunteers, De Long set out on
a thousand-mile journey in his thirty-two-foot coal burner. As
they started on August 2, they should have had good weather.
Instead, they ran into squalls and storms and had to turn back
when within sight of Cape York. Captain, later Admiral, Sir
Alfred H. Markham "considered this boat journey as one of
the most hazardous and venturesome undertakings he had
ever known."[1]

The dangers and discomforts of that trip seem but to have
stimulated De Long's zeal. After reaching New York, he

[1] Correspondence of D. L. Braine, Commander, U.S.N., Commanding
Officer of *U.S.S. Juniata*, orders to De Long, and De Long's report in SecNav
Report, 1873, 200, 223–24, 228–31, George Washington De Long, *The
Voyage of the* Jeannette (ed. by Emma De Long), I, 12–31. Quoted, 32.
Hereafter cited as *Voyage*.

addressed a letter to the Navy Department volunteering his services for another Arctic expedition. In the words of his wife,

> His indomitable energy, strong will, and passion for overcoming obstacles, all tended to develop in him that Arctic fever, which so often fastens upon one who has once known the excitement, difficulty, and peril of northern exploration.[2]

De Long had made the acquaintance of Henry Grinnell while the *Juniata* was preparing for her voyage. Grinnell had given him such information as he had at hand, and loaned De Long charts that had been used by the expeditions he had helped finance. Upon De Long's return, Grinnell invited a group of Arctic explorers to dinner.

At this dinner Mr. De Long asked Mr. Grinnell:

> "Why do you not fit out an expedition to the North Pole? I should like much to take command of one and solve the problem. You have tried so often you ought to try again."
>
> "I am too old a man," replied Mr. Grinnell, "and I have done my share. Younger men must take the matter in hand. There is Mr. James Gordon Bennett. He is the man to undertake such an expedition. You should apply to him."[3]

De Long accepted the suggestion and entered into correspondence with Bennett, who as proprietor of the New York *Herald* had achieved fame by sponsoring Stanley's search in Africa for Livingstone, successfully completed two years earlier. De Long impressed Bennett favorably, but unsettled relations between the United States and Spain stayed Bennett's hand for three years, and only in November, 1876, did they begin to lay definite plans.

The first major step was to locate a suitable ship. The vessel purchased was the *Pandora,* a "bark-rigged steam yacht," which had carried her former owner, Captain Allan Young, into

---

[2] De Long, *Voyage,* I, 37.

[3] *Ibid.,* I, 42–43. Except as specified to the contrary, the following account is drawn from De Long's journals as published in *The Voyage of the* Jeannette.

Arctic waters on several cruises. One of her most desirable features was a two-hundred-horsepower engine.[4]

Congress passed a bill authorizing American registry and the detailing of naval officers to duty aboard her. Another act authorized the Secretary of the Navy to accept the ship, now renamed the *Jeannette*, "for the use of a North Polar Expedition by way of Behring Strait," to fit her, using "any material he may have on hand proper for the purposes of an Arctic voyage," to enlist a crew for " 'special service,' " and to pay the crew temporarily from navy funds, which should later be refunded by James Gordon Bennett. Although the facilities of the navy were to be used and the vessel was to be under naval orders and discipline, Bennett was to meet all costs, the act specifying " 'that the Government of the United States is not to be held liable for any expenditure assumed, or to be incurred on account of said expedition.' "[5]

To hear of the generous co-operation given De Long by both Bennett and the Navy Department must have gladdened the heart of Dr. Hayes, if it did not make him a trifle envious. Such a contrast it was from the previous decades when he and Hall had eaten their hearts out, lecturing and beseeching funds! De Long wrote Bennett quoting the Secretary of the Navy's assurances that De Long should have everything arranged according to his own desires. He should have all the powers of "admirals commanding fleets." He should be accountable to the Secretary directly. "This expedition must succeed," the Secretary had written, "and you shall be prepared and forearmed against all disaffection, insubordination, and disaster."[6] De Long wrote a little later to Lieutenant Danen-

[4] Length, 142 feet; beam, 25 feet; draft, laden with Arctic outfit (Sir John Allan Young's experience), 13 feet; builders' tonnage, 420 tons; 200 horsepower; ". . . barque rigged, rolling topsails and trices up her screw; steams or sails about six knots, and is a neat, tidy little ship," Nourse, *American Explorations*, 370–72.

[5] De Long, *Voyage*, I, 54.

[6] *Ibid.*, I, 56.

hower, his navigator, who was supervising the outfitting at Mare Island Navy Yard, "It is decided by the Secretary of the Navy that all materials are to be given by the yard, and merely the labor paid for." Although she had just been reconditioned in England, almost $100,000 was spent on the *Jeannette* at Mare Island Navy Yard.[7]

Bennett was no less generous. His final instructions, cabled from Europe, contained this heartening message:

> . . . he may push forward to north next spring with perfect confidence, for if ice-bound, I shall spare neither money nor influence to follow him up and send assistance . . . . Should De Long not return next year, or in fact never, the widows of men belonging to expedition will be protected by me. Should like him to tell this to his men upon their departure.[8]

At Mare Island no pains had been spared to put the *Jeannette* into first-class shape for her coming ordeals. The bow was filled in solid to stand the shock of ramming. Knees and braces were placed amidships to withstand the pinching of the ice. New boilers were installed; the machinery was overhauled; new pumps added, and new sails and rigging installed. The bunker capacity was increased 50 per cent, but even then had space for but 132 tons. A deckhouse for the winter was built, then disassembled and stored against the time it was needed. "Everything that the navy yard had on hand was placed at our disposal," De Long wrote.[9]

Scientific observations were given a prominent place in the plans. Edward Ellsberg has said,

> . . . no expedition which had ever gone north before had a stronger ship, a better-equipped vessel, nor a more competent set of officers and men for the purpose, and probably few since. Every scientific instrument then available was carried, and no

[7] *Ibid.*, I, 57; Nourse, *American Explorations*, 371.
[8] De Long, *Voyage*, I, 73–74.
[9] *Ibid.*, I, 60–61.

Arctic commander ever had a keener scent for scientific truth than De Long.[10]

De Long was jubilant. He wrote Bennett:

> We have every appliance for all kinds of scientific experiments. Our outfit is simply perfect, whether for ice navigation, astronomical work, magnetic work, gravity experiments, or collections of Natural History.[11]

The scientific personnel of the party was not without experience. Jerome J. Collins, who was to report the trip for Bennett's New York *Herald*, if no thorough scientist, had received international attention as director of the *Herald's* meteorological bureau for the storm-warning service developed for ships. He received additional instruction at the Smithsonian. Yet his laboratory experience had been so limited that he failed to compare his instruments with standards before departure.[12] Raymond Newcomb, the naturalist, although a youth, had been natural history collector on a summer cruise. Baird, the secretary of the Smithsonian, was familiar with his work, and had recommended him. The surgeon, James M. Ambler, probably had better formal training than the first two, and the report on the geology of Bennett Island is from his hand. Astronomical work would have been the responsibility of the navigator, Lieutenant Danenhower, but for his developing an incapacitating eye infection. To the engineer, George W. Melville, De Long assigned the duty of assembling all hydrographic information on polar currents available in the ship's fine Arctic library.[13]

Meanwhile, another problem had arisen, and De Long was

[10] Edward Ellsberg, "The Drift of the Jeannette . . . ," American Philosophical Society, *Proceedings*, Vol. LXXXII (1940), 890.

[11] De Long, *Voyage*, I, 61.

[12] 48 Cong., 1 sess., *House Misc. Doc. 66* (Cong. Ser. 2243), 838–40, 959–60. For further details, see De Long-Baird and Newcomb-Baird Correspondence in Smithsonian Archives, *Letters Received*, 1879.

[13] George W. Melville, "The Story of the Drift Casks," *Munsey's Magazine*, Vol. XXVII (1902), 366–67.

instructed to give it his immediate attention. Professor Nils Adolf Erik Nordenskjöld in the *Vega* had been about two years under way attempting the Northeast Passage from Europe to the Pacific. De Long's orders from the Secretary of the Navy, R. W. Thompson, gave priority to locating Nordenskjöld. He should "make diligent inquiry," and if he should find "good and sufficient reasons" for believing that Nordenskjöld was safe, he should then proceed on his "voyage toward the North Pole."[14]

Reports had been heard before leaving San Francisco that Nordenskjöld had escaped from the Arctic pack, but De Long stopped at several places along the Siberian coast until he was sure that a vessel which had wintered along the eastern Arctic coast and passed into Bering Sea safely was indeed the *Vega*. He then turned toward the mysterious land that had been seen from afar.

The court of inquiry that later reviewed the causes of the *Jeannette* disaster cited the delay caused by the search for the *Vega* as one of the factors contributing to the *Jeannette's* being so soon trapped in the ice. However, the court did not indicate that it considered those orders inconsistent with the main object of the expedition; neither did it blame De Long for pushing forward. In view of his expectation that he might reach a continental coast north of Wrangel Island and spend the winter exploring by sledges, the court deemed his action appropriate to "the high qualities necessary for an explorer."[15]

De Long's plan to reach the Pole was based on two theories: one—that of Captain Silas Bent, a naval hydrographer—that a branch of the warm Kuro Siwo or Japan Current swept up through Bering Strait and cut a path to the Pole; the other— that of the German geographer, August Heinrich Petermann —which pictured an extension of Greenland to Wrangel Land, like a scarf laid over the top of the planet. Emil Bessels testi-

[14] De Long, *Voyage*, I, 71.
[15] *Ibid.*, II, 893.

Map of Expedition of De Long
in the Jeannette, 1879–81

This map shows only the critical portion of the voyage—that during which the *Jeannette* was trapped in the ice. De Long had set out to test the theory that land stretched from Wrangel Island (as he proved it to be) to Greenland. Had the theory been correct, there would have been relatively little danger in working through the ice.

A detailed track chart would show a number of minor gyrations of the ship, which are omitted here.

One of the difficulties encountered by the survivors of the expedition was that a number of settlements shown on their maps turned out to be a few abandoned huts. Only on reaching Bulun did they find a genuine settlement.

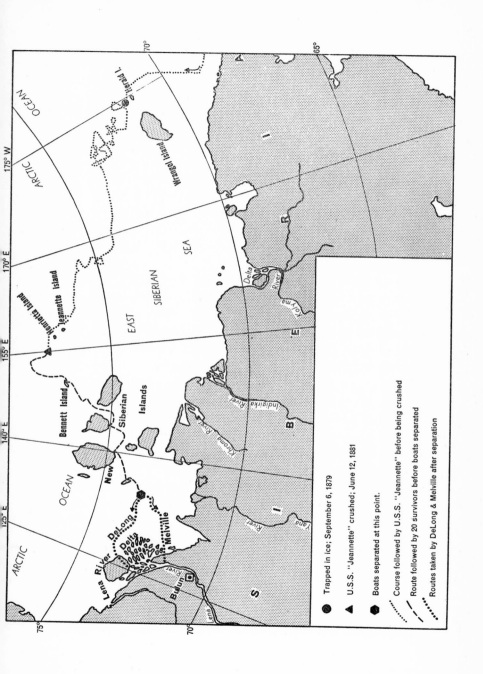

ARCTIC OCEAN

175° W

ARCTIC OCEAN

Emerald I.

70°

Wrangel Island

EAST SIBERIAN SEA

170° E

Delta

Kolyma River

65°

Jeannette Island

Henrietta Island

155° E

Bennett Island

New Siberian Islands

140° E

Indigirka River

Khoma River

125° E

DeLong Delta

Melville

Lena River

Yana River

Bulun River

Lena

75°

70°

- ◉ Trapped in ice; September 6, 1879

- ▲ U.S.S. "Jeannette" crushed; June 12, 1881

- ⬡ Boats separated at this point.

- ⋯⋯⋯ Course followed by U.S.S. "Jeannette" before being crushed

- ─ ─ ─ Route followed by 20 survivors before boats separated

- ·········· Routes taken by DeLong & Melville after separation

fied that on the last of many conversations he had had with De Long, they were agreed, for sound reasons, that it was best to seek the west coast of Wrangel Land and follow it north.[16]

Danenhower had previously testified that De Long had said to him that "putting a ship in the pack [that is, for an all-winter drift] was the last thing to do."[17] Actually, Herald Island was sighted on September 4, and De Long headed into the ice, following the leads of open water. Soon he could glimpse Wrangel Land beyond Herald Island. By September 6, the vessel was practically stalled by the ice, forging ahead painfully by boring and ramming. De Long wrote that he hoped the September storms and the Indian summer promised by the weather-wise would enable him to reach Herald Island for winter quarters. Instead, the pack carried the *Jeannette* past so speedily that a sledge party failed to reach the island.[18]

There followed twenty-one months of drifting in the ice. Day followed day with deadly monotony. Occasionally a bear was seen and trailed, falling a victim to the hunters' rifles. During the summer, birds lent a little variety. The shifting of the ice caused occasional crises. Theatricals and the celebration of anniversaries provided a certain amount of diversion. Food and fuel naturally caused concern. Of these, the fuel was the chief problem, for it was needed for cooking, heating, and operating the pumps. A number of expedients were tried by Chief Engineer Melville, and each saving on the coal account was carefully recorded.

Probably no one was immune to the concern De Long felt about the possibility of escaping alive from the pack, when day after day the vessel was carried north of west, ever farther from land, yet advancing but slowly toward their objective, the Pole itself. One thing had been conclusively proved: that Wrangel Island was no part of a polar continent. Yet De Long was

[16] 48 Cong., 1 sess., *House Misc. Doc. 66* (Cong. Ser. 2243), 665.
[17] 47 Cong., 2 sess., *House Exec. Doc. 108* (Cong. Ser. 2113), 27.
[18] De Long, *Voyage*, I, 113 ff.

galled at the thought that the expedition would be branded a failure in the minds of many: regardless of what they had gone through, they had not reached the Pole. As if in self-justification, he wrote in his journal:

> A full meteorological record is kept, soundings are taken, astronomical observations made and positions computed, dip and declination of the needle observed and recorded, experiments made with ice and snow and surface water, birds shot and skinned, seals hunted, mechanics employed, ship's routine carried out, etc.; everything we can do is done as faithfully, as strictly, as mathematically as if we were at the Pole itself, or the lives of millions depended on our adherence to routine.[19]

So affairs continued into the summer of 1880. Occasionally the ship's drift would be found to have changed toward the east or south. Presently the small advance toward freedom would be checked and the drift continue as before. Summer passed, and on August 13, 1880, the vessel had returned until it was hardly 50 miles west and less than 150 miles north of the position where it was gripped by the ice eleven months before. By November, however, it was fairly in the steady stream of ice, and with but one major exception, moved on an almost constant course toward the northwest. The coast of Siberia receded. In May, 1881, two small islands were discovered and given the names Jeannette and Henrietta.

On June 12, the ice began to nip the *Jeannette* in earnest. Provisions and equipment were put over the side onto the ice and moved back from the ship. The next morning the *Jeannette* sank to the bottom, and the men were faced with a long haul to the coast of Siberia. It was probably fortunate that they were in the longitude of the New Siberian Islands, on which they made several camps. Before reaching them, however, a

---

[19] *Ibid.,* I, 411. A more detailed summary, including hydrographic observations, is given in Danenhower's testimony, 47 Cong., 2 sess., *House Exec. Doc.* 108 (Cong. Ser. 2113), 30.

third unknown island loomed out of the ice before them. With the privilege of discoverers, they named it Bennett Island.

The dramatic portion of the *Jeannette* narrative concerns the escape from the midst of the Arctic Ocean. This emergency had been foreseen. Whether the provision for it had been wise is open to debate. Sacrificing speed to the maximum load of supplies, the party set out for the Lena River Delta with three boats mounted on sleds, and five sleds with stores, a total of 15,400 pounds for twenty-one men to drag. Ten more men were on the sick list and were able to give little help. The well men had to travel thirteen miles to advance the party one mile.

At the end of the first week, the officers discovered that they had not allowed properly for drift. They were then twenty-seven miles farther northwest than at the start. Keeping this information a secret from the crew, they altered course and pushed on. On July 27, they reached Bennett Island. They remained there a week and made important tidal observations. August 20 to 28 found them stalled in the ice. They drifted near enough to one of the New Siberian Islands to reach it; there they camped upon the tundra and shot some wild fowl. Thence they moved to another island of the group, and then to the third, where they shot a deer for their shrinking larder. From that point on, boats were required rather than sledges. On the evening of September 12, a gale began to blow, and the men in the boat with Danenhower and Melville reported that De Long gestured from his boat as if to order wider separation. Melville's boat rode the gale all of the thirteenth with a sack dragging behind as a sea anchor. Heading east and occasionally south, the party struck a river and went up it. They landed on the evening of the seventeenth, after 108 hours in the boat. Two days later, they met natives and soon entered into communication with the outside world.[20]

The boat under Lieutenant Chipp's command was soon lost

[20] Lieutenant Danenhower's account in Raymond Lee Newcomb (ed.), *Our Lost Explorers: The Narrative of the* Jeannette *Arctic Expedition*, 207-44.

to sight of the other two, and nothing more was ever heard of it. De Long's boat was carried to the Lena River Delta at a point well to the west of Melville's landing. Striking shoal water, they abandoned their boat and carried ashore what supplies they could. They then began an overland march, cold, wet, and starved. One by one, the men died. Finally De Long ordered the two strongest men to go ahead and seek aid. When Nindemann and Noros found natives, they were unable to convey the urgency of the situation to them. By the time Russian officials were reached, and De Long's two men had fallen in with Melville's party, it was too late. De Long and his last companion had died before the rescuers got under way. A huge cairn on the Siberian tundra was their monument. (The remains of De Long and his companions were later reinterred in the United States.)

Faithful to his trust, De Long had preserved his journals and observations to the last, and they were brought back by the search party. The youthful Newcomb, through all difficulties, saved his notes and four bedraggled specimens of the rare Ross Gull, delivering them to the Smithsonian Institution.[21] Valuable scientific data had been brought back from an area never before reached.

A limited appraisal of the scientific results is all that can be made here. One of the major geographical achievements was the gaining of information which restricted severely the size of any hypothetical polar continent. The question of an open waterway through Bering Strait to the Pole was settled negatively.[22] Siberia was shown to have a wide continental shelf. The knowledge of Arctic ice currents was materially increased, while the tide observations from Bennett Island confirmed those from similar Arctic Ocean areas.

In the realm of physical measurements, over two thousand observations were taken of the electromagnetic phenomena associated with the aurora. Weather reports were obtained

[21] Smithsonian Institution, *Annual Report*, 1882, 14.
[22] De Long, *Voyage*, I, 373.

from a hitherto blank area on the map, and in such form that they might be correlated with observations from elsewhere. The magnetic measurements helped to fill in a gap, but probably added little surprisingly new or significant.[23] In the long run, the mass of observations was of greater significance than the addition of three islands to the map.

The *Jeannette* Expedition was the occasion for three relief cruises and the inspiration for Nansen's later drift in the *Fram* through the area immediately to the west.

The appropriations act of March 3, 1881, contained authorization for the expenditure of $175,000 for the charter or purchase, equipment and supply, of a vessel to search for the *Jeannette* and "such other vessels," meaning several lost whalers, as might be found in need of assistance. The Secretary of the Navy appointed a board to suggest a plan of action. Most of the board's members had had Arctic experience. Among the witnesses heard were George Kennan, who had been in northeastern Siberia with the Western Union Telegraph Expedition; William Healey Dall, a recognized authority on Alaska; Cleveland Abbé and Lieutenant A. W. Greely of the United States Signal Service, the latter an authority on charting storm tracks and not yet an Arctic explorer in his own right; and Bernard Cogan, a whaling master.

The board recommended the exploration of the Siberian coast and then, as late summer's heat opened the ice, the search of Herald Island and Wrangel Land. Reports indicated that the search vessel might find a harbor on Wrangel Land and spend the winter sending out sledging expeditions.

A whaler already on the Pacific Coast, the *Mary and Helen,* was purchased for $100,000, renamed the *U.S.S. Rodgers* and sent north.[24] She followed the north coast of Siberia as far as

[23] An evaluation of the observations was given by De Long in *The Voyage of the* Jeannette, I, 357. The magnetic observations were among those whose accuracy was low.

[24] SecNav, *Report,* 1881. 47 Cong., 1 sess., *House Exec. Doc.* 1 Part 3 (Cong. Ser. 2016).

The U.S.S. *Jeannette* before she was overhauled and fitted for her cruise through Bering Strait toward the pole.

Ice floes in Kane Basin.

Pack ice in Kennedy Channel, Joe Island in right center.

the ice permitted. A party with dog sledges and Siberian guides was put on the ice to follow the coast still farther in search of information. The *Rodgers* visited Herald Island, to find that the United States Revenue Marine Service steamer *Corwin* had anticipated her and put a party ashore. However, the *Rodgers* had the credit for making the first survey of Wrangel Island, although it had not been anticipated that the *Rodgers* would do any scientific work. While in winter quarters on the Siberian coast of the Bering Sea, she caught fire and was destroyed.

A second cruise was made under Navy Department orders at the suggestion of James Gordon Bennett. This was by the *U.S.S. Alliance,* a small warship. Although the funds appropriated by Congress for the search might have been used, it appears that this was made a part of the regular program of naval cruises.

The *Alliance* was not designed to enter pack ice. For this duty she was given additional protection against scum ice and occasional floes by being sheathed at the bow with live oak and fitted with an iron guard at the stem.

She left Hampton Roads on June 16, 1881, touched at St. John's, and reached Reykjavik, Iceland, on July 9. Bulletins in Icelandic were distributed, giving notice of rewards for reliable information about the *Jeannette*. From Iceland the ship went to Hammerfest, Norway, continuing to Spitsbergen, and then to latitude 80° north, longitude 8° 15′ east, where she was stopped by the ice. She managed to work her way along the pack to longitude 11° 22′ east, whence she retraced her course, reaching New York on November 11.

Unlike the *Rodgers,* the *Alliance* was given detailed instructions for collecting scientific information. Inasmuch as little time was to be spent on land, most of the data were to be hydrographic: the limits of pack ice between Greenland and Spitsbergen were to be noted; the usual barometric and air temperature observations "should be taken with the greatest care"; sea temperatures were to be observed at the surface and five fathoms; a bench mark should be established on Spitsbergen "as proposed by the International Arctic Commission for hypsometrical and tidal observations"; the deep-sea thermometer should be used "especially in the vicinity of the ice-pack"; organisms should be collected by drag nets, for American collections lacked specimens from northern waters; auroras, the degree of phosphorescence, and the specific gravity of sea water were to be observed; and collections of fauna, flora, fossils, and minerals should be made at every convenient landing in Iceland, Greenland, and Spitsbergen. The instructions concluded:

> The above observations, although simple, are highly important to the scientific men of our country and the world, who frequently deduce great results from very small material. Our naval officers should therefore, do everything in their power to aid the cause of science and the progress of useful knowledge.[25]

These instructions appear to have been carried out faithfully, special mention being made in the Secretary of the Navy's *Report* of the collections made while ashore.[26]

A third United States vessel took part in the search for the *Jeannette* during 1881. This was the *Corwin* of the Revenue Marine Service, which took on this search in addition to her regular duties in the Bering Sea and Arctic Ocean. The famous western naturalist, John Muir, was aboard the *Corwin* during this cruise, and the United States Signal Service observer stationed at St. Michaels, Edward William Nelson, came aboard for a part of the voyage to make natural history collections. Inasmuch as the search for the *Jeannette* was incidental, this voyage will be taken up in another setting.

[25] SecNav, *Report*, *1881*, 766.
[26] *Ibid.*, 10.

V

The Schwatka and Howgate Expeditions

IIIIIIIIIIIIIIIIIIIIIIIIIIIIIIIIIIIIIIIIIIIIIIIIIIIII

AT THE SAME TIME that Lieutenant De Long was planning and leading the expedition in the *Jeannette,* two plans were being projected for the exploration of the eastern American Arctic. Lieutenant Frederick Schwatka, United States Army, undertook a search for the records and remains of the Franklin party. Brevet Captain Henry W. Howgate of the United States Army Signal Corps, after several years of lobbying, obtained a grant from Congress for the establishment of an Arctic base or "colony," to use his phrase, from which to conduct explorations over a period of years.

Howgate succeeded in getting two vessels under way, one of which wintered at Baffin Island. His preliminary planning enabled the United States to be first with an expedition in the field when the International Polar Commission invited the United States to co-operate in an International Polar Year, during which a number of expeditions from several countries made simultaneous meteorological and magnetic observations. The Greely Expedition, the product of the Howgate and International Polar Year projects, will be discussed in a subsequent chapter.

Schwatka's interest in the Franklin Expedition had been stimulated by the stories of Captain Thomas F. Barry. Barry claimed that Eskimos at Repulse Bay in 1871–73 and in northern Hudson Bay in 1876 had told of "a great white man" who had visited them many years before. As evidence, he produced a spoon with the Franklin crest, given him, so he said, in 1876.[1]

Schwatka's goal was the region around King William's Land, which Charles Francis Hall had visited a dozen years before. Schwatka seems to have known little of Hall's work. This is understandable, for the book on Hall's expedition was published a year after Schwatka's departure. The limited amount of work that Hall had been able to do would in any case have justified the renewed search.

Judge Charles Patrick Daly, president of the American Geographical Society, was influential in arranging to have Schwatka detailed from the Army to command the party. Morrison and Brown, a shipping and whaling firm of New York, was the major contributor to the expedition. Application was made to Congress for a grant, but as Congress was in special session for limited purposes, the request was not considered, and private subscriptions completed the necessary fund.[2]

The limited scientific equipment of the expedition consisted of a pocket chronometer, a sextant, an aneroid barometer, and books on navigation contributed by James Gordon Bennett. Alcohol thermometers were supplied by the firm of Tagliabue. The entire cost of the expedition was "hardly $5,000 for an expedition of at least two and a quarter years."[3]

Schwatka's party consisted of himself, William H. Gilder, a reporter for Bennett's New York *Herald*, Henry Klutschak, a civil engineer with previous Arctic experience, Frank E. Melms, "an experienced whaleman," and Joseph Ebierbing, Captain Hall's faithful Eskimo companion. Other Eskimos were hired during the expedition, as necessity required.

[1] William H. Gilder, *Schwatka's Search: Sledging in the Arctic in Quest of the Franklin Records*, 3–4, 38. The book was pieced together from articles Gilder wrote for the New York *Herald*. Another whaling captain, Barry's superior in 1871–73, claimed the spoon had been stolen from him. *Ibid.*, 38. Cited hereafter as *Schwatka's Search*.

[2] "Reports on Expedition to Search for Sir John Franklin," 46 Cong., 2 sess., *Sen. Repts.*, No. 528, Vol. V (Cong. Ser. 1982).

[3] Heinrich Klutschak, *Als Eskimo unter den Eskimos*, 14. Cited hereafter as *Als Eskimo*.

The instructions to the party were to search for the "records, remains, or relics of Sir John Franklin or his unfortunate party." Daily observations were to be made, and charts corrected thereby. "Should the expedition for which it is intended prove a failure, make it a geographical success, as you will be compelled to travel over a great deal of unexplored country."[4]

The expedition left New York on June 19, 1878. It spent the winter on Hudson Bay, just a little north of Chesterfield Inlet, at a small bay they named after Judge Daly. The following spring they cut across country west-northwest to Chantry Inlet, crossed the ice to Adelaide Peninsula, and thence to King William's Land. On Adelaide Peninsula and the west shore of King William's Land, they found abundant relics of the Franklin party, which McClintock had missed because of the snow and which Hall had not reached. On their return they followed Back's Great Fish River for a time, then crossed in an easterly direction to their starting point. In August they left Hudson Bay, arriving in the United States in September. The entire expedition was a remarkable feat, the return being more so for having been accomplished in the dead of winter.

In view of its limited equipment and personnel, the scientific results of the expedition were excellent. Klutschak's report is the most satisfactory. He and Schwatka made triangulations on the coast of Hudson Bay in 1878, and in the neighborhood of Adelaide Peninsula the next year. The two triangulations were joined by reconnaissance surveys along the line of march, tied in when possible to astronomically determined positions. Two of the resulting maps adorn his book, and Gilder spoke of a chart having been made "which has already proved useful to the whalers."[5]

Klutschak was a good geographer, but his geological notes were sketchy. He noted land forms and types of soil and rocks, but went no further. He reported on the animal life and noted

[4] Gilder, *Schwatka's Search,* 5–6.
[5] *Ibid.,* 5–6.

Map for the Schwatka Expedition, 1878–80

Schwatka began his explorations southwest of the region of Hudson Bay surveyed by Hall. He was much more fortunate in his investigation of King William's Land than Hall, having gained better co-operation from the Eskimos of the immediately surrounding area. Schwatka was able to search the entire western shore of King William's Land.

Route identifications on this map are of a rather low degree of accuracy. The region between Chesterfield Inlet and Chantry Inlet is hilly, the general elevation being one to two thousand feet. That the return journey was accomplished in the dead of winter is one of the most impressive features of the expedition.

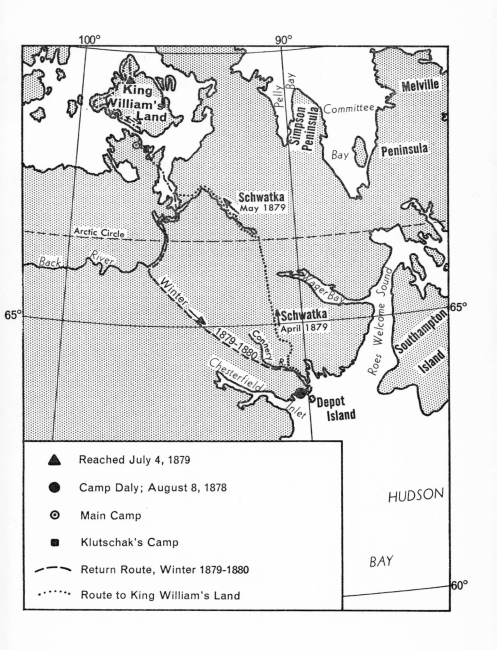

that the flora of the interior was rather rich. The director of the botanical garden at Prague, after examining his collection, reported no novelties.[6] In his volume may be found tables of the meteorological means for the first and last halves of each month, inserted at the appropriate points in the chronicle.

Ethnology was the most attractive subject for the party. Klutschak discussed Eskimo religion, but when his report is compared with those of other observers, it is seen to be biased by his own theological presuppositions. The Eskimo vocabulary he considered defective because of the wide variety of synonyms. For example, different words were used for the same color, depending on the object modified. Other topics he mentioned were the Eskimos' dining habits, domestic arrangements, marriage customs, spear fishing, string figures, musical entertainments, ceremonies, and burial customs.[7]

Schwatka published a series of articles in *Science* devoted primarily to the Eskimos' houses and implements.[8] Gilder devoted twenty pages to a glossary and discussion of Eskimo linguistics.[9]

The amount of sledging that Schwatka's party accomplished would have taken them from Etah to the Pole and back. An expedition with a limited objective, it accomplished that objective and more with a small party and small budget. In contrast, the expedition plans of another army officer were allowed to get out of hand, with results disastrous to himself and unpleasant to his associates.

First Lieutenant and Brevet Captain Henry W. Howgate, property and disbursing officer for the United States Signal Service, planned an expedition that should spend several years

---

[6] Klutschak, *Als Eskimo*, 102.

[7] *Ibid.*, 226–34.

[8] Frederick Schwatka, "The Igloo of the Innuit," *Science*, o. s., Vol. II (1883), 182–84, 216–18, 259–62, 304–306, 347–49; "The Implements of the Igloo," *ibid.*, o. s. Vol. IV (1884), 81–85; "The Netschilluk Innuit," *ibid.*, 543–45.

[9] Gilder, *Schwatka's Search*, 299–318.

in the north. He had represented the Signal Corps on the *Polaris* Board in 1873; this probably influenced him to develop his own project. Two small volumes of scientific observations were the immediate product of his labors. The International Polar Year Expedition to Lady Franklin Bay under Lieutenant Adolphus Washington Greely was the indirect and by far the most important result. For Howgate, the only rewards were disgrace, arrest, and flight.

In early 1877, the House Committee on Naval Affairs recommended a $50,000 appropriation to fit out "an expedition to the north pole, and to establish a temporary colony for purposes of exploration."[10] This the committee endorsed in glowing terms. Letters from Isaac I. Hayes to Howgate, from Joseph Henry to the chairman of the committee, and from Elias Loomis, meteorologist at Yale, were placed in the report. Loomis said, "There is scarcely a problem relating to the physics of the globe which can be fully understood without a knowledge of the phenomena within the polar regions." One extreme or the other of practically all global phenomena, Loomis continued, was to be found in the Arctic: the greatest magnetic intensity, the greatest cold. The cold waves that swept down each winter could be understood only as further information was collected from the Arctic. And the safety of commerce was dependent upon our knowledge of meteorology and magnetism.[11]

Howgate's plan provided for a colonizing party of fifty men, enlisted under military discipline, provisioned for three years, and housed in a portable building. A vessel was to deposit the party and return annually to provision it. There should be three commissioned officers, two surgeons, an astronomer, and several naturalists and meteorological observers. In order to produce the maximum benefit, the observations were to be synchronized with those that other nations, England, Sweden,

[10] 44 Cong. 2 sess. *House Reports*, 4339.
[11] 44 Cong., 2 sess. *House Reports*, No. 181, 7–11.

Holland, and Russia, were preparing and Germany had under way. The committee ended its report with a strong endorsement of the plan, both for the wealth of scientific information to be acquired and for the protection of whalers through meteorological knowledge.[12]

In order to lose no time, Howgate organized a preliminary expedition that should collect the Eskimos and Arctic equipment needed for the project. From undisclosed sources Howgate raised sufficient money to pay $4,000 for the schooner *Florence*, a tiny whaler of fifty-six tons.[13] The various bureaus of the War Department, on instructions from the Secretary of War, furnished rifles and ammunition, meteorological instruments, medicines, and camp equipment. The navy supplied charts and sailing directions.[14]

The scientific work was planned in collaboration with the Smithsonian Institution. For naturalist, Ludwig Kumlien was selected by the secretary of the Smithsonian, Spencer Fullerton Baird,[15] who began his instructions:

> The region you visit is one of the most interesting in North America, and the least explored by the naturalist . . . .
>
> Your principal object should be to make collections of everything in the ethnological, animal, vegetable, mineral, and fossil departments, so that you can prepare a report thereon . . . . In view of this you should make copious notes of the habits, associations, and general conditions of everything that you meet with.[16]

The meteorologist was Orray Taft Sherman, newly graduated from Yale and recommended by Professor Elias Loomis.[17] Howgate issued Sherman's instructions, including therein

---

[12] *Ibid.*, 1–6.
[13] George E. Tyson, *Cruise of the Florence*, 8–9. Henceforth cited as *Cruise*.
[14] Henry E. Howgate, *Polar Colonization*, 41–42.
[15] Tyson, *Cruise*, 5.
[16] Howgate, *Polar Colonization*, 51–53.
[17] *Ibid.*, 55.

"Suggestions for your General Guidance," prepared in the United States Signal Service Office by Cleveland Abbé. They included a long list of meteorological, hydrographic, and magnetic observations that were to be taken.[18]

Command of the vessel was given to George E. Tyson, who had spent a quarter of a century in whaling and who had been aboard the *Polaris* until carried away with the party on the ice floe. His orders read:

> The primary object of the expedition is the collection of material for the use of the future colony on the shores of Lady Franklin Bay . . . . The secondary object of the expedition is the collection of scientific data and specimens . . . . The third, and to the crew most interesting object, is the capture of a sufficient amount of bone and oil to make a profitable return cargo . . . . I must caution you, however, to be on your guard against letting the pursuit of gain interfere in any manner with the successful issue of the two first named objects of the expedition.[19]

The expedition sailed from New London on August 3, 1877, and arrived at its destination, Cumberland Gulf on Baffin Island, a month later. There at the mouth of the Gulf, Tyson found other vessels, which had already claimed the services of the Eskimos for the next spring's whaling. To avoid conflict, Tyson sailed up the Gulf, and soon had an Eskimo colony clustered around the vessel. Only one whale was caught. The Eskimos got the edible portion, the ship's crew got the whalebone, and Kumlien got the skeleton.[20] When the party reached the winter harbor of Annanatook, an observatory was erected, consisting of a canvas tent with a snow hut built around it. There Sherman carried all the burden of observing for a month; after that, two of the crew helped him. The meteorological observations were the most satisfactory. A series of tidal obser-

---

[18] Orray Taft Sherman, *Meteorological and Physical Observations* . . . U. S. Signal Service, *Professional Papers*, XI, 7–8.

[19] Howgate, *Polar Colonization*, 42–43.

[20] Tyson, *Cruise*, 89.

vations was made every three months, but they were frequently interrupted by ice. Magnetic observations were rudimentary, as only a small compass was available. A hundred auroral displays were recorded between November, 1877, and August, 1878. Ground temperatures were taken on several occasions in midwinter, and during the cruise water temperature data were gathered.[21]

Meanwhile, Kumlien was laboring under difficulties. In studying the diseases of Eskimo dogs, he cut his finger while dissecting one, contracted blood poisoning, and very nearly lost his arm. His report included thirty-two pages on the Eskimos of Baffin Island. He found birds breeding far to the north of their earlier-recognized temperate zone habitats. The collection of seals, skins, and skeletons filled "a very important gap in the collections of the National Museum." Other collections were limited: the camp site was not adapted to gathering marine specimens, and the party left too early for the flora.[22]

When the ice began to break up in the spring, Tyson hurried his Eskimo families aboard with their dogs, furs, and sleds, and headed for Disco, where the *Florence* had been ordered to await the projected expedition for Lady Franklin Bay. Kumlien complained that he had not had time to get all his collections aboard—a serious enough complaint. As the *Florence* did not reach Disco until July 31, Tyson had reason for his action. No expedition vessel met the *Florence* at Disco, although word from Denmark of American purchase of the *Pandora* (renamed the *Jeannette*) led Tyson's party to hope for one. Finally Tyson put to sea, restored the Eskimos to Cumberland Sound, and on September 26, 1878, reached St. John's, Newfoundland.[23]

In his report as secretary of the Smithsonian, Baird took

[21] Sherman, *Meteorological and Physical Observations*, 11 *passim*. See also his "Scientific Work of the Howgate Expedition," *North American Review*, Vol. CXXVIII (1879), 191–200.

[22] Smithsonian Institution, *Annual Report*, 1878, 45 ff.

[23] Tyson, *Cruise*.

occasion to compliment Kumlien, especially on his ethnological notes:

> His detailed account of the curious habits and mental characteristics of the Innuit is one of the most complete and finished descriptions ever given of them; clear, succinct, and comprehensive, it is a valuable ethnological pen picture.[24]

Kumlien himself wrote the reports on ethnology, mammals, and birds. Through the National Museum, experts were procured to do twelve other fields. Asa Gray did the botany, W. H. Dall the mollusks, W. H. Edwards the insects.[25]

Meanwhile, the legislative mill was grinding. The Senate Committee on Naval Affairs concurred in the report of the House Committee, submitting the House Committee's report with the Senate measure.[26] Howgate printed and reprinted articles on polar colonization. He compared the safety and comfort of a station at Lady Franklin Bay to that of the forts of the Hudson's Bay Company.[27] Again, he pointed out that the climate was little more severe than that experienced at the weather observatories on Mount Washington and Pike's Peak. A stay of three years would permit the party to become acclimated and provide an extended opportunity to select an open season for the expedition to the Pole.[28] Then, at about the time that the *Florence* set out from Cumberland Sound, the House rejected the proposal, 86 yeas to 127 nays. Howgate's optimism had miscarried.

From the time of the *Florence's* return, Captain Howgate endeavored to get Congress to finance a second expedition.

[24] Smithsonian Institution, *Annual Report*, 1879, 32.
[25] Ludwig Kumlien, *Contributions to the Natural History of Arctic America made in connection with the Howgate Polar Expedition*, 1877–78. U. S. National Museum *Bulletin No. 15*.
[26] 44 Cong., 2 sess., *House Report No. 181*; 45 Cong., 2 sess. *House Report No. 96*; 45 Cong., 2 sess., *Senate Report No. 94*.
[27] "The Polar Colonization," *United Service* (1879), 10ff.
[28] "The Polar Colonization Plan," *American Naturalist*, Vol. XI (1877), 226–32.

He purchased the *Gulnare* in Scotland and had it thoroughly overhauled and braced. Congress authorized its acceptance by the Navy Department, should it be deemed seaworthy.[29] Lieutenant Adolphus Washington Greely, a cavalry officer who had been serving as an acting signal officer, was assigned to command the expedition. Four sergeants were assigned as meteorological observers, including O. T. Sherman of the *Florence* Expedition. Eleven other enlisted men were accepted, all but one being from the Second Cavalry.[30] Long lists of commissary, quartermaster, and engineer supplies were ordered. Supplies not on the subsistence list that Greely wanted were ordered by the Secretary of War for the party's particular use.[31] A memorandum outlining the plan was furnished President Hayes, and his official approval was obtained on April 28, 1880.[32]

General Myer, chief signal officer, appointed a board consisting of J. P. Story, Howgate, and Cleveland Abbé to report a plan for the physical observations. This was duly submitted on April 30.[33] A board appointed to review Howgate's general plan reported on May 27. H. C. Chester, former mate on the *Polaris*, was in charge of fitting out the *Gulnare* and also served on the latter board. Chester was authority for stating "that it is the best adapted for the purposes designed of any vessel that has entered the Arctic seas."[34]

Then the blow fell! The Navy Department refused to accept the *Gulnare*. Howgate, not daunted, provisioned the vessel, put a crew aboard, employed Dr. Octave Pavy, a Louisiana

---

[29] 46 Cong., 2 sess., *U. S. Stat.-at-Large*, XXI, Ch. 72. An Act to authorize and equip an expedition to the Arctic seas, May 1, 1880.

[30] 990 O.C.S.O., Mis. 1881, Encl. 8. The Miscellaneous Files of the Office of the Chief Signal Officer, thus cited, are in the National Archives, Natural Resources Branch. They were in 1950 in wooden file trays marked 700 L[ady] F[ranklin] B[ay].

[31] *Ibid.*, Encl. 12–15, 20–21.

[32] *Ibid.*

[33] *Ibid.*, Encl. 17.

[34] *Ibid.*, Encl. 10, 1.

Creole long interested in Arctic exploration, as naturalist and physician, employed Henry Clay, grandnephew of the statesman, as a second observer, and started the expedition off via Newfoundland. Storms damaged the vessel; her boilers broke down, and she underwent repair in Newfoundland. Other mishaps followed, so that when she reached Greenland, Pavy and Clay remained there, and the vessel returned to the United States.[35]

The curtain was raised on the final act in Howgate's personal drama when on August 6, 1881, the Chief Signal Officer informally advised the Secretary of War that examination of Howgate's accounts as disbursing officer of the Signal Service showed that "he had defrauded the United States of large sums of money . . . ." Howgate fled, was arrested, jumped bail, was rearrested, and indicted for embezzlement and later for forgery. Repeated delays occurred, and in April, 1882, he escaped from a deputy United States marshal and disappeared again.[36]

The cruise of the *Florence*, as with Schwatka's long sledge trip, made positive if limited contributions to science. The principal significance of Howgate's labors, however, was in formulating a program and convincing Congress of its soundness, so that little remained to be done when the call came to embark on the great program of international observations of the years 1881–83.

[35] Smithsonian Institution, *Annual Report*, 1880, 26–27.
[36] 47 Cong., 2 sess., *House Exec. Doc.* 81 (Cong. Ser. 2110).

VI

The International Polar Year:
The Greely Expedition to Lady Franklin Bay

||||||||||||||||||||||||||||||||||||||||||||||

THE GREELY EXPEDITION grew out of the combination of two programs. The first was Henry W. Howgate's plan to establish a "polar colony" at Lady Franklin Bay, Ellesmere Island, from which explorations might be conducted over a period of years. The second program sprang from the enthusiasm engendered by the Austrian discovery of Franz Josef Land in 1873. Karl Weyprecht, codiscoverer of that archipelago, outlined his views on further Arctic exploration in 1875. He believed that the emphasis of polar expeditions should be shifted from geography to physical observations carried out simultaneously at a number of stations.

Weyprecht and Count Johann N. Wilczek prepared a program to submit to the International Meteorological Congress, which was to have met in Rome in 1877, but because of war did not meet until 1879. As the members of the Meteorological Congress had not been authorized by their governments to deal with the question of Arctic exploration, a special conference was called for October 1, 1879, at Hamburg. Delegates from nine nations met at Hamburg and proposed that at least eight stations be occupied for twelve months, beginning in the autumn of 1881. A second conference was held at Bern, where it was decided to postpone the simultaneous observations for a year in order to gain the co-operation of additional countries.[1]

Weyprecht had written to the Chief Signal Officer, Brigadier General Albert J. Myer, who had been authorized by the Secretary of War to enter into correspondence with a view to co-operating with the Meteorological Congress. This led finally to the passage of the authorization on which Howgate had been counting for his *Gulnare* Expedition.[2]

At the Chief Signal Officer's recommendation, the United States Congress on March 3, 1881, appropriated $25,000 to implement the authorization granted in 1880, for an expedition to Lady Franklin Bay on the northeastern coast of Ellesmere Island.[3] The committee that reported the bill to the House of Representatives stressed the scientific objectives of the expedition, and declared that its purpose was to co-operate with those expeditions sent out by other governments in connection with the International Polar Year. The original authorization provided for the establishment of a "temporary station" at or near Lady Franklin Bay, "for the purposes of scientific observation and exploration, and to develop or discover new whaling-grounds." As many as fifty "officers or other persons of the public service" might be accepted as volunteers, and any public vessels might be used as required.[4] The advantage of the Lady Franklin Bay site was that it was a station at a high latitude where comparable observations had been made in 1875–76 by the British Nares Expedition.

To complete the program envisioned by the International Polar Conference, the Signal Corps prepared an expedition to Point Barrow, using regular funds for meteorological observations in Alaska, with $5,000 additional, made available by the Coast and Geodetic Survey. General William Babcock Hazen, newly appointed chief of the Signal Service, was en-

[1] International Polar Commission, *Communications*, Part 2, No. 19, 42–47.
[2] Chief Signal Officer, Albert J. Meyer, to the Secretary of War, May 27, 1880, 990 O.C.S.O., Mis. 1881. (See Ch. V, note 30.)
[3] 46 Cong., 3 sess., *U. S. Stat.-at-Large*, XXI, Ch. 133, 447. *Sundry Civil Expenses* [1882]. March 3, 1881.
[4] *Ibid.*, 2 sess., Ch. 72.

thusiastic about the program and must be credited with making this phase of it possible.[5] The expedition was placed under the command of Lieutenant Patrick Henry Ray.

The instructions furnished Lieutenants Greely and Ray were identical. General instructions were given regarding the maintenance of records; hourly meteorological, tidal, and magnetic observations; photographs; sketches; and "carefully prepared topographical maps."

The detailed instructions embodied large excerpts from those furnished by the International Polar Conference of October, 1879, at Hamburg. In taking "term-day" magnetic measurements, the United States parties should follow the more exact of the methods recommended. Instructions regarding observations and collections in natural history were supplied by Professor Spencer Fullerton Baird of the Smithsonian Institution. The expeditions were also referred to the *Instructions for the Expedition toward the North Pole*, which had been drawn up for the *Polaris*, and to *Suggestions Relative to Objects of Scientific Investigation in Russian America*.[6]

Greely, the leader of the expedition to Lady Franklin Bay, was described later by a loyal subaltern as "a New Englander of the traditional type, meaning the type more often found in tradition than in the flesh—tall, spare, stern, kindly and terribly conscientious." David Brainard continued, "A silent and often taciturn man, his tender heart and unfailing fairness had won for him the affection and the loyalty of his command under very difficult circumstances." In fact, some were neither affectionate nor loyal, but Brainard's characterization shows plainly enough how Greely might have inspired at the same time deep loyalty and hearty dislike.[7]

[5] Greely, *Three Years of Arctic Service*, 4–5.

[6] Adolphus Washington Greely, *Report on the Proceedings of the United States Expedition to Lady Franklin Bay, Grinnell Land.* 49 Cong., 1 sess., *House Misc. Doc.* 393 (Cong. Ser. 2427–2428), I, 100–106.

[7] David L. Brainard, *Outpost of the Lost,* 19, 22. Brainard's journal of the retreat from Fort Conger to Camp Clay clarifies many points in Greely's account.

The personnel of the expedition, besides Greely, consisted of twenty-four volunteers from the army and Dr. Octave Pavy, the surgeon left in Greenland after Howgate's abortive attempt of 1880. Two of the men had enlisted especially for the opportunity: Sergeant Edward Israel, the astronomer of the expedition, and Sergeant George W. Rice, the photographer. Three other sergeants were meteorological observers. Three Eskimos were brought along as dog drivers. Natural history was the province of Dr. Pavy; he had spent 1880–81 in Greenland studying Arctic natural history under Krarup Smith.

The quality of the personnel is evidenced by the posthumous commendation given two of the men for their scientific work. G. E. Curtis, editor of Sergeant Israel's astronomical work, said, "The general accuracy and high character of his work" permitted one to believe that where selection of values was necessarily somewhat a matter of judgment, Israel's figures were "of the highest attainable value," and could not be improved by revision.[8] Greely repeatedly paid tribute to Lieutenant Lockwood's work in organizing and largely increasing the natural history collections after Pavy failed to carry out his duties as naturalist.

Although Congress had granted the use of public vessels, no serious consideration was given to their use. The bulk of the appropriation went for the charter of a Newfoundland steam sealer, the *Proteus*. For work in ice fields she was equipped with an iron prow, extra sheathing on the sides, a self-lifting screw, and spare rudder and propeller.

The ship was sturdy, but other factors were not so favorable. Greely described Robert Lincoln, the secretary of war, as being avowedly hostile.[9] Even after the assignment of Greely to command, formal approval was not issued until April 12, 1881, a month later. Then, in but three days' time, detailed requisitions for food, clothing, and supplies had to be prepared. After

[8] Greely, *Report*, II, 51.
[9] Greely, *Three Years*, 16.

chartering the vessel, only $6,000 was left for special supplies. All standard items of army equipment were available in ample quantities, however.

The voyage along the coast of Greenland and through Smith Sound was made without untoward incident. This should have seemed a favorable omen. At Lady Franklin Bay, near the northeastern corner of Ellesmere Island (Grinnell Land), the supplies were quickly put ashore, for there was danger of the vessel's being trapped. When she sailed for home, three men originally assigned to the expedition returned with her, and Lieutenant Kislingbury just missed getting aboard. A house was assembled at once, and the post named Fort Conger, after the senator who had particularly concerned himself for the welfare of the expedition.

The Greely Expedition was generously supplied with instruments. There were no less than eleven chronometers, about four dozen thermometers, six mercurial and three aneroid barometers. Charles S. Peirce of the Coast and Geodetic Survey had made a pendulum for gravity observations. A galvanometer and long wire were provided for the study of earth currents; a magnetometer and a Fauth unifilar declinometer, for magnetic measurements. Each man was supplied with a three-year diary. Both expeditions carried fine technical libraries, lists of which are available in both Greely's and Ray's reports.[10]

Lieutenant Lockwood and Dr. Pavy were designated as leaders of the principal sledging expeditions, and Sergeant Israel was ordered to train them in making astronomical observations. Lockwood carried out Greely's expectations fully, but "Dr. Pavy made no observations of any character."[11]

Greely's primary interest was in geography.[12] However, the principal purpose of the expedition was to make co-operative

[10] Greely, *Report*, I, 107.
[11] *Ibid.*, II, 59.
[12] "An Expedition to the Northern Magnetic Pole . . . ." American Geographical Society, *Journal*, Vol. XXIV (1892), 256.

physical measurements, and Greely reluctantly subordinated his personal desires. The location of the base likewise limited his opportunity for new discoveries. Greely was at the winter quarters of *H.M.S. Discovery*, less than fifty miles from the *Polaris* winter quarters of 1871–72, and roughly a hundred miles by coast south of the 1875–76 winter quarters of *H.M.S. Alert.*

The Greely Expedition made five major sallies from Fort Conger. Two were made to the east, along the north Greenland coast, by Lieutenant Lockwood. In the spring of 1882, he took the weaker of the two dog teams that had survived the winter and exceeded by some ninety miles the mark established by Lieutenant Beaumont of the British expedition of 1876 under Nares. Lockwood Island, at 83° 24′ north latitude, is his "farthest north." From a height of 2,600 feet, Lockwood looked northward over an unbroken expanse of sea toward the Pole. The following year he was stopped at Black Horn Cliffs by the broken inshore pack, and with difficulty he escaped from the pack as it was being carried offshore.

In the summer of 1882, when Lockwood was pushing toward his "farthest north," Dr. Pavy was sledging toward the north coast of Grinnell Land. The area had been explored by the Nares Expedition, but he hoped to press north from the coast on the trail of fresh discoveries and a new "high." Bad luck dogged his steps, and the breaking up of the ice fields north of Cape Joseph Henry forced him to abandon his plan.

Meanwhile, Greely and one other man set off to the southwest to explore Grinnell Land. They first discovered that Chandler Fjord, reported by the Nares Expedition as a small bay was actually thirty miles long. Turning north up a stream, they came to an ice dam, behind which flowed a river draining a lake "some 500 square miles in area, which at the junction of the two presented an ice-free pool." To the north lay an icecap. The lake he named for General Hazen.

Greely made a second journey into the area the following

month and discovered that his valley lay between two icecaps. In 1883, the indomitable Lockwood made a third trip into the area. He discovered on the west side a long fjord that almost bisected the island. This he named after his commander.

These journeys covered an area of six thousand square miles. A remarkable feature was the finding of ice-free valleys where numbers of musk oxen grazed. Sir Joseph Hooker had expected Greenland and Grinnell Land to be "instead of ice-capped, merely ice-girt islands."[13] The truth, however, is that Grinnell Land and the southern portion of Ellesmere Island, likewise, are ice-capped, but with wide ice-free margins.

The principal oceanographic observations were of sea temperatures and tides. Temperatures were observed aboard the *Proteus* on the way north; later at Fort Conger they were observed at the surface, thirty-three feet, and sixty-six feet, three (later five) times monthly.[14]

Simultaneous tidal readings were made at Capes Beechey and Baird, Distant Cape, and Fort Conger. Later, in September, 1882, parties made readings at Cape Cracroft, Distant Cape and Conger. It was thus possible to form a picture of the tidal sequence.[15] The tidal observations were reduced and discussed by A. S. Christie of the Coast and Geodetic Survey. One of his most interesting conclusions was that the tide at Fort Conger originated between Greenland and Spitsbergen, and somewhere south of Conger met the tide coming up through Baffin Bay.[16]

In January, 1882, sixteen days were devoted to geodetic work, forty-eight sets of pendulum observations being made.[17] Even on the return trip, when food was scarce and energies were low, the pendulum was carried with the party in order to permit proper recalibration after the observations. Then, ironically,

---

[13] Greely, *Handbook of Polar Discoveries*, 1907 ed., 235.
[14] Greely, *Report*, II, 379–85.
[15] *Ibid.*, I, 44.
[16] *Ibid.*, II, 699–700.
[17] *Ibid.*, I, 14–15.

it was found that the stone cap for the original pedestal at Washington had been removed, and an essential portion of the suspension had been left at Fort Conger.

Geological collections were made at a number of points, including Fort Conger and Capes Baird and Cracroft. Specimens included fossils, shells, rocks, lignite, coal, and, from Fort Conger, a keg full of rock crystals, coal fossils, and "rosin." Just south of Cape Baird, Sergeant Brainard discovered fossil trees over one foot in diameter eight hundred feet above sea level.[18]

One especially interesting phenomenon was the permafrost soil, although no systematic observations comparable to those of the Ray Expedition (described in the next chapter) were made. One reading, taken three feet below the surface on August 11, 1881, showed 26° Fahrenheit. At one point, a landslide disclosed solid ice ten or twelve feet beneath the surface. "It was plain that the ice was of very considerable extent." Flowers growing on the clay covering showed that the ice had long been buried. Greely theorized that it might be the remnant of a glacier or perhaps sea ice caught in a sudden uprising of the land.[19]

A comparison of Greely's official report with the British instructions for Arctic geological observations which he carried does not leave one with a particularly high opinion of this phase of the expedition.[20] No serious effort was made to study the glaciers in the vicinity. The study of the soil and ground ice was casual rather than systematic. There seems to have been no realization of the possibilities of stratigraphy along the fjords and creeks. It is unfortunate that no enterprising young geologist was secured for the expedition in the same way that Israel was employed as astronomer.

[18] *Ibid.*, I, 45, 314–15.
[19] *Ibid.*, II, 379.
[20] Great Britain, Admiralty, *Manual of the Natural History, Geology, and Physics of Greenland . . . Ed. by Prof. T. Rupert Jones, together with instructions suggested by the Arctic Committee of the Royal Society for the Use of the Expedition.*

In May, 1883, Greely ordered Lockwood to relieve Pavy of the natural history collections, except for the botanical collections, which Greely took upon himself. Lockwood arranged and increased the collections, "numbered and labeled all specimens, arranged and packed them in the best manner," thus repairing some of the deficiencies caused by Pavy's slackness, lack of system, and insubordination. All were prepared so that the collections might be loaded aboard ship in an hour's time. Greely likewise paid tribute to Sergeant Elison, whose "habits of application and untiring zeal, added many fine specimens of birds," and to Sergeants Brainard and Gardiner for their fossil collections.[21]

When no ship came, and the expedition had to fight its way down the channel, all the collections were abandoned except for an incomplete set of botanical duplicates carried back by Greely and Brainard. Drawings of mollusks and jellyfish and a photograph of a single fish were brought back. Specialists were reluctant to commit themselves on the basis of drawings and a few notes. However, J. Walter Fewkes believed he had identified a new jellyfish (medusa), which he designated *Nauphanta polaris* Fewkes.[22] The Greely-Brainard botanical specimens and Greely's notes on mammals, however, made a worth-while contribution to the known ranges of a number of species.[23]

The meteorological observations constituted the largest single task of the expedition. As the commanding officer and three of his sergeants were experienced observers, this phase was carried out with a high degree of dependability. Regular hourly observations were taken on the exact hour of Washington Civil Time. These were continued through two full years. One of the few unusual features was an effort to determine the evaporation from an ice cube during the winter

[21] Greely, *Report*, I, 47.
[22] *Ibid.*, II, 39–45.
[23] *Ibid.*, II, 1–18.

months. Between October and the end of February, the net loss was insignificant. The mean annual precipitation was but 3.88 inches. [24]

The humidity observations "were practically valueless," since a coating of ice on the wet bulb appeared to act as insulation. "The patent Klingerfusser hygrometer furnished the expedition proved absolutely worthless."[25] Measurements of solar radiation were frequently lost because the solar thermometers were graduated only to 0°F., while the terrestrial radiation thermometers likewise failed, being scaled to a minimum of only −40° F.[26]

Magnetic observations were made hourly. Twice a month, term-days were held, when the variation (declination) was read every five minutes; and for one hour, it was read every twenty seconds. As only one magnetometer was available, absolute measurements of intensity had to be made the day after the term-day.[27] A detailed analysis of the observations appeared in the *Report*.[28] Auroras were sought at each observation. From September to March of the two-year period, auroras were seen 6.5 per cent of the time.

> In general, it may be said that the auroras at Fort Conger were colorless and quiescent, and that magnetic disturbances were not generally coincident with auroras of this class . . . . Again, colored auroras and those of rapid changes of form and position seemed to be more frequently contemporaneous with magnetic disturbances.[29]

Among the miscellaneous activities of the expedition was an effort to determine the speed of sound at low temperatures. Another activity was the collecting of Eskimo artifacts from dwelling sites far from the nearest contemporary tribe of

24 *Ibid.*, II, 366–70.
25 *Ibid.*, II, 238.
26 *Ibid.*, II, 371–78.
27 *Ibid.*, I, 30.
28 *Ibid.*, II, 548 ff.
29 *Ibid.*, II, 386.

Eskimos. These were photographed and reproduced in six plates in the *Report*.[30]

Thick ice in Kennedy Channel during the late summer of 1882 made it obvious that no relief ship would reach the party that year. As supplies were on hand for two more years, there was no immediate danger of hardship. They had lost a good many dogs, which hampered exploration. Worse, several members of the party were insubordinate. Among those who should have known better were Pavy and Lieutenant Kislingbury. The latter actually "withdrew" from the expedition at the very first, but did contribute by his hunting. The expiration of the enlistments of several of the men while no possibility of relief was in sight caused dissatisfaction to spread.

The second winter passed in due course, and August rolled around, at which time Greely was under orders to retire from the base, even though a year's food remained. On August 10, 1883, the party set out with all boats available, the steam launch *Lady Greely* towing the others. Up to August 21, they could have turned back to Fort Conger. That day Sergeant Brainard wrote in his journal, "We have crossed the Rubicon and to turn back now is out of the question." On August 27, he wrote, "We have managed to travel southward about 200 miles, but actually we have gone 400 miles to get here. Winter has set in extraordinarily early." Here an extra effort might have saved them, for Jens and Sergeant Rice thought they had stopped just a mile short of open water.

Winds for several days carried them north with the ice field faster than they advanced south. Counsels were divided. Greely wanted to head for the Greenland shore, thirty miles distant, where help was fairly certain. He delayed out of deference to his officers, and as the drift carried them away from that shore, the opportunity, if it ever existed, was lost. Again several wanted to keep on the move, working from floe to floe, but Greely decided to wait until the ice was better for travel.

[30] *Ibid.*, I, 535 ff.

On September 10, the launch was abandoned, and the two boats remaining were hauled over rubble and around bergs. On September 12, only the lighter boat was retained. On September 29, the party reached the western shore south of Cape Sabine. In summarizing the experience, Greely said:

> The retreat from Conger to Cape Sabine involved over four hundred miles' travel by boats, and fully a hundred with sledge and boat . . . after fifty-one days and five hundred miles of travel, I landed near Cape Sabine not only my party, in health and with undiminished numbers, but its scientific and private records, its instruments and its baggage, with arms and ammunition sufficient, in a land fairly stocked with game, to have insured our lives and safety.[31]

Then began a discouraging round of searching the caches known to be in the vicinity. The first blow was perhaps the worst. Sergeant Rice and Jens went to Cape Sabine, and returned thence with a letter written by Lieutenant Garlington of the 1883 relief expedition. The note announced the sinking of the *Proteus* on July 23, the voyage of her escort, the *U.S.S. Yantic*, with supplies for Littleton Island, and the expected visit of a Swedish steamer to Cape York. The location of 750 rations on Cape Sabine was described. Although a careful reading of the text of the letter shows that a variety of possibilities existed, Greely went by the determination of Garlington's tone and his concluding promise to "endeavor to open communication."[32]

The fact of the matter was that the *Yantic* reached Littleton Island and sailed away without caching any provisions. At Cape Sabine, Garlington's party rifled the stores and removed the boat left by the relief expedition of 1882. The condition in which Greely's men found the cache was described by Brainard:

[31] Greely, *Three Years*, 439–526. Quoted, 526. See also Greely, *Report*, I; Brainard, *Outpost of the Lost*, 54–111, quotations from 59, 66–67.
[32] Greely, *Three Years*, 539–40.

We eagerly overhauled the cache, but were much disappointed to find so little. Of vegetables, raisins, lemons, clothing, boxes, looking-glasses, etc., there was a profuse display. Also about twenty pounds of Durham tobacco and ten of plug. A portion of this was issued to the smokers, the others receiving a quantity of raisins instead.[33]

The *Yantic* reached St. John's, Newfoundland, on September 12, 1883, carrying word of the loss of the *Proteus* and the failure to relieve Greely.

The exact sequence of events leading to Secretary Lincoln's decision against sending another relief expedition immediately is not clear. On September 14, George Tyson wrote, offering to take a ship north in the early spring.[34] On the same day George Melville, who had aided in the rescue of the *Polaris* party and had later escaped across the ice of the Arctic Ocean from the *Jeannette,* offered to set sail at once and lead a party from Cape York to Littleton Island in midwinter.[35] On September 15, James Laws, surgeon with the expedition to rescue Kane in 1855, wrote Lincoln opposing an immediate attempt.[36] At the same time Garlington wired from St. John's, proposing to return north at once on a whaler manned by navy volunteers.[37] On September 17, a news dispatch told of Emil Bessels' and George Kennan's advising William E. Chandler, secretary of the navy, that a relief expedition at that time could not succeed. Meanwhile reports were coming from St. John's that "All our old sealing and whaling masters are surprised that immediate steps have not been taken to rescue Lieutenant Greely and his party from starvation and death."[38] A rumor had it that Lincoln had agreed to send a sealer, then reversed

[33] Nourse, *American Explorations,* 550.
[34] Tyson to Lincoln, Sept. 14, 1883. 9521 O.C.S.O., Mis. 1883.
[35] Copy in 6346 O.C.S.O., Mis. 1883. See also George W. Melville, *In the Lena Delta,* 417-19.
[36] Laws to Lincoln, Sept. 15, 1883. 6195 O.C.S.O., Mis. 1883.
[37] Garlington to Chief Signal Officer, Sept. 15, 1883. 6059 O.C.S.O. Mis. 1883.
[38] New York *Herald* (Sept. 17, 1883), 4; (Sept. 19, 1883), 7.

himself after talking to Chandler.[39] In any case, Lincoln rejected the gallant offers of the brave and accepted the counsels of the fainthearted.

After the survivors of the Greely Expedition were rescued by Commander Winfield S. Schley in 1884, Lincoln was blamed for the loss of seventeen American lives. Schley produced statements, presumably obtained in Greenland, to prove that rescue the previous winter would have been impossible. Melville, who had sailed as Schley's chief engineer, still believed in the practicability of his original plan, and close examination shows that Schley's evidence did not invalidate it. Schley's supposed facts, however, fell to the ground when directly contradictory evidence from neutral Danish sources was produced by the defense attorney during the court-martial of General Hazen.[40]

Hardly had the decision to delay further relief attempts been reached in Washington, when Greely reached Cape Sabine and, finding Garlington's promise to relieve him, decided to await rescue there. He moved from his first camp to the cache from the *Proteus* wreck, sending parties through the winter to strip every cache within reach.

The best hunters were out continually. "Shrimps" so tiny that several thousand made a pound, sealskin, almost anything organic was eaten. Nonetheless, the men literally starved to death, one by one. It is one of the most tragic stories in Arctic annals. Two decades later Peary was in the same vicinity and found much more game. One hesitates to express a judgment based only on the printed record, yet from the account of the number of seals and walruses lost, because of the failure to

[39] Thomas Jefferson MacKey, *The Hazen Court-Martial*, 53.

[40] *Ibid.*, 34. The undocumented statements of MacKey, 25 ff., indicate that in Lincoln's consultation of the Arctic authorities available, he failed to come to grips with "the only practical question, which was, whether a steam-sealer despatched from St. John's by the 18th or 20th of September could reach Cape Sabine or Littleton Island that autumn?" See also Greely, *Three Years*, 572; Melville, *In the Lena Delta*, 417–19; Winfield S. Schley, . . . *The Greely Relief Expedition of 1884* (49 Cong., 2 sess., *House Misc. Doc. 158*, [Cong. Ser. 2428]), 69. [Bound with Greely, *Report*, II].

use harpoons and floats, and from the lack of accounts of the long, persistent stalking characteristic of Eskimo seal hunts, the evidence suggests that the Greenland hunters had learned to rely too much on rifles and lacked the skill shown by the Smith Sound Eskimos. Peary's parties were successful in obtaining plenty of musk oxen, while Greely's party did not appear to be aware of the potentialities of the mainland.

Peary's criticism of the party's failure to cross Smith Sound, as he himself had done, was less well founded. It had been attempted on February 2 by Rice and Jens. They started for Littleton Island, but were stopped two miles from shore in the main channel. During the whole winter Brainard had watched the ice carefully, and believed that at no time was the Sound completely frozen. Hence this criticism is contradicted by the evidence.[41]

On February 18, 1884, Commander Winfield S. Schley received the command of a squadron to be sent to Greely's rescue. Three naval vessels and a collier were provided. Dogs and drivers were to be secured in Greenland. Chief Engineer Melville attended to many of the details. Both cloth and skin clothing were ordered. Supplies and equipment ranged from 500-pound anchors to chamois-lined, blue flannel undershirts and mustard spoons. The total expense of the expedition, including the cost of the ships purchased, aggregated $750,000 before allowances for materials returned intact.[42] This presumably did not cover the value of the *Alert*, provided as a gift from Great Britain.

The *U.S.S. Bear* was ready first, and proceeded to Upernavik, where she was joined shortly by the *U.S.S. Thetis* and the collier *Loch Garry*. On May 29, the *Bear* and the *Thetis* left the *Loch Garry* behind to await the *Alert*. The vessels worked and rammed their way through the ice, frequently in the vicinity of a group of steam whalers, the crews of which had

41 Brainard, *Outpost of the Lost*, 179–88.
42 Schley, *Greely Relief Expedition*, 69 and elsewhere.

their eyes on the bounty offered by Congress for the relief of the party.

At Cape York no word could be obtained of the whereabouts of the expedition. Schley pushed the *Thetis* on, working through the ice in the mouth of Smith Sound. Learning from Eskimos that no whites had been seen during the winter at the Cary Islands, he decided to push on with all dispatch for Cape Parry and Littleton Island. Having no success there, Schley waited only long enough for the *Bear* to catch up. Sailing north "in a moderate gale," they reached Payer Harbor on Bedford Pim Island and sent four parties out to visit the neighboring islets. "About 8 p.m. cheers were heard above the roaring winds, but could not be located accurately." More cheering and then a seaman came with word of a message from Greely left in a cairn on Brevoort Island. Other records and instruments were found a few minutes later by the party at Stalknecht Island.

The steam cutter of the *Bear*, under Lieutenant Colwell, was ordered around Cape Sabine to Wreck Camp on the north side of the island. "If any of the party were alive he [Colwell] was to inform them that their relief was close at hand. At the same time he was instructed to administer food with the greatest care until the surgeons should arrive." Within two hours of the first discovery, the cutter and both ships were on the scene.[43]

Greely later recounted:

> By the morning of the 22nd we were all exhausted, and it was only through the energy of Frederick or Brainard, I do not remember which, that we obtained, about noon, some water. That and a few square inches of soaked seal-skin was all the nutriment which passed our lips for forty-two hours prior to our rescue . . . .
>
> Near midnight of the 22d I heard the sound of the whistles of the *Thetis*, blown by Captain Schley's orders to recall his parties.

[43] Schley, *Greely Relief Expedition*, 31–43.

I could not distrust my ears, and yet I could hardly believe that ships would venture along that coast in such a gale.

Greely asked Brainard and Long if they had the strength to stir out. They said they would do their best. Brainard returned, discouraged, having seen nothing. Long went a little farther on to set up the distress flag, which had blown down. At first he could not see the ship whose whistle they had heard. Stumbling out a second time, he saw the two vessels at a distance, with the steam launch lying offshore. In his anxiety and haste he staggered and tumbled down the ice cliff to the cutter. His story was out in a moment, and the men hurried to the lone tent where six men lay.[44]

The sight that met the eyes of the rescuers was a tiny camp, perhaps a hundred feet back from the beach, slightly above the water. The gales that had been raging had blown the tent over on the men, and they lacked the strength to raise it. Near by were the graves of others, the later burials so shallow that parts remained uncovered. Debris and pitiful bundles of effects lay about the camp, each marked by its owner in the hope that some memento might reach home.

Rescue came just in time, for the survivors had developed the swollen joints and faces seen in their comrades within forty-eight hours of death.

They were taken gently aboard the vessels, the bodies of the dead removed, and everything of significance stowed aboard before 3:00 A. M. By midafternoon the ice began to set into Payer Harbor from Kane Sea, and the ships quickly headed south through the ice fields. On July 2, the vessels, now joined by the *Alert* and the *Loch Garry*, ran out of the ice and reached Upernavik. The rescue vessels had been in the ice continuously from May 19, and had navigated some 1,300 miles under extremely trying conditions. At St. John's, Portsmouth, and New York, they were given an enthusiastic wel-

[44] Greely, *Three Years*, 712–14.

come, the North Atlantic fleet at Portsmouth having dressed ship with every available flag and pennant to receive them.[45]

Although only six of the party reached the United States alive, the written records were brought back intact. For almost a year Greely had been at work arranging and reducing his reports and observations against the possibility of just such a retreat. He had taken along his most valuable instruments, not even abandoning the heavy pendulum.[46] In 1902, Peary removed all the records and collections from Fort Conger that were fit to be moved. Much of the material had been left in barrels outside the house and was in wretched condition.

The Lady Franklin Bay station was the most northerly of those co-operating in the International Polar Year. Its physical observations, the principal ones desired, had been made and returned safely. From that standpoint it was a genuine success. Joseph Everett Nourse, who through his editing of Hall's journals and study of Arctic exploration had qualifications for judgment, commended the selection of Lady Franklin Bay as a site, as well as the planning and provisioning of the expedition. George Kennan, famed Siberian traveler, said that if the Greely party had found the supplies which they were entitled to expect, the expedition would probably have been without casualty, and "their Arctic record, in point of skilful management and success, would have been unparalleled."[47]

The scientific staff of the relief expedition likewise received its meed of praise. Three naval ensigns had been "well trained at the Smithsonian Institution in the methods of instantaneous photography, in taxidermy, and in the collection of minerals and fossils." Although they had to gather what they could in brief moments ashore, the natural history collections and the "numerous photographs of the country, of the natives, and the ice" were finer than had been anticipated.[48]

[45] Schley, *Greely Relief Expedition*, 43-59.
[46] Greely, *Report*, I, 36, 61.
[47] Nourse, *American Explorations*, 593.
[48] Smithsonian Institution, *Annual Report*, 1884, 15.

VII

The International Polar Year: The Ray Expedition to Point Barrow

IN ORIGIN and the details of organization, as well as in its relatively prosaic history, the expedition to Point Barrow led by Lieutenant Patrick Henry Ray was in marked contrast to Greely's. The first mention found of establishing a station in northernmost Alaska is in the letter from Weyprecht to General Myer, dated May 5, 1879, proposing United States co-operation in the International Polar Year. An intermediate station, between the proposed Russian station at the mouth of the Lena and the Danish station proposed for west Greenland, "is of the utmost importance." There had been two nine-month series of meteorological, magnetic, and auroral observations at Point Barrow, the station of the *Plover* in 1852–53 and 1853–54. Wrote Weyprecht:

A new wintering would furnish the first existing data on the secular changes of terrestrial magnetism from the regions of the large perturbations. The position of this point is very favorable also to meteorological observations.[1]

Myer replied that a polar expedition was outside the De-

[1] Weyprecht to Myer, chief signal officer, U.S.A., dated Trieste, May 20, 1879. 1005 O.C.S.O., Mis. 1881. Unless otherwise specified, the MS files on the Ray Expedition thus cited are in the Natural Resources Branch, National Archives. At the time of this study, they were in a wooden file tray marked Mis. 588 Pt. Barrow.

partment's scope, but "the establishment of a station of observation at Point Barrow . . . is quite within the province of this office." The feasibility and requirements of setting up the proposed station were being examined, and if found practicable, Myer was confident that the Department would cooperate in the proposed system of observations.[2]

The practicability of the location, from the standpoint of natural history, was investigated by Secretary Baird of the Smithsonian. Edward William Nelson, the joint Signal Service observer and Smithsonian collector at St. Michaels, replied to Baird's query, giving information on the physical requirements of the station and expressing the opinion that useful collections and observations could be made of waterfowl, "fishes, marine mammals, and the natives."[3]

The United States Coast and Geodetic Survey promised its co-operation in a letter from the superintendent, C. P. Patterson, to General Hazen on February 21, 1881. Patterson's successor, J. E. Hilgard, disputed the agreement. The language of Patterson's offer is given below:

> I am prepared to say that this Survey is ready to expend for the establishment, fitting and support of the tidal and magnetic observers &c., at the proposed station at or near Point Barrow during the fiscal year ending June 30th, 1882, the sum of $5,000, and I am ready to cooperate with you in any way for the establishment of this station. It should be maintained for five years at least.[4]

The correspondence relative to establishing a station at Point Barrow was turned over to Lieutenant Greely for summary, review, and recommendations. Greely turned to William Healey Dall for estimates of equipment, provisions, and costs.

[2] Dated Washington, D. C., Sept. 8, 1879. MS copy filed with 1349 O.C.S.O., Mis. 1879.

[3] Dated July 7, 1880. Copy in 1709 O.C.S.O., Mis. 1880, filed with 1349, Mis. 1879.

[4] Copy in 2828 O.C.S.O., Mis. 1881, Encl. C. Original may be 588 O.C.S.O., Mis. 1881.

Dall estimated the costs at $10,000, excluding wages, transportation, and scientific equipment, items for which a special budget might not be required.[5] Greely recommended that the station be established,

> with a view to its personnel taking, in addition to the regular meteorological observations [of the Signal Service], the physical observations agreed on at the Hamburg conference of Oct. 1st, 1879. The station should be established during the coming summer . . . be provisioned for two years, and maintained for five years.

The Coast and Geodetic Survey should be invited to participate, and the chief signal officer should attend the St. Petersburg conference of the International Polar Commission scheduled for the summer of 1881.[6]

On April 4, 1881, Hazen wrote a letter to Secretary Lincoln, presenting the plan and correspondence regarding the station and citing the prior approval of his predecessor, Secretary Ramsey, and the commitments made at that time to the international group by Hazen's predecessor, General Myer.[7] The delay encountered by the Greely Expedition was now felt by the Ray Expedition, for five weeks later, on May 10, Secretary Baird wrote Hazen an account of his interview with Lincoln on the preceding Saturday.

> I think I succeeded to some extent in impressing him with the scientific and practical importance of the Point Barrow mission . . . . I think he was better satisfied of the propriety of making a station, not in telegraphic communication with the central office, when he found that the Act of Congress gave authority to establish meteorological stations, and also the fact that several

[5] Dall to Greely [Feb.–Mar.], 1881, Encl. with 733 O.C.S.O., Mis. 1881.

[6] Greely to Hazen, Washington, D. C., March 7, 1881, 733 O.C.S.O. Mis. 1881.

[7] Chief signal officer to Secretary of War, dated Washington, D. C., April 4, 1881. 2828 O.C.S.O., Mis. 1881.

stations, almost as isolated as Point Barrow, like St. Michaels & the Aleutian Islands, have been carried on for some time.[8]

Lincoln granted authorization on May 13, with minor provisions regarding personnel and funds.[9]

The actual details of financing the expedition need not be discussed here, except to say that the United States Signal Service supplied the larger share of the cash. Dissatisfied with the conduct of the expedition, Hilgard interpreted the Survey's commitment as being an initial lump sum rather than an annual contribution and displayed bad temper when an effort was made to work out a nominal adjustment.[10]

Ray's scientific instructions were the same as Greely's. He was to follow the recommendations of the Hamburg International Polar Congress in regard to "meteorological, magnetic, tidal, pendulum, and such other observations as were recommended." Collections were to be made of animal, vegetable, and mineral materials, all of which were to be the property of the government. The collections in natural history and ethnology were to be turned over to the National Museum.[11]

The personnel of the expedition consisted of First Lieutenant Patrick Henry Ray; Acting Assistant Surgeon George Scott Oldmixon; Sergeant James Cassidy, meteorological observer; Sergeants John Murdoch (A.M., Harvard) and Middleton Smith, naturalists and observers; Captain E. P. Herendeen, interpreter and storekeeper; Mr. A. C. Dark, astronomer and magnetic observer (assigned by the Coast and Geodetic Survey); one carpenter; one cook; and one laborer: ten men in all, less than one-half the size of the Greely party.[12] Several of these

[8] 1619 O.C.S.O., Mis. 1881.

[9] Secretary of War to chief signal officer, 1646, O.C.S.O., Mis. 1881.

[10] Hilgard to Hazen, dated Washington, D. C., Jan. 23, 1884. 420, Mis. 1884. See also memorandum of Cleveland Abbé regarding the letter.

[11] Patrick Henry Ray, *Report of the International Polar Expedition to Point Barrow, Alaska, (1881–83)* . . . . 48 Cong., 2 sess., *House Exec. Doc. 44* (Cong. Ser. 2298), 8. Henceforth cited as *Report of International Polar Expedition*.

[12] *Ibid.,* 6.

men were relieved during the two years of the expedition. Nonetheless, Ray, like Greely had cause to regret the haste with which it was necessary to select the personnel. His principal objection was to the quality of some of the scientific work accomplished. He apparently did not have the disciplinary problems that confronted Greely.[13]

Cassidy, Murdoch, and Smith were detailed for instruction, along with Israel of the Greely Expedition, to the Coast and Geodetic Survey in Washington. There they learned the use of the sextant, the altazimuth, and the magnetic instruments which they were to take with them, as well as methods of computation. A. C. Dark, nominee of the Coast and Geodetic Survey, received his instruction in astronomical observations at San Francisco.[14] Aside from Murdoch, the naturalist and observer, official reports do not indicate that these men had had any particular formal training for their tasks. As United States Signal Corps observers, however, they were chosen from a group of men with practical experience. The training was admittedly less than was desirable.[15]

The set of magnetic instruments furnished for the first year by the Coast and Geodetic Survey was incomplete, for differential instruments could not be obtained in time.

The expedition sailed out of the Golden Gate on July 18, 1881, two years and ten days after the *Jeannette*. After an uneventful voyage, they met the United States Revenue Marine Service steamer *Corwin* at Plover Bay, Siberia, during her search for the *Jeannette*. On September 8, Point Barrow was sighted. After scouting several positions, a site for the expedition's house was selected some three-fourths of a mile northeast of one of the two native villages.

Most of the time was spent close to the observation station. During 1882, Ray made a short expedition paralleling the

[13] *Ibid.*, 21.
[14] *Ibid.*, 446.
[15] *Ibid.*, 445.

shoreline to the southeast. In 1883, he, with A. C. Dark and some Eskimos, made a journey with dog sledge for a longer distance southwest into the interior. On this basis he was able to prepare a sketch map of the immediate hinterland.

The relief schooner, *Leo*, appeared on August 2, 1882, bearing three additional Signal Corps observers: Sergeant J. E. Maxfield and Privates Charles Ancor and John Guzman. Cassidy was returned to the States. An additional year's supplies and new magnetic instruments formed the cargo.

The following year, the Coast and Geodetic Survey sent an observer with the *Leo* to make pendulum observations and to redetermine the latitude and longitude. Circumstances conspired against him, for the *Leo* brought orders to Lieutenant Ray to abandon the station, damage to the vessel on the way north made immediate departure necessary, and bad weather ruined the few days at his disposal.

The expedition embarked amidst raging gales. Shortly the *Leo* sprung a leak. She was successfully careened at Unalaska and made watertight. On October 7, she reached San Francisco, having overcome the hazards of her difficult voyage.[16]

The standard observations on meteorology, magnetism, and tides may be passed over briefly. The meteorological observations were continued for twenty-two months. In addition to the regular observations, soil temperatures were taken in a shaft at depths down to 37.5 feet. The lowest soil temperature recorded was −5°F., just under the surface, in December; the highest, 17.5° F., at sixteen to eighteen feet the following November. The temperature at the bottom of the shaft remained at 12° F. for months at a time. In making the excavation, temperature observations were combined with stratigraphy and the digging out of a meat locker.[17]

The Ray Expedition was able to make a number of satisfactory observations on electrical currents in the earth's surface.

[16] *Ibid.*, 34.
[17] *Ibid.*, 339.

However, efforts to correlate them with the aurora borealis were unavailing.[18]

In the fields of ethnology and natural history more favorable circumstances produced results superior to those of the Greely Expedition. The latter had only been able to pick up Eskimo artifacts of quite uncertain date, photograph, and describe them. Its main accomplishment had been to extend the known area of former Eskimo habitation. The Ray Expedition was more fortunately situated, for two Eskimo villages were close at hand. Although they had been visited by explorers and whalers for decades, there had been no such extended opportunity for observation. Handicapped by the language barrier, nonetheless Ray turned in a worth-while "ethnographic sketch," to which John Murdoch contributed supplementary materials. Later, Murdoch produced a volume on the ethnology of the Point Barrow Eskimos.[19]

Tradition was supplemented by physical evidence that the neighborhood had been the site of Eskimo villages for a long time. Wooden goggles were found at a depth of twenty-six feet in the soil. A few legends and religious beliefs of the Eskimos were recorded. A vocabulary was diligently collected and set down according to established rules. A detailed census was made, and ethnographic measurements were taken. The *Report* contains a catalog of the collections and drawings of some thirty items.

Ray, like other students, remarked on the Eskimos' lack of government and on their seemingly inconsistent notion of property rights. Things definitely cached or stored were safe without any protection. But items "adrift" were instantly appropriated; if their return was demanded, they were yielded, apparently without hard feelings.[20]

[18] *Ibid.*, 685–86. Descriptions of the magnetic instruments, with instructions for mounting, may be found on 446–54.

[19] John Murdoch, "Ethnological Results of the Point Barrow Expedition," U. S. Bureau of American Ethnology, *Ninth Annual Report*, 1887–88.

[20] Ray, *Report of International Polar Expedition*, 37–88.

The reports on mammals contained little that was new. Twenty-five species were listed. Much of the information was gained from the Eskimos, particularly regarding the animals' ranges.[21] The collection of insects was extremely limited, and it reached the National Museum in bad condition. Several new species were tentatively identified.[22] Ignorance of proper methods of collecting and preserving fungi led the taxonomist to whom they were submitted to report that "specific determination is in their present condition impossible."[23]

Other phases of natural history fared better. Eighty-one species of marine invertebrates were identified, of which the largest group was the sixty-one species of mollusks classified by William Healey Dall. Asa Gray of Harvard wrote up the botany and commented, "This collection probably comprises most of the Phanerogamous plants growing at that arctic station; some of them not before received by us from that region, rich as our herbarium is in Arctic American plants."[24] John Murdoch, who was primarily responsible for making these collections, wrote up the report on ornithology. Most of the collecting was done within fifteen miles of the station. He felt that the collection was a "tolerably complete representation" from the area.[25]

Was this a routine expedition compared with Greely's? Was Greely's task fundamentally more difficult? Were the scientific achievements of one vastly ahead of those of the other?

Ray was in a location well known to whalers, and usually accessible during a short part of each year. Relief vessels did come through regularly. Not until Peary built the *Roosevelt* for the purpose was Smith Sound conquered with regularity. Likewise the terrain of the Alaskan Arctic coast presents few difficult stretches for sledging, whereas Smith Sound presents

---

21 *Ibid.*, 92 ff.
22 *Ibid.*, 134–35.
23 *Ibid.*, 192.
24 *Ibid.*, 191.
25 *Ibid.*, 104–28.

a long series of high cliffs and intersecting fjords. Hence there is little likelihood that retreat from Ray's position would ever have presented such a problem.

Greely's task was fundamentally more difficult. He had a harder area, a more ambitious program, a larger party, and more troublemakers. Such a program surely required more time for preparation than Greely was allowed. Nevertheless, the expedition would have been considered a success but for the fatalities. Greely blamed others' cowardice and hesitance for his lack of supplies. Peary blamed Greely's own leadership.

The reports of the Ray Expedition are more satisfactory than the Greely reports. The loss of the Greely collections is in large measure responsible for this. Because of Pavy's incompetence in natural history, the Greely collections would probably have turned out to be no better than Ray's. Knowledge of the Alaskan interior was important, but had never been the cause of endless theoretical discussions such as the questions of the northern continental extension of Greenland and of an "open polar sea." Greely made more of a contribution to the major problems of Arctic research of his day. The Ray reports were better, so far as consistent work, ingenuity, and effective coverage of the area are concerned.

VIII

Peary's Greenland Expeditions

||||||||||||||||||||||||||||||||||||||||||

IN 1886, the names of Adolphus W. Greely and George Melville, De Long's engineer, would probably have been the first to come to one's mind among living American Arctic explorers. William Healey Dall's or Patrick Henry Ray's might well have been the first in Alaskan exploration. Frederick Schwatka might have been thought of in connection with his search north of Hudson Bay for records of the Franklin Expedition. By late 1909, two other names were on every tongue: Robert Edwin Peary and Frederick Cook. The lasting one was Peary.

Peary traveled farther in the north and added more to the knowledge of Arctic geography and travel techniques than any other man of his generation. He was industrious in collecting the standard scientific observations. His own technical skill was greatest in surveying and taxidermy. He surrounded himself with competent observers for carrying out the bulk of the scientific program. Geographical discovery was his prime objective and the field of his greatest achievement. There was reason for the feeling of Sir Clements Markham and others that Arctic programs had too often become athletic events rather than scientific studies. The other side of the story was expressed by Peary from time to time. Where he had gone, others could learn to follow. Moreover, he was able to report the best areas for studying the phenomena of interest to a particular scientist. Through Peary's explorations, Thomas

Chrowder Chamberlin was able to go directly to the area best suited for his glacier studies. Other scientists going north for the summer on Peary relief cruises were dropped off to study ethnology, natural history, geology, or geography where it best suited their purposes.

Contrary to a widespread impression, no Peary expedition was financed or made official by the United States government. Leave on reduced pay for his expeditions was in later years granted reluctantly by the Navy Department. The United States Coast and Geodetic Survey supplied instruments repeatedly and sent an observer one summer, while in 1908–1909, Peary was detailed to the Coast and Geodetic Survey so that he might draw full navy pay during that one expedition. This is the sum of the official assistance Peary received.

Few of the scientific reports of the expeditions came from Peary's hand. The first information from his expeditions usually consisted of letters to the New York *Sun*, for which he was paid. The American Geographical Society *Bulletin* printed extracts from these. Later, he submitted reports containing full notice of his geographical accomplishments, which were published in the same journal. Mrs. Peary published *My Arctic Journal* after her return in 1892 from her first winter in Greenland. This received a warm reception. In 1898, Peary published *Northward Over the Great Ice*, an account of his journeys over the icecap between 1886 and 1895, and of his removal of the Cape York meteorites between 1895 and 1897. This was followed by *Nearest the Pole*, in 1907, and *The North Pole*, in 1910. His summary of Arctic techniques was published in 1917 as *Secrets of Polar Travel*.

The volumes on his explorations parallel closely the reports published in the American Geographical Society *Bulletin*. His volume, *The North Pole*, was written on railway trains between lectures and lacks the accuracy of his serial, "The Discovery of the North Pole," in *Hampton's Magazine*, January–September, 1910. In view of the bulk of the material dealing with the Peary expeditions, it is fortunate that William Herbert Hobbs, a distinguished geologist with experience in Greenland, has written a scholarly biography of Peary.[1]

Robert Edwin Peary was born in 1856, and spent most of his youth in Maine. He was graduated in civil engineering from Bowdoin College in the Class of 1877. In 1879, he entered government service as a draftsman in the Coast and Geodetic Survey in Washington. After rigorous examinations he was commissioned in the Civil Engineering Corps of the United States Navy in 1881. He spent a good share of the next four years on surveys and plans for the proposed Nicaragua canal.

About that time Peary ran across a pamphlet on the inland ice of Greenland that recounted Nordenskjöld's experiences in 1870. He wrote, "A chord, which as a boy had vibrated intensely in me at the reading of Kane's wonderful book, was touched again."[2] He went on to plan his own investigation of the icecap, which at that time was thought to be perhaps not a cap, but a narrow belt within which flowers and trees might grow in ice-free valleys.

Peary presented his scheme before the National Academy of Sciences on April 23, 1886. A single season would suffice, he thought, to penetrate from the west to the unknown east coast of Greenland. One might cross the southern section of Greenland, then circle the tip at Cape Farewell. Or one might start much farther north near Whale Sound and lay a course northeast to the coast around the 80th parallel. "This, I believe, is the way by which not only the crossing of Greenland but the delineation and closing of its coast-line will be accomplished."[3]

The financial arrangements for Peary's first expedition were

---

[1] William Herbert Hobbs, *Peary*, 334n. Hobbs did not have access to the Peary manuscripts. Peary's daughter, Marie Peary Stafford, is custodian of the manuscripts. These consisted originally of forty-three cases of material, but some have been damaged by water. Mrs. Stafford plans to put them in order and eventually make them accessible to research. Various letters, Mrs. Stafford to the writer.

[2] *Ibid.*, 59. This was probably the story of Kane's own expedition, 1853-55.

simple; they were never to be so again. To his own slender reserves was added $500 borrowed from his mother.[4] Later arrangements furnish some clue to the growing difficulty and complexity of the task. In 1891, somewhat less than $10,000 was raised, a member of his party (John M. Verhoeff) contributing $2,000, the American Geographical Society, the Columbian Exposition, and the New York *Sun* $1,000 each. In turn, the Exposition was to receive an ethnological exhibit, and the *Sun* a series of letters. Professor Angelo Heilprin, curator of the Philadelphia Academy of Sciences, organized a summer cruise of scientists that finally raised the funds for the vessel. Various friends made small contributions, and Peary put in "a few thousand dollars of my own."[5] A second auxiliary expedition was organized to share the expenses of the relief ship in 1892.

In 1893, the funds required were considerably greater. Mrs. Peary contributed the royalties from her books. The American Geographical Society again contributed $1,000. The *Sun* raised its offer to $2,000. Friends supplied two or three thousand more. Needing far more than that, Peary approached the Pond Lecture Bureau and succeeded in convincing Major Pond that a lecture series should be arranged, late in the season though it was. Despite the heavy burden of organizing duties, Peary delivered 168 lectures in 96 days, realizing $13,000 for his efforts. As funds were still insufficient, due partly to the Panic of 1893, a friend suggested that the public be permitted to tour the expedition's vessel at twenty-five cents apiece. The needed amount was thus raised by exhibitions at Philadelphia, New York, Boston, and Portland.[6]

From 1893 to 1897, funds were raised by gifts and auxiliary expeditions. In 1895, the burden fell on Mrs. Peary alone, as Peary was still at Whale Sound. Mrs. Peary was under consider-

---

[3] R. E. Peary, *Northward over the Great Ice.* I, xxxv.

[4] Hobbs, *Peary*, 62.

[5] Peary, *Northward*, I, xl–xlii; Hobbs, *Peary*, 86.

[6] Peary, *Northward*, I, xliv–xlv; Hobbs, *Peary*, 124.

able stress for some time until Morris K. Jesup, president of the American Museum of Natural History, guaranteed the balance.[7]

Realizing that the element of financial uncertainty greatly hampered his program, Peary proposed in 1897 that $150,000 be raised and deposited in a trust fund for expenditure on a polar campaign over a period of ten years. He modified the plan and appealed to wealthy friends, a number of them affiliated with the American Geographical Society or the American Museum of Natural History, asking that twenty-five men should each guarantee $1,000 a year for four years.[8] The Peary Arctic Club was thus informally organized in the autumn of 1898, and in January, 1899, it perfected its organization. The numbers were never sufficient to the needs, and Peary's expenses outran his anticipations. Although the steamer *Windward* was a gift of Alfred Harmsworth (later Lord Northcliffe), repairs to her came high. Building the *Roosevelt* in 1905 cost $50,000, and repairs to her in 1907 cost an additional $75,000.[9] Nevertheless, a large share of the burden of arrangements was now off Peary's shoulders. He felt that he could keep at it until his goal was won. And he no longer needed to worry about rescue expeditions being forthcoming.

In 1897 Peary could write,

> The Government has never appropriated, nor been asked to appropriate, a dollar for any of my Expeditions. Nor has the Government had any responsibility in connection with my work. It has, however, kindly given me my time, *i.e.*, allowed me the leave necessary to enable me to prosecute my plans.[10]

For part, if not all of the time, Peary received leave pay.[11]

[7] Peary, *Northward*, I, xlv–xlvii.
[8] H. L. Bridgman, "Departure of the *Windward*" American Geographical Society, *Bulletin*, Vol. XXXIV (1902), 273.
[9] Am. Geog. Soc., *Journal*, Vol. XXIX (1897), 118–20; Peary, *The North Pole*, 13–17.
[10] Peary, *Northward*, I, lvi.
[11] Hobbs, *Peary*, 86.

In December, 1904, the American Geographical Society appealed to the Navy Department to send a cruiser to Peary's relief. It was turned down coldly. The Secretary of the Navy said neither a suitable vessel nor the funds were available.[12]

Peary's Arctic career may be followed through two major stages. His first concern was with the Greenland icecap; by 1897, his thoughts were on the Pole. From 1886 to 1895, he explored the inland ice, finding that it was truly a cap, and he reached the coast sufficiently far north to make it virtually certain that Greenland did not join any polar continent. From 1895 to 1897, he was sidetracked with the problem of bringing three remarkable iron meteorites from Cape York to the American Museum of Natural History.

When the American Geographical Society, on January 12, 1897, awarded Peary its Cullum Medal, he made his first public announcement of his campaign for the North Pole. He pointed out that Fridtjof Nansen, by his drift across the polar sea in the *Fram*, and Frederick G. Jackson, by his explorations of the area between Europe and Greenland, had eliminated all routes but Smith Sound from consideration. He explained the technique of living and travel that he used thenceforth without major modifications until he achieved the Pole in 1909.[13]

The first four of the eleven years that Peary was engaged in reaching the Pole, he spent continuously in the north. His vessel, the *Windward*, was not particularly adapted for ice work, and she was never able to deliver him north of the Bache Peninsula area, 250 miles south of Fort Conger. This was four hundred miles south of the base from which Nares started toward the Pole. Success came only after Peary had a ship designed for the duty. Twice he and Captain Bob Bartlett

---

[12] "The Greenland Scientific Expedition of 1895," Am. Geog. Soc., *Bulletin*, Vol. XXVII (1895), 126–28.
[13] Am. Geog. Soc., *Journal*, Vol. XXIX (1897), 118–20.

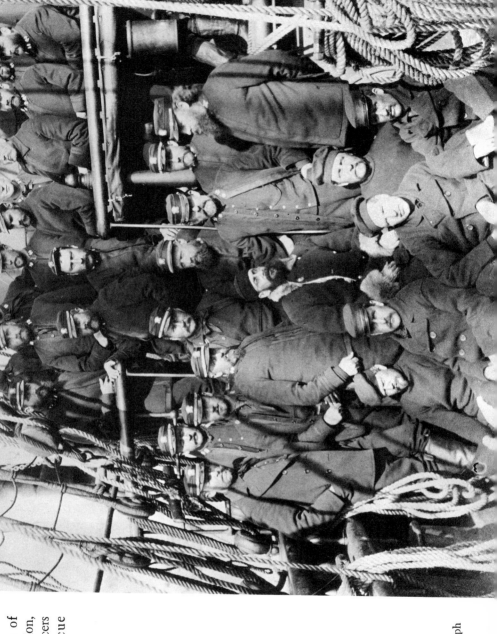

The six survivors of the Greely Expedition, surrounded by officers of Schley's rescue squadron, 1884.

U.S. Navy photograph

The site of Fort Conger (upper left) as seen from the air, looking east.

fought the *Roosevelt* north through the ice and wintered her on the northernmost coast of Ellesmere Island.

In 1886, on his first trip, Peary went alone, with skis, snow-shoes, and ice creepers, with untested equipment in unknown territory, and speaking neither Danish nor Eskimo. He landed at Godhavn, Disko Island, from a whaler. Thence he ferried to the mainland at Ritenbenk in an umiak (skin boat), and there secured a companion, Christian Maigaard. They began the climb up the glacier onto the icecap on May 26. In the next three days they gained an altitude of three thousand feet. There a snowstorm trapped them for three days. Pressing on again, a new storm arose on the fifteenth that held them prisoners until the nineteenth of July. They then had but six days' provisions left, so Peary took a careful observation of the sun, and they began their return to the coast. They had pene-trated inland one hundred miles, a greater distance than any-one had yet traveled on the icecap. Lashing the sledges together and hoisting a sail, with a hatchet for a rudder, they sped toward the coast. Both had narrow escapes in the crevasse area but reached the village unharmed. Peary improved the time until the whaler called for him by examining a near-by glacier and a notable fossil bed.

The trip had achieved its principal objectives. A practical knowledge had been obtained of travel and ice conditions, equipment had been tested, and a new record set for icecap travel. The interior plateau had at last been reached, and lessons learned on where to approach the cap and how to travel over it.[14]

Five years elapsed before Peary was free to return to his Arctic ventures, during which time he became second in com-mand of Nicaraguan canal surveys, and achieved a reputation both for solid work and for initiative.

[14] R. E. Peary, "A Reconnoissance of the Greenland Inland Ice," Am. Geog. Soc., *Journal*, Vol. XIX (1887), 288–89; Peary, *Northward*, I, 39–40.

By the summer of 1891, interest in the canal had faded, and Peary again turned his thoughts to Greenland. Fridtjof Nansen had meanwhile anticipated him by crossing Greenland at a low latitude. The other and more difficult plan propounded in 1886 and elaborated in 1887 still lay open: a journey from Whale Sound, at the northern limit of assured navigation, northeasterly to the far coast. This was the critical test of his belief that the inland ice was truly an "imperial highway," and the heights of the icecap's edge the best place for a survey.

The principal problem that Peary set out to solve was the actual extension of Greenland to the north. Geographers, hydrographers, meteorologists, and geodesists were all concerned, and theories were in sharp conflict. Next to the attainment of the Pole, with the information that would be elicited thereby, Peary considered this the most important geographical problem of the polar regions. Its solution might well point out the most practicable route to the Pole. And withal, much might be added "to our knowledge of the geography, geology, glaciation, ethnography, meteorology, and natural history of the Arctic regions."[15] In 1895, at the close of this phase of his explorations, Peary had to reiterate that his primary objective had not been the Pole, "as many imagined," but the solution of the Greenland enigma. "The discovery of the Pole itself was a secondary object and conditional upon the northern extension of Greenland or adjacent lands north of it."[16]

The 1891 plan was to land a party of five or six in June or early July, at or near Whale Sound, in the lower reaches of Smith Sound. During the summer, a house should be erected, game shot, and a reconnaissance made over the inland ice to the southern angle of Humboldt Glacier, where a cache should be laid down. Equipment should be made ready during the winter, and skiing practiced. Early in the spring a caretaker

[15] R. E. Peary, "A Proposed Exploration of Northern Greenland," Am. Geog. Soc., *Journal*, Vol. XXIII (1891), 169.

[16] Remarks by Peary in "The Reception of Mr. Peary," Am. Geog. Soc., *Bulletin*, Vol. XXVII (1895), 375.

should be left at the base, and if conditions were favorable, the entire party should go as far as the head of Petermann Fjord, ninety nautical miles past the Humboldt cache. There the supporting party would turn back, and the main party would continue across the heads of the next three main fjords, heading then for the presumed northern terminus of Greenland, four to five hundred miles from the Humboldt Glacier cache.[17]

The smoother inland ice would be used in preference to the more dangerous sea ice. The party would be kept at a minimum size. Because of the better ice, the sledges and equipment could be lighter and more compact. The leader would be in the van to set the pace and to make the vital decisions.[18] Direct advances would be made through each segment of the route; the small party would permit selectivity and ease of leadership—to Peary a vital element of the plan—and no risk would be run with the sea, wild beasts, vermin, or fevers.[19]

The tiny *Kite's* passengers must have surprised many a Greenlander as she headed north with a crowd of professors, Newfoundland dogs, lumber for a house, supplies and equipment of all sorts, and one tall, handsome woman. Mrs. Peary, wedded two years, was not going to be left behind. Angelo Heilprin of the Philadelphia Academy of Sciences was in charge of the scientists going up for the summer. Dr. Frederick Cook, of later notoriety, was the surgeon and ethnologist. Eivind Astrup was a champion Norwegian skier. And Matthew Henson, colored factotum of Peary's, was there, Peary's constant companion and most dependable dog driver during his expeditions.

While the ship was fighting the ice, a floe struck the rudder such a blow that the men holding the wheel were thrown

[17] Peary, "A Proposed Exploration . . . ." Am. Geog. Soc., *Journal*, Vol. XXIII (1891), 162–63.

[18] Peary, *Northward*, I, xxxviii–xxxix.

[19] Peary, "A Proposed Exploration . . . ." Am. Geog, Soc., *Journal*, Vol. XXIII (1891), 162–63.

away from it. The heavy tiller swung around, pinning Peary to the deck house and breaking his leg. Three weeks later, when a satisfactory site had been located on Whale Sound and the men began erecting the building, Peary could be restrained no longer. At his demand, he was strapped to a board, lowered into a boat, and carried ashore.

As the party needed dogs and Eskimo seamstresses to work up furs into clothing, a boat was sent out on a scouting expedition to find them. Soon several families were ensconced near Red Cliff (as often spelled "Redcliffe") House, and during the winter others were invited there. This group of Eskimos had been almost completely cut off from contact with whalers. They lacked guns, and metal was at a premium. Not only did Peary provide these, but then, as afterwards, he made it a point to secure ample food for his Eskimo allies, aiding them in their hunts. At the same time, the Eskimos provided abundant ethnographic material.

On May 3, Peary, his leg now healed, and Astrup, Gibson, and Cook set out. When the supporting group was to turn back, all volunteered to continue with Peary. Astrup, the most experienced skier, was selected. The remainder turned back on the twenty-fourth, leaving Peary and Astrup with fourteen dogs and twelve hundred pounds of equipment. On June 26, mountains appeared to the northeast, and several days later a trenchlike depression could be seen beyond the nearer range. Peary turned southeast, roughly paralleling the depression. Descending to four thousand feet, they found a moraine made up of rough boulders that rendered walking most difficult. Although there were clumps of flowers, birds, and musk oxen, it was no Arctic Eden. Peary said, "A region of such utter barrenness I never saw before."[20] They managed to shoot several of the oxen and replenish their food supplies.

After twenty-six miles of miserable going, they found themselves atop a 3,800-foot precipice that dropped down to a great

[20] Peary, *Northward*, I, 334.

fjord. Across from them they saw an entrance that appeared to connect with the depression they had been paralleling. Peary at one time said it "appeared" to connect; again, he said, "Looking to the west, we saw the opening of the fjord that had barred our way." The next explorers could find no fjord, and Peary was criticized for bad reporting. Peary was not as careful of his statements as he might have been; neither was Astrup. However, they reported what they had expected to find, for General Greely had written Peary in April, 1891, regarding the fjords of the northwest coast that Lockwood and Brainard had seen, "There is the strongest possible circumstantial evidence to prove that one of these fiords separates the northern part of Greenland."[21] Peter Freuchen and Lauge Koch, who later explored that area, explained the discrepancy.[22] There was indeed such a trough that may in recent geological times have been a fjord, but now is a low valley.[23]

On July 6, the homeward trip was begun, and it was completed, despite snowstorm and loss of dogs, on August 4. The *Kite* was there to receive them, and there was yet time to finish the survey of Inglefield Gulf begun the year before.

The other members of the expedition had not been idle. John M. Verhoeff wrote up a résumé of the meteorological observations made between August, 1891, and March, 1892. "These notes," Peary commented, "give but little idea of the

---

[21] Adolphus W. Greely, "Polar Probabilities of 1894," *North American Review*, Vol. CLVII (1894), 295–96.

[22] Peary, *Northward*, I, 346; Hobbs, *Peary*, 113–19.

[23] Peary was bitterly criticised, especially in Denmark, for having claimed that a channel existed. It was stated that Ludvig Mylius-Erichsen, counting on finding that channel, had thereby lost his life. On the basis of surveys, both by land and by air, Lauge Koch has shown that Peary's sketch maps were quite satisfactory under the circumstances. He has analyzed Peary's and Astrup's statements in detail. He concludes, "It has later proved that Amdrup's supposition regarding Mylius-Erichsen's journey to Kap Glacier cannot be maintained. And however appalled Denmark was by the fate of Mylius-Erichsen and his companions, it is an injustice towards Peary to make him responsible for their bad luck." Lauge Koch, "Survey of North Greenland," *Meddelelser om Grönland*, Vol. CXXX, No. 1 (1940), 1–364. Quoted, 185.

Map of Peary's Expedition, 1891–1909

Peary's first venture in Greenland was too far south to be shown here. It was a trip over the icecap a hundred miles inland from the Danish-Eskimo settlement of Ritenbenk.

One of the most striking features of Peary's explorations, by comparison with others, is the great area covered by Peary. It would be even more impressive if the map were on a scale that permitted tracing each time that Peary covered the route from Cape Sabine to the Fort Conger region.

For sheer audacity, Peary's two trips to northeastern Greenland rank with anything he did later. Crevasses, adverse weather, and the absolute lack of game animals except at either end of the journey, make this comparable to the dangers of open leads and drifting ice that he encountered on his way to the Pole.

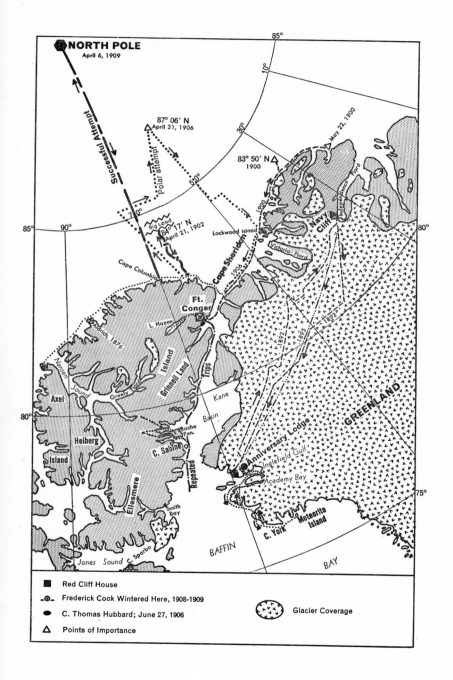

NORTH POLE
April 6, 1909

87° 06′ N
April 21, 1906

83° 50′ N
1900

May 22, 1900

Successful Attempt

Polar attempt

Big Lead
84° 17′ N
April 21, 1902

Lockwood Island

Navy
Cliff

Cape Columbia

Cape Sheridan

Victoria Fiord

Independence Fiord

1906

1900

85°

90°

Ft.
Conger

L. Hazen

Sverdrup 1876

Nansen
Sound

Axel

Greely

Grinnell Land

Trips

Kane

Basin

1892

1895

1892

GREENLAND

Heiberg

Island

C. Sabine

Bache
Pen.

Repeated

Anniversary Lodge

Inglefield Gulf

Academy Bay

Smith
Bay

Ellesmere

Jones Sound   C. Sparbo

C. York

Meteorite
Island

BAFFIN

BAY

85°

80°

80°

75°

■ Red Cliff House

-◉- Frederick Cook Wintered Here, 1908-1909

● C. Thomas Hubbard; June 27, 1906

△ Points of Importance

◯ Glacier Coverage

minute and voluminous observations made by Verhoeff, observations which were his pride, and with which no stress of weather was ever allowed to interfere."[24] Shortly before the expedition's departure, Verhoeff started off over a glacier by himself, and was never heard of afterwards.

Although Cook was credited with the bulk of the anthropological work, the report on it in Peary's volumes appears to have been written by Peary himself. Photographs and anthropological measurements were taken. Population statistics were gathered. Social customs and family relationships were recorded. No outstanding characteristics were noted that differentiated these from other Eskimo groups. Their lack of bows and arrows had been noted earlier.[25]

For the inland ice journey, Peary carried a "Traveller's" transit, a sextant and artificial horizon for use if the transit was damaged, three pocket chronometers which he kept suspended in a case around his neck, three aneroid barometers in a common case, compasses, thermometers, one pair of binoculars, one camera, and two odometers. Wind, drift, vibration of the mount, freezing of the mercury in the artificial horizon, vibration of the atmosphere, refraction, and damage to the eyes, all made accurate observations for position difficult. With the four-inch boat compass lashed to the sledge load or pushed ahead of them on skis, and with the odometers to measure distance, the men navigated by dead reckoning, thereby reducing the number of observations required, and kept moving through days of fog.[26]

The principal contributions of the expedition were geographical. It had practically confirmed the insularity and the approximate northerly extension of Greenland. The explorers had found ice-free areas to the north. A major addition had been made to knowledge of the topography of the icecap. New

[24] Peary, *Northward*, I, 429 ff.
[25] *Ibid.*, I, 479–509.
[26] *Ibid.*, I, lxiv–lxvii.

glaciers had been discovered, and methods for future explorations established.

Having forced ajar the door to an unexplored corner of the world, the Pearys in August, 1893, were again in Greenland a few miles from Red Cliff House, on Bowdoin Bay, building headquarters known for sentimental reasons as Anniversary Lodge. The party was larger, and the quarters much finer than in 1891. Among the fourteen whites were a surgeon, a meteorologist, a taxidermist, an artist, and a nurse for Mrs. Peary. Before the Arctic night was well upon them, an additional member joined the expedition. Marie Ahnighito Peary was born in September.

The pattern of life had been established on the previous expedition. The Eskimos flocked around. Meteorological observations were made steadily. The base was set up as a first-order weather bureau station. The barograph and thermograph made a continuous record at the base and operated satisfactorily later on the trip over the ice.[27]

Peary's plan was to use the Eskimos as a supporting party, turning them back shortly. The whites should continue in one party to Independence Bay, where he had reached the coast in 1892. One party should follow the coast to the north, another to the south, while the base party should explore the Independence Bay area.[28]

A line of caches was begun by Astrup in the autumn, but a succession of storms that forced the party to "hole up" on the ice for as much as a week at a time halted the work before mid-November. A trip in February to free a cache from snow almost caused the loss of Hugh J. Lee and delayed the start. On March 6, 1894, eight whites, five Eskimos, and eighty dogs set forth. Peary, following several days behind, found two of the men sick and convoyed them to the lodge. Another was frostbitten, and the doctor took him back. Others were suffer-

[27] *Ibid.*, II, 177.
[28] *Ibid.*, II, 93.

ing from frostbite, but it was the loss of dogs to *piblockto*, the characteristic Greenland madness, that brought the party to a halt on April 10, after covering 128 miles of the 500-mile journey. As he now lacked men, time, and supplies for his original program, Peary cached a large supply of pemmican and headed homeward, establishing a second cache en route. Peary blamed his failure chiefly on frequent storms, violent wind, and long periods of cold, and secondarily on his failure to appreciate the dogs' need for shelter on the icecap.[29]

The most ambitious trip made after the early return from the inland ice was one in search of the Cape York meteorites. English and Danish expeditions had found that the Eskimos were using meteoric iron for knife blades, but the Eskimos had been chary of information. Before the Peary expeditions, this source had been replaced by utensils received from whalers; Peary had added substantially to their stocks of such treasures.

With Lee and one Eskimo, Peary set out for the Cape York villages. There he found a guide who led him to the meteorite called the "Woman," lying some five hundred yards up a ravine from the shore. The smaller meteorite, the "Dog," could not be found in the deep snow. The location of the largest of all, the "Tent," was pointed out on an island seven miles away. After a venturesome trip of two hundred miles, in three successive marches, Peary reached home. When the *Falcon* came north to relieve the party, Peary made an effort to reach the meteorites by ship, but failed to come within twenty-five miles of the spot.[30]

The personnel of the auxiliary expedition of 1894 included six "scientific gentlemen," including Mrs. Peary's brother, Emil Diebitsch; Thomas C. Chamberlin, professor of geology at the University of Chicago and formerly president of the University of Wisconsin; and Professor William Libbey, Jr., of Princeton.

[29] *Ibid.*, II, 66–120.
[30] *Ibid.*, II, 133, 145–48, 151, 155. Hobbs furnishes a much more detailed and colorful account of the trip, based on Hugh Lee's unpublished diary. See Hobbs, *Peary*, 167–76.

The time of departure was a critical one for Peary. He was determined to winter at Anniversary Lodge and try again. Two of the 1893 party were invalids, Mrs. Peary and baby Marie were scheduled to leave, and it became only too obvious that few of the others had any desire to remain. Matthew Henson was the only one he was sure of. All others he had asked had refused him. The last one was Lee. Yes! "I'll stay with you." Peary could scarcely believe his ears, and had to be reassured. For a time all was joy; later, gloomy hours were to assail him.[31]

After an autumn spent in hunting and a winter in preparation and training for the trip, the three Americans and six Eskimos set out across the cap on April 1. The Eskimos were to help get the sledges up the steep incline at the edge of the ice; none was to go past the big cache 128 miles out. Alas, the cache at thirty miles, containing biscuit, pea soup, and oil, could not be found. At forty-two miles, the barest tip of the pole revealed the smallest cache: ten cases of biscuit and one and one-half cases of milk. The big cache containing fourteen hundred pounds of pemmican could not be found. With supplies short and the dogs half-fed, they pushed on. On May 6, with Lee and the dogs unfit to travel, land was seen ahead. Peary and Henson made a three-day trip and reached the moraine, but located no musk oxen. Now a crucial decision had to be made: to struggle back almost without food, or to gamble on finding musk oxen. If they chose the latter and lost, there would be no hope for them. All were agreed, however, that it was the thing to do.

Musk oxen were found at the cost of great effort, and the strength of the party was renewed. Having come this far, they faced the question of whether they could carry out further

[31] Peary, *Northward*, II, 155; Hobbs, *Peary*, 142, for Lee's account. A copy of the diary of F. W. Stokes, artist of the expedition, is among the papers of Evelyn Briggs Baldwin, the meteorologist of the expedition. Entries for April 20 and 26 show how the men lacked understanding of Peary's intentions, and how in turn he must have been troubled, not knowing on whom he could count. Baldwin MSS (Library of Congress).

explorations. Even had their sledge been able to withstand the crossing of the moraine and sledging over sea ice, the men were in no condition for it. A better view of the area, which disclosed a huge mountain to the north and corrected Peary's notion of the trend of the southern shore of Independence Bay, was their only reward. They returned to the base at Bowdoin Bay, thoroughly exhausted and discouraged, with the last biscuit gone and but one dog remaining.[32]

If the geological results were scant, there was some compensation in being able to put aboard the rescue vessel *Kite* the two smaller meteorites. The *Kite* brought north four scientists, including Professor Rollin D. Salisbury of the University of Chicago and Professor L. L. Dyche, who was making collections for the American Museum of Natural History.[33] Peary's first report, published in the New York *Sun* with the dateline St. John's, September 21, said:

> The mapping of the Whale Sound region and the studies and ethnological collections of the Arctic highlanders have been completed. Another year's meteorological records have been obtained and the *Kite* brings back two of the most interesting meteors in the world.[34]

An editorial note described Dyche's zoological collection as "the most valuable collection ever brought from the Arctic regions." Dyche had collected "nearly 4,000 specimens of birds, eggs, and animals in the neighborhood of Holsteinborg, besides which there were also secured during the *Kite's* cruise, 24 walruses, three narwhal, 25 seals, 13 polar bears, and a number of other animals."[35]

The 1896 and 1897 summer cruises, although interesting both because of securing the huge "Tent" meteorite and be-

[32] Peary, *Northward*, II, 437–524. The Hobbs account, *Peary*, 151–66, is an adequate summary and contains additional material supplied by Lee.
[33] *Ibid.*, II, 536–37.
[34] Reprinted in Am. Geog. Soc., *Bulletin*, Vol. XXVII (1895), 306.
[35] Peary, *loc. cit.*

cause of the work of the parties that accompanied Peary, must be counted as minor, both in program and results.

In 1896, Ralph S. Tarr headed a group from Cornell University, while A. E. Burton of the Massachusetts Institute of Technology led another group. Burton's group was landed at Umnak Fjord in southwestern Greenland, while Tarr's went to the Devil's Thumb area of Melville Sound. Albert Operti went along to make museum figures of the Eskimos.[36] Although unable to bring back the "Tent," Peary secured two live polar bears and "a hundred cases of collections" for the American Museum of Natural History.[37]

The 1897 voyage had two dozen passengers organized into three groups. That of Professor Schuchert of the National Museum was landed at Umanek, except for Robert Stein of the United States Geological Survey, who was landed at Nugsuak with several Eskimo companions. The second group was landed at Cape Haven, while the third accompanied Peary. This time Peary was successful in bringing away the largest Cape York meteorite.

Peary summed up the results of his dozen years' efforts in Greenland, first, as pioneering through which scientists following in his steps had been able to reap an abundant harvest; second, as collecting which had "more than doubled the amount of scientific material and information from the Arctic regions, in the museums of this country"; third, as raising substantially the living standards of the Cape York Eskimos; and fourth, as establishing new techniques in Arctic explorations: use of the Arctic night for journeys, use of very small parties, maintenance of health through fresh meat. Thus he had shown that Arctic exploration could be conducted economically and without loss of life.[38] Peary had in truth not discovered these facts regarding Arctic exploration. Hall certainly knew the

[36] Am. Geog. Soc., *Journal*, Vol. XXVIII (1896), 171.
[37] *Ibid.*, 279.
[38] Peary, *Northward*, I, lviii–lx.

advantages of small parties and fresh meat. Kane's men had conducted many excursions through the Arctic night. Peary was to learn that large parties are sometimes necessary. But Peary did bring these things home to a new generation and rekindle the interest in the north that had been quenched by recent American losses.

IX

Peary's Campaigns for the Pole

||||||||||||||||||||||||||||||||||||||||||||||||

PEARY'S SCHEME for financing a drive to the Pole, year by year, has been described. The first major contribution toward his new program was Alfred Harmsworth's gift in 1898 of the *Windward*. She was to have been re-engined in England, for she was woefully underpowered. A machinists' strike delayed any action, and she was finally sent to the United States, where some refitting was done.

Meanwhile, word of the gift aroused opposition within the Navy Department. Peary was ordered to Mare Island; his response was a request for five years' leave, which was ignored. Charles A. Moore, a prominent New York Republican, then went to see the Secretary of the Navy, John D. Long, on Peary's behalf. It was reported that the Secretary received Moore gladly, but that on hearing the request, the blood rushed to his face and he shouted, "Anything but that, Moore!" Moore then went to President McKinley and obtained the desired order.

This incident involves a lot of good things being done for bad reasons. Peary had then been on leave the better part of eight years. There was certainly no clearly formulated departmental, presidential, or Congressional policy favoring such leave for scientific purposes. Yet the actual reasons for denying the request, according to William H. Hobbs, were compounded of envy at Peary's repeated leaves and ignorant acceptance of British criticism of his use of dog sledges. McKinley's action, taken as some small reward to a political supporter, would better have been in public recognition of the nation's obligation to Peary for his contributions, and of the navy's need for the geographic, hydrographic, and meteorological data he was supplying.[1]

Peary proposed to go by ship as far north as possible along the Greenland coast, for example, to Sherard Osborn Fjord on Robeson Channel. There a colony of Eskimos led by whites would be established, as Captain Howgate had planned in 1877. Caches would be laid to the northernmost tip of Greenland. Then a dash to the Pole would be made by the leader with two of the best Eskimos. If bad ice conditions caused failure one year, the supply ship, which should succeed in reaching them every second year, would keep them in supplies. Dogs would furnish a means of retreat across the inland ice to Whale Sound if necessary.[2]

Meanwhile Captain Otto Sverdrup, the skipper of Fridtjof Nansen's *Fram* during its drift north of Siberia, announced his own plan to seek the North Pole by way of Smith Sound. Aside from duplication of effort and questions of priority, the principal problem was that both parties were counting on getting dogs and assistance from the Smith Sound Eskimos. Peary's plan had been in print since early 1897, and had appeared in the *Georgraphical Journal* of London in February, 1898. Sverdrup claimed to have conceived his plan in 1896, but he did nothing to publicize it until he was on the point of departure in midsummer, 1898.[3]

Then began a rather undignified race to get ahead of Sverdrup. The *Windward* was not ready for the trip, so Peary headed north on the *Hope*. Ice slowed the *Hope*, so that the

[1] Hobbs, *Peary*, 194-96.
[2] Peary *Northward*, I, xlix–liii.
[3] Hobbs, *Peary*, 198–99, 198n., 207. See also George C. Hurlbut, "Mr. Peary's Plan and Captain Sverdrup." Am. Geog. Soc. *Bulletin*, Vol. XXIX (1897), 453. The paths of Peary and Sverdrup crossed but once. Peary's conduct showed that he still harbored resentment. This lingering antagonism has been blamed for Sverdrup's quick endorsement of Frederick Cook's fraudulent claim to the conquest of the Pole.

Peary sledging party: first detachment starting from Red Cliff House for the head of McCormick Bay and the Inland Ice, April 30, 1892. Present are Dr. Cook, Gibson, Astrup, five Eskimos, and twelve dogs.

Photograph by Robert Edwin Peary; courtesy of the National Geographic Society

The *Roosevelt* in the ice in Wrangel Bay, August 31, 1905.

Windward was not far behind her as they neared Melville Bay. Transferring to the *Windward*, the party headed to Smith Sound. On August 18, they were stopped by ice near Cape D'Urville, to the north of Bache Peninsula across the mouth of Princess Marie Bay. They were eighty miles north of Etah and on the opposite side of Kane Basin.

On the night of August 21, 1898, ice formed and did not melt again. On September 12, Peary unloaded a year's supply of provisions at Cape D'Urville. All hope of moving the ship now vanished, and Peary began to revise his plans to fit the new situation.

Meanwhile Sverdrup was turned from his original objective by ice in Kennedy Channel. Instead, he explored the islands to the west of Ellesmere, making some outstanding journeys and a valuable contribution to knowledge.

Peary's first task was to secure fresh meat for the winter. Establishing caches to the north would have to wait until the ice was solid along the channel, when advantage could be taken of the winter moons. Meanwhile, there was an excellent opportunity to survey the area from Cape D'Urville south to Cape Sabine on Bedford Pim Island. Beginning on September 18 with a reconnaissance, Peary proved Bache "Island" to be a peninsula and Hayes "Sound" to be far different from the representation of Greely. Peary declared flatly that it was non-existent. Grinnell Land was thus shown to be a northern extension of Ellesmere Island. Hunting and exploration were continued until October 20. Bear, walrus, and musk oxen were secured in a good hunt.

The journey to Fort Conger was started on December 20. It was reached on January 6, 1899, after a terrific struggle with rough ice. On gaining the fort, Peary found his feet badly frozen. He could not be moved until mid-February. It was apparent that he would lose most of his toes. As walking was out of the question, he was put on the sledge and hauled 250 miles back to the ship. The last amputation was performed on

March 13. On April 19, Peary was back on the trail, headed for Conger, where Henson and some of the Eskimos had preceded him.

On May 4, the party began a vain search for a route across to northern Greenland. The ice in Robeson Channel was too broken to cross, so they returned to Conger and on May 23 started back to the ship with the scientific records and private papers abandoned by Greely sixteen years before.

Peary wasted no time in idly bemoaning his misfortune. On June 29, he led a party out to complete the survey of the bays on either side of Bache Peninsula. Ascending a glacier that entered the more northerly bay, he looked down from 4,700 feet altitude "upon the snow-free western side of Ellesmere Land, and out into an ice-free fjord, extending some fifty miles to the northwest." On his return, he found the *Windward* free of the ice. Leaving a cache at Cape Sabine, the party sailed south to Etah. There they met the *Diana*, Captain Samuel Bartlett commanding, which had been sent to their assistance by the Peary Arctic Club.

Aboard the *Diana* was Professor Libbey of Princeton, who had been on the summer expedition of 1894 and who was back again with three assistants to study biology and oceanography. Another voyager was Robert Stein, who had been north in the 1897 party. Stein and his companions proposed to winter on Ellesmere Land.[4]

Peary cited as accomplishments of the year his survey of the Bache Peninsula area, which altered the maps materially, crossing of the Ellesmere Land icecap, recovery of the Greely papers, and the establishment of a continuous line of caches from Cape Sabine to Fort Conger on which the next season's work might be based.[5]

[4]Amer. Geog. Soc., *Journal*, Vol. XXXI (1899), 279.

[5] R. E. Peary, ". . . Work Done in the Arctic in 1898–1902" [Report to the Peary Arctic Club], Am. Geog. Soc., *Bulletin*, Vol. XXXV (1903), 496–534. The account of the years 1898–1902, as given here, is based primarily

The winter of 1899–1900 was spent at Etah. As opportunity permitted, dog food was sledged across to the first cache at Cape Sabine. The march to Fort Conger was begun on February 19, 1900. The party was in three divisions, leaving Etah one week apart. Peary was in the third party, which made the journey of some four hundred miles in twenty-four days.

Again the Greenland route was tried. Leaving Conger on April 11, they had to cut "a continuous road" from Cape Sumner to Polaris Boat Camp. They crept past Black Horn Cliffs on the thinnest of ice. To Peary's joy, Cape Washington, seen by Lockwood and Brainard of the Greely Expedition, was not Greenland's northernmost point. The triumph of that discovery was still to be his, for on reaching Cape Washington, yet another headland lay to the east and slightly to the north. This he named in honor of Morris K. Jesup, president of the Peary Arctic Club.

Peary was now at the point for beginning his march due north. Although a water sky loomed ahead, the party started out over the ice. They reached the edge of the pack after four marches, on May 16, and were forced to turn back at latitude 83° 50'. On reaching the cape again, they swung east, to complete, if possible, the circuit down to Independence Bay. Fog halted them, and with food exhausted, they started back. Musk oxen and Arctic hares were available along the route, else they could not have delayed.

At Peary's farthest southeastern point, he believed he recognized a mountain that he had seen in 1895 to the north of Independence Bay.[6] He had proved that no land lay to the north or northeast for a considerable distance, "with every indication pointing," as he stated, "to the belief that the coast along which we traveled formed the shore of an uninterrupted

on this article. See also Peary's *Nearest the Pole* and, of course, Hobb's biography, whose maps for this period are especially good.

[6] Lauge Koch produces evidence to show that Peary was mistaken in his identification of the mountain. However, Peary almost completed the circuit of north Greenland.

central Polar sea, extending to the Pole, and beyond to Spitz-bergen and Franz Josef Land groups of the opposite hemis-phere."[7]

The winter of 1900–1901 was spent in the vicinity of Fort Conger. Much of the time the party stayed in igloos in the field to be near the food caches and save hard hauls. In the spring Peary set forth with Henson and one Eskimo for the north. "On reaching Lincoln Bay," he wrote, "it was evident to me that the condition of men and dogs was such as to nega-tive the possibility of reaching the Pole, and I reluctantly turned back."[8]

Peary now turned south to seek his supply ship. Meeting a party of Eskimos sent north from the ship to find him, he learned that the *Windward* had been at Payer Harbor all winter with Mrs. Peary and their daughter aboard. The 1901 relief ship, the *Erik*, reached the *Windward* shortly after Peary did.

Headquarters for the winter of 1901–1902 was established on Payer Harbor; and in February, supplies were again sledged to Conger. Returning parties brought the Greely instruments and other government property back to Payer Harbor. After four days at Conger, the northbound party set forth. On April 6, 1902, they left shore from Cape Hecla, north Ellesmere Island. On the twenty-first, after making slow progress over old floes that had been grounded and upended, they turned back, having reached latitude 84° 17′. Payer Harbor was regained on May 17. The only significant achievement of the summer was a survey of Dobbin Bay, lying a few miles to the north of their base. When the *Windward* arrived, Peary and Henson returned to the United States.

Peary's four-year stay, from 1898 to 1902, resulted in sub-stantial geographical accomplishments. If the most notable achievements were his rounding the tip of Greenland and his

[7] Peary ". . . Work Done in the Arctic in 1898," Am. Geog. Soc., *Bulletin*, Vol. XXXV (1903), 522.
[8] *Ibid.*, 523.

close approaches to the Pole, his surveys of Ellesmere Land should not be lost to sight. In no other field than geography can anything outstanding be recorded, except for the limited extension of previous knowledge of the surface and drift of the polar ice pack. Even the relief vessels failed to bring north the hosts of eager scientists that had accompanied and helped finance earlier trips.

With characteristic resilience, Peary soon had new plans formulated. If he could start north early in the spring from the farthest coast itself, he might well reach the Pole. The Nares Expedition had wintered a vessel at Cape Sheridan on the north coast of Ellesmere Island and brought it out. The problem was to find a ship suited to the task. Nansen had shown, with the *Fram*, that a vessel could be built that would elude the pinching of the ice by sliding up over it. Powerful ships could buck and break fairly heavy ice. But there was no ship in the world that combined those qualities. So Peary set out to raise funds for a ship of his own. The builders he secured had sufficient faith in him to begin purchasing and seasoning the wood before the money was in sight. His dream ship he named the *Roosevelt*, in token of the rugged qualities she should possess in common with Theodore Roosevelt.

The designers gave the vessel a raking stem and filled her bow in solid for icebreaking. In cross section, she was rounded, flaring out up to the rail. "The archives of shipbuilding fail to show a vessel so strongly framed as the *Roosevelt*."[9] She had a one-thousand-horsepower engine, with a bypass by which high-pressure steam from the boilers could be injected directly into the low-pressure chamber, doubling the power for emergencies. Her shaft was worthy of a vessel three or four times her size. The propeller and rudder likewise were designed for heavy duty and easy repair.[10]

[9] "Ships," American Society of Naval Engineers, *Journal*, Vol. XVII (1905), 574–76.
[10] Peary, *The Secrets of Polar Travel*, 3–39. This contains an interesting discussion of the characteristics of a number of Arctic vessels.

With a vessel designed to fit his developing conception of the requirements for polar travel, Peary also saw the need for a large supporting party. Thus, when he headed up Kennedy Channel in late 1905, his decks were covered with Eskimos and their equipment. The *Roosevelt* turned in a splendid performance under Captain Bob Bartlett's competent direction, but suffered severe damage to her stern. On September 5, she reached the *Alert's* old quarters and was secured two miles to the west, at Cape Sheridan. A camp was established ashore to avoid the possibility of losing supplies should the ship be crushed. Hunting parties were sent out into the field, and eventually most of the Eskimos divided among the camps, to check, if possible, the spread of *piblockto* among the dogs.

The base for the northward dash was established at Cape Moss, and caches were established at approximately fifty-mile intervals across the ice. Expecting to meet "unbroken homogeneous ice," Peary set up his supporting parties as relays, each outfit to be responsible for one section of the road. Then Peary would travel along the line, and at the farthest point load up, take the best dogs and most reliable Eskimos, and dash for the Pole. Peary found the polar sea quite different from his anticipations. It was rough, storm torn, and full of leads. He left shore on March 6, 1906. April 21 found the party at latitude 87° 06'. They had run into an area of cracks and leads which they had little hope of surmounting.

On turning back, they were slowed first by storms. Then they were halted for five days beside an uncrossable lead. Observations showed that they were drifting eastward, although the Eskimos believed the shift was toward the west. Finally, young ice was found to be forming on the lead. Spreading out in a skirmish line, they gingerly slid one snowshoe ahead of the other until all were at last across the lead. A moment later the thin ice parted. After crossing a welter of ridges, they found the going became easier, and finally the

Greenland coast was sighted. They had come perilously close to being carried out to sea. Arctic hares and musk oxen were now found for provisions. From the time they reached the Greenland coast, no extraordinary difficulties were encountered by them.

After returning from his unsuccessful attempt to reach the North Pole, Peary decided to survey the gap in the coast line of Grant Land (farthest northwest corner of Ellesmere Island), between the points attained by the Nares Expedition in 1876 and by Sverdrup's party in 1900.

He set out on June 2, only a week after his return from the north. Over much of his track, fog prevented his taking bearings or sun sights, so he had to pace the distance. Crossing the channel, he climbed a peak on the north of Axel Heiberg Island (named originally Jesup Land by Peary). Thence he believed he saw another land looming to the northwest. This he named Crocker Land. Later explorers failed to find Crocker Land. Discovery in the 1940's of floating ice islands several hundred feet high furnished a reasonable explanation of Peary's report. Between July 3 and 30, Peary waded through the thaw water on the ice, three hundred miles back to the ship.

The vessel returned to the United States after more wild encounters with the ice. She was so damaged that a major overhaul was necessary.

Peary began his final trip in 1908. Because of its success it has drawn a great deal more attention than its predecessors. Peary wrote two major accounts of it. All his surviving party leaders also wrote accounts at one time or another: Captain Bob Bartlett, George Borup, Matthew Henson, and finally Donald MacMillan. Matthew Henson and four Eskimos went with Peary all the way to the Pole.

This trip was very much like that of 1906, except that weather and ice conditions were more favorable. Peary had already discovered that the light sledges that worked well on the inland ice were not the type required for crossing the ice ridges of the polar sea. The sledges he designed for this trip were exceptionally long, many of them twelve feet, with high, solid runners. Having discovered in 1906 that his parties must allow for ice drift, he kept all together as much as possible, with a minimum of relaying. Then he sent one group after another back to shore. Each party was under a person competent to make astronomical observations, since the Eskimos' instinct could not be counted on. Then, if movement of the ice "faulted" the back trail, the parties would not be lost. Ross Marvin, while returning to shore with his supporting party of two Eskimos, lost his life.[11]

Peary made camp in the vicinity of the Pole on April 6, 1909, taking observations for position then and again the following day. He sledged over the area, back and forth, so he certainly reached the Pole within the limits of normal navigational error.

Reaching the North Pole itself was the great achievement of the expedition: a feat of physical endurance, of courage, of organizing material resources, and of inspiring men. It also settled beyond reasonable doubt the geographical characteristics of a large area. Geography, however, was not the only science to benefit from the expedition.

The scientific program, for which Peary had been assigned to duty with the Coast and Geodetic Survey, had been begun in November. Donald MacMillan was given orders to proceed to Cape Columbia to take tidal readings for a lunar month. He should at the same time make hourly observations of temperature, atmospheric pressure, and weather and hydrographic

[11] The Eskimos reported that Marvin had gone through thin ice on a lead. This was believed for seventeen years, until one of the Eskimos, when converted to Christianity, confessed that Marvin had been shot after threatening to go on and leave one of the Eskimos, who had been lagging behind. Hobbs and members of the expedition surviving at that time were skeptical of the story. The transcription of an interview between Rasmussen and the two Eskimos concerned, however, makes it sound quite plausible. Greely Collection (National Geographic Society library, Washington, D. C.), Notebook Acc. No. 13439. Compare Hobbs, *Peary*, 347, citing New York *Times*, Sept. 25, 1926.

notes. Borup and Marvin were likewise kept very busy with observations.[12]

On the trip north, Peary started with two 100-fathom reels of wire for soundings and a "clamshell" for bottom samples. Bottom samples to the 110-fathom line were saved,[13] others having been lost at the time of Marvin's death. As one of the wires broke off, the soundings that had been carried on regularly were discontinued until a final sounding at the Pole, where the depth exceeded the length of the line. Sun sights were taken under considerable difficulties, Peary sparing his own eyes against the time when all assistants trained in that work had turned back.[14]

After MacMillan and Borup got back to the ship with their parties, they began the assignment that had been given them —to go to Cape Jesup, Greenland, to make tide observations. They had high hopes of geographic discovery as well, but this was cut short by a letter from Peary, written after his return to the ship at the end of April. They were to concentrate on the tide observations and push a line of soundings north over the ice every ten miles up to the 85th parallel. Additional instruments were sent them, including a pocket sextant and artificial horizon, a sea thermometer, a pocket aneroid barometer, and maximum-minimum thermometers.[15]

About the time that this party returned, Dr. Goodsell left the ship at Cape Sheridan to hunt in the neighborhood of Lake Hazen and Ruggles River. He returned on June 15 with geological, botanical, and zoological specimens, including musk oxen and the beautiful white caribou which was named

[12] Donald B. MacMillan, *How Peary Reached the Pole*, 124–25; George Borup, *A Tenderfoot with Peary*, 89.

[13] Peary to F. W. Perkins, October 18, 1909, with accompanying "Notes on Sounding." Coast and Geodetic Survey File, National Archives, 14 S.H.S. 1908–09 P.

[14] Peary, *The North Pole*, 248–49.

[15] Borup, *Tenderfoot*, 231–32.

for Peary.[16] MacMillan was sent independently to make tidal observations in the neighborhood of Fort Conger.[17]

The result of Peary's last two expeditions was to destroy the myth of land at the North Pole and, in view of the deep soundings obtained, to eliminate the possibility of any large land masses over a considerable area. Additional evidence was obtained regarding the Arctic ice pack, Arctic tides, the size and shape of the continental shelf, and the northern coastline of Greenland and the American Arctic Archipelago.

This ended Peary's active explorations, although not his plans. On February 1, 1910, he proposed to place the *Roosevelt* and all the equipment from his last expedition, along with $10,000 he received from a popular gift, at the disposal of the National Geographic Society for an expedition to the Antarctic at a point opposite Captain Robert Falcon Scott's base. Peary suggested that the Society raise $50,000 and the Peary Arctic Club the remaining $25,000 to $50,000. As the Society's building program had taken its ready cash, an appeal was made to the membership. Several thousand answers to the appeal netted only $10,000, so the board of managers resolved to return all subscriptions to the donors. Even after Amundsen's and Scott's successful trips to the Pole, Peary was still anxious to send a small party, proposing that it remain at the South Pole for a year making scientific observations.[18] Only with the International Geophysical Year 1957 did the scientific world begin to catch up with Peary's vision.

16 Matthew Alexander Henson, *A Negro Explorer at the North Pole*, 156–57.
17 MacMillan, *How Peary Reached the Pole*, 240 ff. The tidal observations are arranged and discussed in Rollin A. Harris, *Arctic Tides*, 10–30.
18 Hobbs, *Peary*, 398. "The South Polar Expedition," *National Geographic Magazine*, Vol. XXI (1910), 161–70; note to members, *ibid.*, 365.

X

Did Dr. Frederick Cook Reach the Pole?

||||||||||||||||||||||||||||||||||||||||||||

FREDERICK COOK was a native of New York. He was educated at the University of the City of New York and the College of Physicians and Surgeons. He accompanied Peary to Greenland in 1891–92 as physician and ethnologist. In 1893, he was commander of an expedition on the yacht *Zeta*. The following year he took quite a large party to south Greenland on the steamer *Miranda*. The vessel was wrecked, and the party had to be rescued. On the Belgian Antarctic Expedition of 1897–99, Cook was surgeon, anthropologist, and photographer, according to the *Manual* of the Arctic Club of America. In 1903, he organized an expedition to climb Mount McKinley. Finally, in 1907, financed by a wealthy sportsman, he and several other men were taken to Etah, in north Greenland, and left there. Like Amundsen, in his famous dash to the South Pole, Cook announced his true destination—the North Pole —only at the last moment.

At Etah, Cook employed four Eskimos to go with him. His route lay along the west side of Ellesmere Island. According to one account, the two Eskimos who were with him on the last stage of his journey were but sixteen or seventeen years old, though their lack of maturity may be immaterial to the result.

They proceeded north up the channel between Ellesmere Island and Axel Heiberg Island, then, Cook claimed, headed for the Pole over comparatively smooth ice, reaching it on April 21, 1908. Only when they had returned to Ellesmere

Island did they run into serious difficulties that made their return to Etah a living hell. Cook spent the winter on Devon Island, reaching Etah in the spring of 1909.

At Etah, Cook was picked up by a Danish vessel and carried to Denmark. There he was given a royal welcome by throngs headed by the Crown Prince. Banquets were held in his honor, and he was thoroughly lionized. Then from Labrador came a loud and discordant note. Peary's vessel had reached the first telegraph station, at Indian Harbor, on September 6, and he had announced his own victory. Telegraphic communication, however, broke down, and only on September 8 did a one-hundred-word dispatch to the New York *Times* contain the famous statement that Cook "has simply handed the public a gold brick."

Who was right? If the Danes had been taken in by a swindler, there would be many red faces in Copenhagen. Two notable Danish Arctic experts had vouched for Cook, one being Dr. Knud Rasmussen, the other being Otto Sverdrup. Rasmussen had returned to Denmark on the same ship with Cook.

Cook at first took the gentlemanly line, "There is honor enough for all." W. T. Stead, a famous British journalist who was covering the Cook story, was impressed by his straightforwardness and his childlikeness. This quality seemed to appeal to many. In the United States there were some who would side with Cook simply to discredit Peary. The most notable of this group was General A. W. Greely, whose competence Peary had severely impugned. Commodore W. S. Schley was another. The ramifications of the controversy need not be elaborated here. It is important to point out, however, that a great deal was written by people who were uninformed or half-informed, and who made up their minds on evidence largely, if not entirely, beside the point.

Who went with Cook on his journey? Four Eskimos part of the way, two Eskimos all the way. Were they trained to take sun sights? No. Was the Eskimos' testimony ever asked? Yes, at least twice. George Borup, one of Peary's lieutenants, reported that when the *Roosevelt* reached Etah, Peary's men tried to get the Eskimos to admit that they had made a ten or fifteen days' march over the ice, but the Eskimos insisted that they had been but two days' march out of sight of land. Moreover, Cook's sledge was there. Reported Borup, it was flimsy, but by no means badly damaged, which was far different from the Peary party's experience.[1]

The second taking of evidence was even more positive. Donald B. MacMillan took two of Cook's Eskimos over the same ground several years later when he was searching for "Crocker Land." They identified the route and again insisted that they went but a day's march onto the ice, built an igloo, slept in it two nights, and returned to shore. The Eskimo lads also identified the pictures published by Cook. Several captioned as being taken at the Pole were, according to Eskimo testimony, taken the following spring on the east coast of Ellesmere Island. Musk-ox boots shown in one picture of the "Pole" had actually been made the winter following the claimed date, at Cape Sparbo on Jones Sound.[2] Knud Rasmussen, who had supported Cook, had the opportunity to cross-examine Cook's Eskimos and disprove Borup's and MacMillan's claims. Possibly other Cook supporters had the same chance. The writer has found nothing to change MacMillan's conclusions.

One must then turn from Cook's companions to his documentary evidence. Evelyn Briggs Baldwin, who had originally supported Cook, went over his printed account and pointed out a host of inconsistencies.[3]

A bit of evidence that would be difficult to fake successfully —authorities differed over the possibility—was Cook's original

[1] Borup, *Tenderfoot*, 300–301.

[2] MacMillan, "New Evidence that Cook Did Not Reach the Pole," *Geographical Review*, Vol. V (1918), 140–41.

[3] Baldwin to Clark Brown, January 25, 1916, Baldwin MSS (Library of Congress.

record of his astronomical observations to determine his location. The Consistory of the University of Copenhagen, which had honored Cook, asked him to submit his original notebooks. Instead, he submitted typed sheets purporting to be copies of the original notebooks, which Cook said he had forwarded to the university. The original notebooks seem never to have arrived. The typed sheets failed to furnish *"such guiding information as might show the probability of the said astronomical observations having been really performed at all . . . the material sent us for investigation,"* the Consistory reported, *"can furnish no proof whatsoever that Dr. Cook has reached the North Pole."*[4] Men who knew navigation characterized Cook's descriptions of his astronomical methods as absurd.

When corroborative evidence is shaky or falls to the ground, an attorney will concentrate on establishing the credibility of his chief witness. Since Cook claimed that Peary's supporters hounded him to federal prison in the 1920's on charges of fraud, we shall make our crucial test one that arose before 1909. Cook had claimed to have reached the top of Mount McKinley, Alaska, on his 1903 expedition. His claim was challenged, and the Explorers' Club of New York appointed a committee to investigate the charges. The investigation was repeatedly delayed to permit Cook to give his side of the story. He appeared before the committee with an attorney, agreed on a time for a hearing, but failed to keep the appointment. Other members of the expedition were heard, and on December 24, 1909, the committee, which included his close friend, Anthony Fiala, reported adversely to Cook's claims.

The Explorers' Club, including friends of Cook's and foes of Peary's, voted *unanimously* to expel him. The Arctic Club, which had been founded by comrades of Cook on the *Miranda* cruise, likewise dropped him, as did the Council of the Brooklyn Institute of Arts and Sciences. Here are three "juries,"

---

[4] Italics in the original. Translation quoted in Hobbs, *Peary*, 482–83.

which cannot be considered predisposed against Cook, each of which in effect found him guilty of knowingly making false claims.[5]

One must reluctantly conclude that there is no positive evidence that Cook reached the Pole, and rather carefully substantiated evidence from his companions that he did not come anywhere near the Pole.

[5] Hobbs, *Peary*, 380–82.

XI

The Routes via Spitsbergen and Franz Josef Land

IIIIIIIIIIIIIIIIIIIIIIIIIIIIIIIIIIIIIIIIIIII

THE PEARY SAGA has obscured a number of expeditions, some of which, for money invested, scientific program
undertaken, and achievement, were more important than individual expeditions of Peary's. Having lost out to Peary in the
race for the Pole, other Arctic explorers and their efforts have
been almost forgotten. For instance, the physical observations
of the Fiala–Ziegler Expedition excel any of Peary's, although
its natural history collections are not the equal of Peary's.

Most of the expeditions discussed heretofore have lain in
the quadrant between 20° and 110° west longitude. The
Alaskan expeditions to be discussed in the succeeding chapter
were confined almost entirely to the sector 140°–180° west
longitude. The five expeditions to be described here were based
on Spitsbergen or the Franz Josef Archipelago, between 10°
and 70° east longitude. Thus there is a certain geographical
unity to this group of expeditions.

Probably all these expeditions were stimulated by Peary's
work. Whether or not, it is true that, except for Walter
Wellman's first expedition, the leaders were schooled in the
Peary techniques and traditions. Wellman had Evelyn Briggs
Baldwin, meteorologist for Peary in 1893–94, as second in
command during his second expedition. Then Baldwin became
the leader of the first Ziegler Expedition. Anthony Fiala, who
had been photographer for Baldwin, led the second Ziegler
Expedition. Ernest de Koven Leffingwell and Einar Mikkelsen

formed a friendship on the Baldwin–Ziegler Expedition which resulted in their own expedition to the Alaskan Arctic.

The failure of the *Jeannette* and *Polaris* Expeditions had by no means eliminated the idea of polar exploration from all American minds but Peary's. George Melville had been back from the *Jeannette* Expedition but a few months when he volunteered for the rescue of the Greely party. He closed his narrative of the events with his own proposal for an expedition toward the North Pole. From his experience with the *Jeannette*, Melville believed no vessel could be made strong enough to withstand the pressure of the ice, even if given a solid hull. Hence he proposed a land route via Franz Josef Land, his information (wrongly) indicating that it stretched to 84°, almost 150 miles farther north than the true value.[1]

Another proposal for Arctic research belongs chronologically to this group. W. H. Gilder had been with Frederick Schwatka on his search in the vicinity of King William's Land for the remains of the Franklin Expedition. He had been aboard the *U.S.S. Rodgers* and had crossed Siberia in the search for De Long. Between 1890 and 1892, he was busy gaining support for an expedition to the region of his first journey, with the purpose of determining more exactly the location of the North Magnetic Pole. Gilder sounded out the United States Coast and Geodetic Survey; in turn, its chief, Thomas Corwin Mendenhall, requested the advice of the National Academy of Sciences; the Academy requested the expert on Mendenhall's staff, Charles A. Schott, to prepare a plan for such a survey. The Academy recommended "a cordon of stations, stretching from Alaska to Newfoundland." Possibly because this was not what Gilder had in mind, the plan seems to have been dropped at that stage.[2]

Like Gilder, Walter Wellman combined geography with

[1] George W. Melville, *In the Lena Delta*, 479–82.
[2] "An Expedition to the Northern Magnetic Pole . . . .," American Geographical Society, *Journal*, Vol. XXIV (1892), 218, 224–25, 233.

Map of Spitsbergen;
Walter Wellman, 1894, 1906, 1907, 1909

Wellman's first voyage to Spitsbergen took him by ship to the Seven Islands in the far north of the archipelago. His luck did not hold, for he lost his ship and was fortunate in being picked up.

Wellman's airship base was on Danes Island, at the northwest corner of the archipelago, just a few miles from the old Dutch whaling base of Smeerenburg.

Another point of interest is Longyearbyen or Longyear City, named after an American mining engineer. It is now the Norwegian administrative headquarters for the islands.

Remote though these islands seem to most Americans, there has been whaling and fishing activity in the vicinity for almost four centuries.

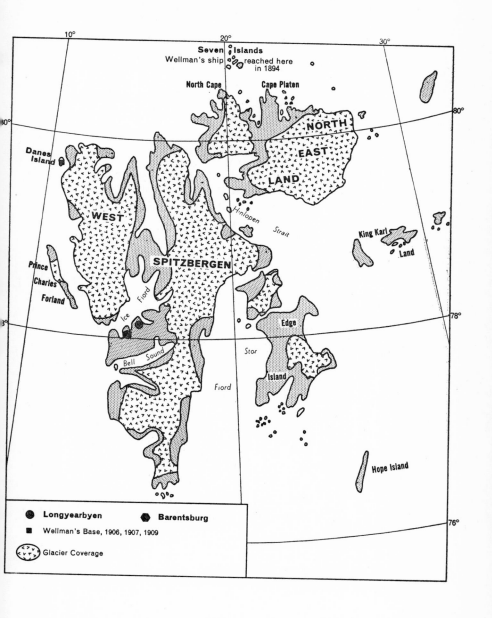

Seven Islands
Wellman's ship reached here in 1894

North Cape   Cape Platen

NORTH

EAST

LAND

Danes Island

WEST

SPITZBERGEN

Hinlopen

Strait

King Karl

Land

Prince
Charles
Forland

Ice

Fiord

Edge

Bell Sound

Stor

Island

Fiord

Hope Island

● Longyearbyen   ⬡ Barentsburg

■ Wellman's Base, 1906, 1907, 1909

Glacier Coverage

journalism. His term as president of the National Press Club of Washington, D. C., had been his chief distinction up to 1894, when he set off blithely for the North Pole. His plan to use Spitsbergen for a base came from reading Parry's account of the British expedition of 1827, which had made a modern "farthest north" record broken first by Lockwood and Brainard in 1882. Wellman went to Norway in 1893 to investigate the possibility of setting up an expedition. Encouraged by Norwegian skippers who had sailed around Spitsbergen,

> I returned to America, secured the necessary capital, organized an expedition, chartered an old ice-steamer in Norway—she was named the *Ragnvald Jarl*—and built three boats of aluminum for use on the trip, with special sledges and other equipment designed to facilitate travel over the polar pack in the summer of the year.[3]

Wellman's scientific staff was to consist of Professor O. B. French, Charles G. Dodge, and four professors from the University of Christiania. He planned to take fourteen men and sixty dogs over the ice toward the Pole, one-half of them turning back after twenty-five days, the remainder making a "dash to the pole."

On the eve of his departure from New York, Wellman brashly informed the New York *Tribune*, "Our objective is to find the truth about these polar regions. Whether there is, as some authorities assert, an open polar sea, or whether there is nothing but ice covering both sea and land."[4]

At first, fortune smiled. The *Ragnvald Jarl* sailed from Tromsö, Norway, on May 4, 1894, and found the ice gone a month earlier than usual. The Seven Islands, at the extreme tip of the archipelago, were reached. The polar pack could be

---

[3] Walter Wellman, *The Aerial Age*, 16–17. For a description of the boats, see Clements R. Markham, "Address to the Royal Geographical Society," *Geographical Journal*, Vol. IV (1894), 12.

[4] Quoted in "Geographical Notes," Am. Geog. Soc., *Journal*, Vol. XXVI (1894), 73–74.

seen a few miles to the north. The ice party left the ship with sledges, dogs, and boats, following land ice in the hope of finding a good spot to cross the ridged and craggy boundary of the polar pack.

Then a storm came down from the northwest, heaping the pack ice mountain high. Messengers overtook Wellman with the heart-rending information that the violence of the storm had crushed the heavy ice barrier sheltering the *Ragnvald Jarl*. Wellman returned to find the ship a total wreck. Much of the stores and sufficient material for a hut had been salvaged. It was agreed that the ship's captain should take a small boat south in search of a vessel.

Wellman returned to the northbound party and sledged eastward for several days. There was so much water that they decided to shoot the dogs and take to the boats. At Platen Island they renewed their attempt to get a foothold on the pack. By now it was the end of May, and pools of water on the floes added to the difficulties of ice travel. Recognizing the futility of their efforts, they began the retreat, pushing the boats over the slush ice toward the hut at Walden Island. There they waited with the ship's crew week after week. As the ice gave no evidence of permitting a ship to reach them that season, the whole party started working the boats south over the ice floes. At the edge of the pack they found a sealing schooner that had come north to look for them.[5]

A member of a yacht party that had picked up Wellman's dispatches at Danes Island, reporting to the Royal Geographical Society, described Wellman as "a plucky young American leaving his editorial chair in Washington and, without any practical acquaintance with ice navigation . . . starting off helter-skelter to make a rush for the North Pole."[6] If there was a large measure of truth in the statement, yet that was not

[5] Wellman, *Aerial Age*, 17–34.
[6] Quoted in "Geographical Notes," Am. Geog. Soc., *Journal*, Vol. XXVI (1894), 391–93.

the entire truth. Several of Wellman's Norwegian allies had had Arctic experience, and his aluminum boats showed imaginative planning.

After his return from Spitsbergen, Wellman conferred with leading French balloon makers and seriously considered ballooning across the Pole. The financial requirements delayed planning, and the more he considered it, the less he liked the idea.[7] In 1897, a Swede, Salomon August Andrée, tried ballooning, but failed to reach the Pole and apparently lost his life as a result of carbon monoxide poisoning while "safe" within a tent.

By 1898, Wellman had come to a deeper appreciation of Arctic problems and the men that set out to solve them than was expressed in his New York *Tribune* interview of 1894. Acknowledging that the trip to the Pole was an athletic feat— and justifying it as quite as worthy of applause and reward as any other athletic event—he had also arrived at a thorough realization of the variety of scientific problems involved. For the *American Review of Reviews* he wrote,

> [The first expedition to reach the Pole] will return with valuable information concerning the magnetic and electrical forces of the earth, now so little understood, concerning meteorology and geology, the forms and extent of unknown lands, if any exist, the depth of the sea and the currents thereof, the organic life of our own and past ages, and the great problem of glaciation, which involves the history of the human race.[8]

Wellman asked the National Geographic Society formally to endorse the aims and purposes of the expedition projected for 1898, to appoint a scientific advisory committee, and to contribute funds which should be refunded if the expedition were successful. The Society appointed a committee as requested. Among its distinguished members were A. W. Greely,

[7] Wellman, *Aerial Age*, 35–39.
[8] Walter Wellman, "Arctic Exploration and the Quest of the North Pole," *American Review of Reviews*, Vol. XVII (1898), 178–79.

long since a general and chief of the United States Signal Corps; George W. Melville, now an admiral; and Alexander Graham Bell.

The committee recommended that three scientific observers be added to the expedition. This was promptly done. Evelyn B. Baldwin, an employee of the United States Weather Bureau on furlough, was appointed second in command. Quirof Harlan, a physicist and photographer of Washington, D. C., and Dr. Edward Hofma, physician and naturalist, completed the scientific roster.[9]

The National Geographic Society raised $1,000 of the $12,000 that came from contributors. The remainder of the $27,000 needed came from unspecified sources, probably in large measure from advances on promised magazine articles. Contributors listed included such wealthy New Yorkers as J. Pierpont Morgan, W. K. Vanderbilt, and Morris K. Jesup.[10]

The Weather Bureau supplied meteorological instruments: two aneroid barometers, a barograph, maximum and minimum thermometers, a thermograph, two anemometers, two psychrometers, record books, and the like. Time did not permit the ordering from Paris of a barograph and thermograph in aluminum cases.[11]

The Second Wellman Polar Expedition sailed from Tromsö, Norway, in the steamer *Frithjof* on June 26, 1898. Having found on his first expedition that Belgian cart dogs became psychotic after a short stay in Spitsbergen, Wellman put in to Archangel for Siberian dogs. Then the party sailed for Franz Josef Land, but the ice was much worse than in 1894. Once

[9] "The Wellman Polar Expedition," *National Geographic Magazine*, Vol. IX (1898), 373–75. Walter Wellman, "On the Way to the North Pole," *Century Magazine*, Vol. LVII (1898–99), 534. On Baldwin's status, see letter from Willis L. Moore, Chief of the Weather Bureau, to Baldwin, May 19, 1898, in Baldwin MSS (Library of Congress).

[10] "The Wellman Polar Expedition," *National Geographic Magazine*, Vol. X (1899), 481.

[11] Weather Bureau to Baldwin, Washington, D. C., April 26, 1898, Baldwin MSS.

they put back to Norway for coal, and only on July 30 did they land at Cape Tegetthoff in Franz Josef Land. There were four Americans and five Norwegians in the party.

Immediately, Baldwin was sent out with a party to establish a northern outpost. A ton of condensed rations was deposited for the northern sledging party; walruses were killed as winter rations for forty dogs.[12] Meanwhile, Wellman followed with the bulk of the provisions, moving about three miles a day. By August 15, he realized that the ice surface was too bad for further travel. He instructed Baldwin to leave two men to feed the dogs and guard the supplies, and to return to the main base with the remainder.[13] Two Norwegian volunteers were appointed to spend the winter guarding the cache.

This time Wellman and the main party set out on February 18, 1899, when they could be much less exposed to the danger of moving ice fields and open water. On reaching the advance base, "Fort McKinley," they found that one of the Norwegians had died. As the soil was frozen, the only way to protect the dead man's body from animals was to lay it back in one corner of the hut. That his companion had not gone insane in the two months of solitary vigil, Wellman attributed to his reciting poetry from his well-stocked mind.

On March 17, the party started north. Wellman figured they could make the Pole if they were willing to take a chance on getting back. If they could move one mile an hour, ten miles a day, for 100 to 115 days from late winter to the beginning of summer, the victory would be theirs. But Wellman found that the five men, each with sledge and dog team, could make but six miles a day.

They had gone only three days' journey when Wellman seriously bruised and wrenched his leg. As the party pressed forward, the leg got worse rather than better. Then, on March

[12] Wellman, *Aerial Age*, 41–49; "Geographical Record," Am. Geog. Soc., *Bulletin*, Vol. XXXI (1899), 378.

[13] Wellman to Baldwin, Cape Tegetthoff, August 4, 1898; Wellman to Baldwin, Cape Tegetthoff, August 15, 1898, Baldwin MSS.

22, disaster struck again in the form of an icequake in the midst of a storm. They barely rescued the tent, sleeping bags, and cooking gear from one floe before it upended. Three sledges were saved, but a third of their dogs, all their dog food, and a large part of their own supplies had vanished into the depths of the sea. It was obviously foolish to go on. Later, when Wellman realized that his leg might have given out so far from base that he could not return, the icequake seemed almost providential.[14]

After the party returned to the main base, a group set out under Baldwin's leadership to explore the Franz Josef Archipelago. This party discovered a new island, and named it in honor of Alexander Graham Bell, president of the National Geographic Society.[15]

Meanwhile, physical observations had been going forward. Aboard ship on the way north,

> Each observation consisted of readings of the wet and dry bulb thermometers, water thermometer, salinometer, aneroid barometers . . . ship's barometer . . . anemometer . . . observations were made as to the direction of the wind, the amount of cloudiness, and the kind and direction of clouds.

Observations were promptly commenced ashore. Then, on the autumn trip to "Fort McKinley," Baldwin cradled many of his precious instruments in a basket lashed to the sledge and made a series of observations at that point. The instruments were returned to the main base in October, and observations were continued at that point for the remainder of the expedition.[16] Hofma prepared a report on the flora and fauna,[17]

[14] Wellman, *Aerial Age*, 102–103.

[15] "Geographical Record," Am. Geog. Soc., *Bulletin*, Vol. XXXI (1899), 378.

[16] Evelyn B. Baldwin, "The Meteorological Observations of the Second Wellman Expedition," *National Geographic Mazagine*, Vol. X (1899), 514–16.

[17] Wellman, "The Wellman Polar Expedition," *National Geographic Magazine*, Vol. X (1899), 492.

while Harlan interested himself primarily in magnetism and the aurora. Just less than 150 records of auroras were made between October 7 and March 13. Typical observations gave a description of the form, color and movement, location in the constellations, and meteorological conditions.[18]

At the sacrifice of chronological order, the two expeditions financed by William Ziegler of Royal Baking Powder wealth will be passed over for the time being, while consideration is given to Wellman's last and greatest effort to reach the Pole.

Wellman's progressive outlook had first been shown with aluminum boats. Now, between 1899 and 1905, he tried to develop a motor sledge weighing 150 to 200 pounds to replace dogs. The men should ride from one ice ridge to the next, where they would pick up the units in the train of sledges and manhandle them over to the next smooth stretch. In 1901, Wellman purchased a steam whaler, in which he hoped to start north in 1902. However, these plans came to naught.[19]

Then Wellman became intrigued by Santos-Dumont's airship, and in 1905 was impressed by two airships built for the French government. They had a top speed of twenty-seven miles per hour with a forty-horsepower motor. Why not fly one of these to the Pole?

Wellman submitted the idea to Frank B. Noyes, editor and publisher of the Chicago *Record-Herald*. The Wellman Chicago *Record-Herald* Polar Expedition corporation was formed just before New Year's, 1906, and Wellman set out immediately for France to contract for the airship.

After consulting French experts, Wellman drew up the specifications. The distance to the Pole was six hundred miles. Allowing a 50 per cent safety factor, a cruising range of eighteen hundred miles was required. With the airspeed reduced to

18 Evelyn B. Baldwin, "Auroral Observations on the Second Wellman Expedition Made in the Neighborhood of Franz Josef Land," *Monthly Weather Review*, Vol. XXIX (1901), 107–15.

19 Wellman, *Aerial Age*, 120; "Geographic Notes," *National Geographic Magazine*, Vol. XII (1901), 203.

fifteen knots, the weight of the fuel and motor could be kept down to seven thousand pounds. Still, a much larger gasbag for the greater lift was needed than for the French military craft. The building time allowed for Wellman's airship was four months.[20] The campaign, however, was planned for two years, so that initial failure would not halt the work. Wireless stations were to be set up at Hammerfest and Spitsbergen, while the airship was to carry a third set. The cost of the airship was estimated at over $250,000.[21]

Meanwhile, Wellman began to erect an "airship hall" of steel framing and sail cloth at Danes Island, Spitsbergen. The contractors failed to make delivery date, and the airship was delivered at Spitsbergen without contractors' trials. Repeated mechanical failures occurred in the engine. Finally, the car began to shake to pieces. Winter was approaching, so a caretaker party of three was left at the base, and on September 4, the expedition returned to Europe.[22]

A new airship was built for 1907. It was the second largest in the world. Melvin Vaniman, an experienced balloon builder, became Wellman's right-hand man. The frame of the new car was, at Vaniman's suggestion, made of tubular steel. The balloon was lengthened to 185 feet, while the car was 115 feet long. The total height was 65 feet. The gasbag was made of a triple layer of silk and cotton, with three coatings of rubber. Losses of gas were estimated at 1 per cent a day, while Andrée's fine balloon had lost 3 per cent. Total lift was almost 19,000 pounds. A 70-horsepower, 750-pound Lorraine-Dietricht motor replaced the earlier 40-horsepower motor. As balloons ordinarily start out with extra weight that can be jettisoned, Wellman made a "serpent" weighing 1,400 pounds of leather "sausages," each one filled with provisions.

[20] Wellman, "By Airship to the North Pole," *McClure's*, Vol. XXXIX (1907), 191–200.

[21] "Walter Wellman's Expedition to the North Pole," *National Geographic*, Vol. XVII (1906), 205–207.

[22] Wellman, "By Airship to the North Pole," *McClure's*, Vol. XXXIX (1907), 194–200.

Wellman had again asked the National Geographic Society to appoint a representative. In 1906 and 1907, Major Henry Blanchard Hersey, inspector in the United States Weather Bureau, was appointed. He served as meteorologist, navigator, and finally as executive officer. His meteorological observations for 1906 were reported in the *Monthly Weather Review.*[23]

Once at the North Pole, Wellman proposed to anchor the airship, which he had named the *America*, climb down, and perform a series of observations proposed by the National Geographic Society and other organizations.

Should accidents cause a landing, Wellman was prepared with ten sledge dogs, sledges, a small boat, equipment, and food for ten months.

From late June to September 2, Wellman waited for favorable mechanical and meteorological conditions. After one of the stormiest summers in years, a break came in the weather, and the party took off. The airship behaved well in the minutes devoted to test. Then it "slowly rounded the north end of Foul Island in the teeth of the wind." Gaining confidence, Wellman ordered the start for the Pole. But the wind increased—to twelve miles an hour. Snow began to fall, and then the compass failed. They put about and tried to find the ship from which they had cast off. After two hours aloft, they landed on a glacier. Two vessels had been following their course, and the crews rescued the aeronauts and the most valuable of their equipment.[24]

The presidential election of 1908 called Wellman home to America to his old job as correspondent. But in 1909, while both Peary and Cook were on expeditions based on Ellesmere

[23] "Meteorological Work at Camp Wellman, Danes Island, Spitsbergen, *Monthly Weather Review*, Vol. XXXV (1907), 63–68.

[24] Harry De Windt, "The Race for the Poles," *Living Age*, Vol. CCLVI (1908), 207–208. Wellman, *Aerial Age*, 134–35, 168–77. Wellman, "Will the *America* Fly to the Pole?" *McClure's*, Vol. XXIX (1907), 243–45. "Test of Wellman's Airship in the Arctic Regions," *Scientific American*, Vol. XCVII (Sept. 28, 1907), 223.

Island, Wellman returned once more to Spitsbergen. The principal improvement in the *America's* construction was the addition of a second motor.

On August 15, 1909, the *America* again set out. If all had gone well, it should have reached the Pole in two days. Everything appeared to operate satisfactorily, so the airship was turned north. Just as it was set to leave the coast, its large leather "serpent" dropped off. The crew not only lost their food, but had to compensate by releasing gas. As a substitute was needed to prevent the airship's hitting the ground, a steel cable that unfortunately had a loop in the end, was dragged. This caught against all sorts of projections. They were forced to turn back, and finally reached a Norwegian survey vessel that took them in tow. The rising wind forced them to lower the airship to the water's surface. The men were taken off, and the hulking bag was towed back to the beach.[25]

Back in Europe, Wellman learned that Peary had at last reached the Pole. The glory taken from that conquest, Wellman turned his attention to crossing the Atlantic by air, with results similar to his Arctic efforts. Like S. F. B. Morse, Wellman was a promoter rather than an engineer or scientist; yet in this case insufficient honor has been paid to his imagination and energy.

Evelyn Briggs Baldwin, Wellman's lieutenant on his second expedition, had no sooner returned from Franz Josef Land than he began planning an expedition of his own to the Pole. No prospects seemed brighter than his, for he had been trained under Peary in 1893–94 and tested as a party leader under Wellman. William Ziegler, baking power baron, provided such generous financing for the expedition that three vessels were available, two for the main expedition to Franz Josef Land and a third to lay down an emergency cache on Shannon Island off east Greenland in case breaking up of the ice should prevent the sledging party's return to its base.

[25] Wellman, *Aerial Age*, 187–92.

Baldwin claimed no financial reward from Ziegler. Rather, he laid careful plans to capitalize on his anticipated fame. Like Wellman, he planned to sell his story, contracting with *McClure's*. Like Peary, he endorsed various products, signing a contract with the Kato Coffee Company for a royalty of one-quarter of a cent a pound up to $10,000 for the use of the trade-mark "Baldwin Coffee." He had already gained experience on the lecture platform. And to avoid being undercut, he made each of his party sign an agreement that they would neither lecture, write, take pictures, nor even carry a camera without his consent.

Although he planned primarily a polar expedition, Baldwin was provided with excellent scientific equipment and a good staff. The Signal Corps lent twenty-six items valued at $234.05. The Coast and Geodetic Survey loaned a surveying camera and magnetic instruments. Deep-sea sounding apparatus was purchased. The gravity pendulum was a model built to operate in vacuum. The National Museum furnished nets, sieves, dredges, and preservatives.

Chief of the scientific party was Ernest de Koven Leffingwell, a pupil of A. A. Michelson at the University of Chicago, who was prepared to do meteorological, magnetic, and astronomical observations. Francis Long, one of the Greely Expedition survivors, had continued to work as a meteorological observer, and was one of the few who was paid more than the nominal wage of $25.00 a month. There were three physicians who acted also as naturalists. And a photographer, Anthony Fiala, was also to serve as chief assistant.[26] The three physicians were expected to return "valuable physiological data upon the effects of Arctic environment."[27] Continuous meteorological records would be made. The aurora would be observed, and by means of simultaneous observations from two stations con-

[26] The paragraphs above are based on a variety of letters, bills, and contracts in the Baldwin MSS (Library of Congress).

[27] "Geographical Record," Amer. Geog. Soc., *Bulletin*, Vol. XXXIV (1902), 25-26.

nected by telephone, the height of clouds and of the aurora should be determined. Absolute magnetic readings would be made on Mondays while each Tuesday a term-day would be held, and observations on the horizontal intensity and the variation made every five minutes. Observations would be made on low stars to determine the index of refraction of air at low temperatures. Geodetic, tidal, and photographic work would go on, while Franz Josef Land would be surveyed by triangulation and by topographical camera.[28]

Despite his attention to scientific observations, Baldwin proclaimed that neither science alone nor merely the establishment of a new "farthest north" would suffice. The Pole alone would do, and July 4, 1902, was the date set for reaching it.[29]

Feeling that other parties had failed for lack of dogs, Baldwin had no less than four hundred of the snarling Siberian huskies and fifteen ponies from Siberia for his use. Like Peary, he planned to make dog eat dog in order to stretch the food supply.

From Andrée, whose balloon flight he had sought to join in 1897, he borrowed the idea of getting back messages by means of floats. A number of 3,000-cubic-foot balloons were carried, each of which supported a series of buoys. As the gas escaped, the bottom buoy would touch the water and be released, the balloon springing up and traveling with the wind until the descent to the sea surface released another.[30]

In midsummer, 1901, the steamer *America* set forth with the main party, consisting of seventeen Americans, six Russian dog drivers, and the Swedish ship's crew.[31] For about one year nothing was heard from the expedition. Then, despite its three years' supply of provisions, the party suddenly appeared at

[28] Evelyn Briggs Baldwin, "How I Hope to Reach the North Pole," *McClure's*, Vol. XVII (1901), 422.
[29] *Ibid.*, 418.
[30] *Ibid.*, 422.
[31] Am. Geog. Soc., *Bulletin, loc. cit.*

Tromsö, Norway. Early dispatches carried word of the establishment of three large food caches, the inability to proceed north in 1901 as far as desired, the shortage of coal, and the loss of ponies and dogs.[32]

The story, as it was told in the newspapers and the geographical journals, was that Captain Johansson of the *America* had refused to take orders from the ice pilot, had quarreled with Baldwin and his appointed party commanders, splitting the party into opposing Swedish and American camps.[33]

Further glimpses of the truth come out in the Baldwin manuscripts. While the *America* was still being outfitted in Dundee, Leffingwell wrote Baldwin that the Swedish officers misunderstood the position of the Americans simply because the Americans had pitched in at waiting tables and doing dirty work. "I am sure that the officers do not mean wrong but do not have the perception to see a gentleman beneath working clothes." Leffingwell said that the chief engineer, H. P. Hartt, was stirring up trouble and should be dismissed.[34]

After the ship returned, testimony agreed that the captain— or sailing master, as he had signed on—and the chief engineer led one faction against Baldwin and the Norwegian ice master. That Baldwin also was at fault, for what reason it is not apparent, is indicated from the sympathetic testimony of one of the party:

> Nothing is ready for announcement as yet but it is all over with the commander. It is terrible to witness but I am powerless to aid him even if I had not cause to fearlessly do my hard duty . . . . His punishment is terrible but it had to be and I find it hard to write of it calmly.

Baldwin returned to New York, was summarily relieved of

[32] "Geographical Record," Am. Geog. Soc., *Bulletin*, Vol. XXXIV (1902), 328. "Geographic Notes," *National Geographic Magazine*, Vol. XIII (1902), 358–59.

[33] *National Geographic Magazine*, loc. cit. "Geographischer Monatsbericht." *Petermanns Geographische Mitteilungen*, Vol. XLII (1902), 216, 268.

[34] Leffingwell to Baldwin from Dundee, n.d., Baldwin MSS.

Mr. and Mrs. Robert Edwin Peary

The *U.S.S. Vincennes*, Commander Ringgold, first commanding officer of the U.S. North Pacific Surveying Expedition, 1853-56.

Building sledges between decks.

his position by an angry Ziegler, and Anthony Fiala appointed in his place. Baldwin believed that William Champ, Ziegler's private secretary, had poisoned Ziegler against him. He also claimed that Bridgman, secretary of the Peary Arctic Club, had been interested in preventing any one but Peary from reaching the Pole, and hence had charged that the Baldwin–Ziegler Expedition cost a million dollars, when the real cost, including supplies cached, was but $142,000.[35]

The scientific results were disappointingly small. Collections were made for the National Museum. Motion pictures were tried with some success.[36] A few observations were incorporated in the volume of scientific results of the Fiala–Ziegler Expedition edited by John A. Fleming.[37] Leffingwell portrayed his disappointment. He had been appointed head scientist and told

> to prepare a complete scientific program . . . being assured that I should be furnished with ample assistance . . . . I was equipped with an outfit with which I hoped to cast the results of all previous expeditions into the shade.

Instead, he often found himself in the role of deck hand, kept at busy work. He had done little but map the route of a one-hundred-mile sled trip.[38]

The entire personnel of the expedition that Ziegler sent out under Anthony J. Fiala was American, although some search was necessary to find experienced Arctic seamen. There were eight men with some scientific pretensions: William J. Peters of the United States Geological Survey and second in command; Francis Long, the weather observer; Russell W. Porter,

---

[35] Baldwin MSS. For last paragraph, see MS of speech to "Science Club." Cf. New York *Herald*, Magazine Section, Sept. 6, 1909.

[36] *National Geographic Magazine, loc. cit.*

[37] *The Ziegler Polar Expedition, 1903–1905 . . . Scientific Results . . . .* Henceforth cited as *Scientific Results.*

[38] "A Communication from Leffingwell," *The University of Chicago Magazine,* Vol. VII (1915), 76–79.

Map of Franz Josef Land Expeditions

Three major expeditions from the United States sought this area: that of Walter Wellman in 1898–99, the first Ziegler Expedition under E. B. Baldwin in 1902–1903, and the second Ziegler Expedition under Anthony Fiala in 1903–1905. The last was by far the most extensive. Its tracks are shown on the accompanying map.

The place names given here are the original German and English names. A person making comparisons with some recent maps may become confused in trying to match up the names. As Franz Josef Land is now claimed by the Soviet Union, certain agencies have tried to transliterate the names as given in the Cyrillic alphabet on Soviet maps. But these in turn have been Soviet efforts to translate from the Roman alphabet, the rules applied to English names seemingly having been designed originally for transliteration from German. In other words, the result is an approximation of a Russian trying to read English from what he has learned of German pronunciation. Thus (Alexander) Graham Bell Island becomes Ostrov Grehm Bell, Cambridge becomes Kembridj, and so forth.

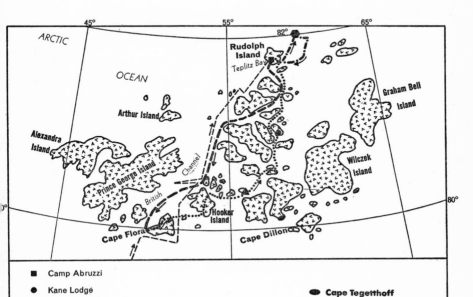

45°   55°   65°

ARCTIC

OCEAN

Arthur Island

Alexandra
Island

Prince George Island

Channel

British

Cape Flora

Rudolph
Island
Teplitz Bay

Graham Bell
Island

Hooker
Island

Wilczek
Island

Cape Dillon

82°

80°

■   Camp Abruzzi

●   Kane Lodge

▲   Camp Ziegler   ⬢ **Cape Tegetthoff**

⬡   Northernmost point reached by Fiala during polar attempt; March 22, 1905

✿   Glacier coverage

∫   Route of Fiala's ship, "America", to Teplitz Bay, 1903

∫   Retreat route, May 1904

∫   Return to Camp Abruzzi, September-November, 1904

∫   Polar attempt, March 1905

R. R. Tafel, John Vedoe, and three physicians.[39] Leffiingwell at first applied, but fearing that he would fare no better than he had with Baldwin, withdrew his application.[40]

Instruments were furnished by the Coast and Geodetic Survey, the Weather Bureau, and the Signal Corps:

> Dr. L. A. Bauer, Director of the Department of Terrestrial Magnetism of the Carnegie Institution of Washington, devised the plan of observation best suited to the limited [magnetic] outfit and conditions to be encountered, which plan experience proved successful. He [had] further suggested the general scheme of reduction of this portion of the observations.[41]

The expedition set out in the summer of 1903. Fighting heavy ice up the British Channel, the *America* finally reached Teplitz Bay, the site of the Duke of the Abruzzi's base. No sooner were the ponies taken ashore—equipment was much the same as on Baldwin's expedition—than they stampeded, and five were lost to the near-by glacier's crevasses. It soon became apparent to the ship's captain that the bay would not be a safe wintering place. To move to ship, however, would so weaken the manpower of the expedition that it could not hope to accomplish its objectives. Fiala decided to take responsibility for the possible loss of the ship and ordered it to remain. Most of a cache established in 1902 by Baldwin was moved to the new camp, materially fortifying it. An observatory was set up, a house built for the shore party, and a wire laid over the ice to carry power from the ship's generators.

On October 22, a storm struck that carried the *America* from her moorings. Some four days later, after a terrifying experience, she was back at her anchorage and almost instantly frozen in. On November 12, the ship was squeezed; on December 21, she was crushed so thoroughly that she would sink the moment the ice released her. Everything possible was carted

[39] *Scientific Results*, v.
[40] "A Communication from Leffingwell," *loc. cit.*
[41] *Scientific Results*, vii.

one mile over the ice to the shore, and the tiny quarters were enlarged to take care of the influx.

The final sledging plan provided for a main party of six men and three supporting parties. The men to form each return party would be selected on the march. One hundred and thirty-five days were allowed for the round trip at full rations. The men who wished to go were put to work making their own fur clothing. Meanwhile observations continued, an Arctic newspaper was started, and sledges were prepared. In the January night, a huge disturbance carried the ship to the bottom, together with the coal in its hold and a provision cache. It was found that the entire front of the glacier had "calved" and generated a small tidal wave.[42]

On March 7, 1904, the northern party left Camp Abruzzi, but breakdowns forced them to return. The ponies were found ready and willing, but needed a different type of sledge. They started again on March 25. At the end of the second day, the sledges were in such deplorable condition that Fiala decided he could not go on until repairs were made, which meant, in view of the near approach of spring, the postponement of the effort for another year.

A large share of the party found that they had seen all they wanted to see of Franz Josef Land. These men went south some seventy miles to Cape Flora, where the chance of a relief ship's reaching them was greater than at Camp Abruzzi. A number of small trips were made, for discovery, surveying, or looking for the relief ship. The ice remained, and no ship reached them.

Fiala had taken personal command of the fainthearted southern contingent. During the summer William J. Peters led a survey party south. In the autumn they started north again separately. Peters and his party were almost carried away on the ice when a storm caught them crossing a channel, while

---

[42] Anthony J. Fiala, *Fighting the Polar Ice*, 66. The following narrative is taken from 48–196.

Fiala himself was almost lost in a crevasse when crossing a glacier. Joining forces at Camp Ziegler, they returned together to Abruzzi, leaving two men to dig out the supplies buried at Camp Ziegler, against the spring's needs.

The winter passed busily and reasonably happily at Camp Abruzzi, as the faithful band prepared for the spring attempt on the Pole. Fiala had decided to take but one man, "a strong obedient sailor, Duffy by name, who would rather be on the trail than in the house." One hundred days' food would be taken for the men, one-half that for the dogs, with the supporting parties adding a week's rations. As the supporting parties would be spending the summer sledging supplies from the cache at Camp Ziegler south to Cape Flora, their strength had to be husbanded.[43] On March 22, they reached the 82nd parallel, but they were far from breaking the record for "farthest north." Progress had been painfully slow over bad ice. While there was hope of better ice ahead, nothing within view from the highest ice crag looked better. And then another factor entered: the temperature had risen, and an early thaw was in prospect. Finally, if no relief ship should arrive in 1905, every bit of food possible would be needed at Cape Flora; hence every team would be needed to haul it. Likewise, the southern party needed the leader's impetus to get in the supplies and do the necessary hunting. Fiala decided to return.

Camp Abruzzi was put in order. Instruments and supplies were hauled south to Camp Ziegler, where the instruments were set up for another series of observations. The supplies at Ziegler were in turn moved south to Cape Flora. Meanwhile at Cape Flora and at Camp Ziegler, preparations for the winter went on, while men were sent from Ziegler south to Cape Dillon, a more likely spot for a ship. On July 30, word reached Fiala at Camp Ziegler that the relief ship had reached Cape Dillon that morning, would proceed to pick up the party at Cape Flora, and then return to Dillon for the remainder. So concluded the second Ziegler expedition.

43 *Ibid.,* 166–67.

The death of Ziegler put an end to this series of expeditions, although Fiala at the close of his narrative said he wanted to try again, using the experience gained. That experience Fiala summarized as follows. He had come to favor an ice drift, such as the *Fram's*. He gave excellent reputations to the Siberian ponies. After his experience with the Baldwin–Ziegler Expedition's quarrels and the faintheartedness of some of his own party, he stressed especially the importance of moral character in the personnel. A winter's trip through the mountains he thought would be an excellent means of discovering staying qualities and temperament of candidates. So long as it was possible, any one acting dissatisfied should be dismissed. Said Fiala:

> In Arctic research—as in all undertakings—Christian character is the chief desideratum. The Polar field is a great testing ground. Those who pass through winters of darkness and days of trial above the circle of ice know better than others the weaknesses of human nature and their own insufficiencies. They learn to be more tolerant of the mistakes of others and read more understandingly the words of the great Master of Life.[44]

The Fiala–Ziegler Expedition was the exact reverse of many of the Peary expeditions. Geographical discovery was practically nil; in compensation, physical observations were carefully made on the basis of a systematic plan. Publication of the scientific results was unified, rather than fragmentary. Financing was the work of one, rather than the contributions of many. Perhaps as a result of that, the Ziegler expeditions were more poorly advertised than the Peary or Wellman expeditions. Nevertheless, 630 closely packed pages of scientific results bear witness to the faithfulness of the scientific observers.[45]

[44] *Ibid.*, 234.

[45] A limited amount of supplementary data and an uncomplimentary appraisal of Fiala are contained in typed copies of the journal of H. H. Newcomb, the veterinarian of the expedition. It should be used with caution. Baldwin MSS.

XII

Explorations in Northern Alaska

||||||||||||||||||||||||||||||||||||||||||||||||||

ALASKA IS a political unit because the chances of history marked it as the outer limit of the forces of expansion of the Russian Empire (save for an outpost and ranch north of San Francisco). The United States purchased the Russian claims, and so acquired a more intimate relation to the Alaskan Arctic than to any other Arctic area. Alaska was hers to govern, hers to protect, hers to exploit—and first of all, hers to explore.

For the present purposes, all Alaska is divided into three parts. The southern coast consists of range after range of mountains, where fishing ports and native villages cling to the less precipitous slopes. For a century the skins of sea otter and other aquatic mammals furnished the stock in trade; then the more prosaic salmon became king. Communication has always been by sea. Trails across the mountains have been almost nonexistent. To the east the fierce Thlingets had their home, while as one neared the Alaskan Peninsula the Aleuts lived in subjection to the Russian traders.

North of the Alaskan peninsula, on the Bering Sea, the Aleuts, their cousins the Eskimos, and the Indians of the Yukon met. The Eskimos held most of the coast, while inland their culture and that of the Indians mingled perhaps more than the blood of the peoples. Here the predominant geographical feature is the Yukon. Forming the great interior basin of Alaska, the Yukon provided for the Indian tribes a highway at right angles to that of the Eskimos along the coast.

The geographical division between the central and northern sections of Alaska is the Brooks Range, whose crest approximates the 68th parallel of latitude. The tree line closely follows the one hundred-foot contour along the southern foothills of the range, cutting the area between the range and the Arctic Circle very nearly in half. The Arctic claims as its own much of the coast of the Bering Sea south to the Yukon Delta.

As the exploration of Alaska is a story with a unity of its own, the present plan of telling but a part of the story necessarily involves arbitrary omissions. A particular effort will be made to portray faithfully the part of the United States government in these explorations, and sufficient material will be supplied to form an idea of the problems and trends in exploration. Limitations of space will preclude the mention of all but a few workers.

The first United States government expedition vessel to enter Bering Strait was the *U.S.S. Vincennes* under Lieutenant-Commanding John Rodgers. The United States North Pacific Surveying Expedition of 1853–56, of which the *Vincennes* was a part, like Commodore Perry's expedition to Japan, Kane's to Greenland, and Page's to Paraguay, had felt the driving force of J. P. Kennedy, secretary of the navy. "The outfit, manning, and instructions were both liberal and sagacious, and their respective Commanders warmly acknowledged their obligations for his scientific zeal as well as official courtesy."[1]

The act of Congress passed in August, 1852, provided for a "survey and reconnaissance for naval and commercial purposes" of the portions of Bering Strait, the North Pacific, and the China seas that were frequented by American whalers and traders.[2] That a hydrographic survey in Siberian and Arctic waters was urgently needed can be seen from the data furnished

[1] Nourse, *American Explorations*, 110.
[2] G. W. Littlehales, "The Navy as a Motor in Geographical and Commercial Progress," American Geographical Society, *Journal*, Vol. XXXI (1899), 137.

to the Senate by the Secretary of the Navy: Captain Roys had passed through Bering Strait in 1848 and had filled his vessel with whalebone and oil within a few weeks. The next year, 154 venturous American vessels followed him, with similar numbers in 1850 and 1851. During two of the years, the value of American ships and cargoes amounted to almost $17,500,000.[3] The quality of existing charts is indicated by one of the officers who recorded that he sailed repeatedly over the places where mountains were shown on the charts. American whalers along the Siberian coast, wrote Alexander Habersham, a member of the surveying expedition, "annually lose one or more of their fleet simply from the want of good charts."[4] And Rodgers could find neither Plover Island nor Kellett Land in the positions indicated on charts.

Secretary Kennedy instructed Commander Cadwallader Ringgold, first leader of the expedition, to conduct scientific research as well as hydrographic surveys. The scientific staff of five was headed by William Stimpson, a pupil recommended by Agassiz, and an authority on marine invertebrates.[5] One of the officers, Lieutenant J. M. Brooke, was the inventor of an improved deep-sea sounding apparatus. Instructions stated in the broadest terms enabled the scientists to seize the best opportunities as they were presented. In Nourse's words:

> All were expected to co-operate harmoniously in the prosecution of physical investigations, embracing those of temperature at different elevations, and in different latitudes, with specific references to barometrical, hygrometrical, and [ther]mometrical observations, and those of the aurora borealis, of parhelia, and the mirage.[6]

War in China delayed the accomplishment of the original

[3] 32 Cong., 1 sess., *Sen. Exec. Doc.* 55 (Cong. Ser. 619), 9.
[4] Alexander Habersham, *The North Pacific Surveying Expedition*, 325.
[5] Ringgold to Kennedy, Nov. 11, 1852. Letters to Kennedy, XI, No. 107.
[6] Nourse, *American Explorations*, 109–10. A list of the astronomical and surveying instruments is given in Frederic D. Stuart, Journal, Ship *U.S.S. Vincennes . . . 1853-4*, MS (War Records Branch, National Archives).

mission of the expedition; not until 1855 did it reach the North Pacific. By that time Rodgers had succeeded Ringgold in command. On July 7, the *Vincennes* and *Fenimore Cooper* reached Petropavlovsk. The *Vincennes* sailed thence into Bering Strait, surveyed the Siberian harbor of Glasenappe, and left a party and steam launch for additional surveying. Rodgers then stood north through Bering Strait and past Herald Island, but no land, let alone a continent, could be seen to the north, although the visibility was splendid. He then returned and put a party ashore on Herald Island. Still no land to the north could be seen from its heights. Turning west, Rodgers looked in vain for the reported Plover Island and Wrangel Land. With many specimens from the Arctic and Bering seas, the vessel headed for San Francisco.[7]

While the *Vincennes* cruised the Arctic, the *John Hancock* extended the charts of the whaling grounds in the Sea of Okhotsk and the Gulf of Amur. Alexander Habersham, the writer of the only contemporary volume in English on the cruise, related the encounters with both whalers and Russians. William Gibson in the *Fenimore Cooper*, meanwhile, was ordered by Rodgers to survey the Aleutian Islands. He was to look for harbors, "and particularly to coal, which is of the first importance to our trade with China." Coal beds had been rumored on Akun and Unga. Adak should be particularly examined for harbors. "As this is a point, through which the great circle nearly passes between San Francisco and Shanghai," Rodgers said, "you will perceive at once its importance."[8]

Stimpson summarized the natural history collections immediately after the *Vincennes* reached San Francisco. The collection of mammals was small, but, with one exception, it was an Arctic group from the neighborhood of Seniavine Strait (a short distance southwest of Bering Strait). About one-half the

[7] Littlehales, *op. cit.*, 137–44.

[8] John Rodgers to William Gibson, commanding U. S. Schooner *Fenimore Cooper*, dated Petropaulski, July 12, 1855, North Pacific Surveying Expedition Letters, John Rodgers, Vol. II (National Archives).

birds were representatives of thirty-four species taken at Senia-vine Strait or Kamchatka. None of the thirty species of reptiles came from that area. Of the eighty-seven species of crustacea, seven were attributed to Kamchatka and ten to Seniavine. The proportions were about the same for the other zoological classes.[9]

The anthropological materials consisted of two Chukchi skulls and several native vocabularies collected by Lieutenant Brooke and John Baer, one of the marines landed with the party at Glasenappe Harbor, Seniavine Strait.[10]

If the principal work of the expedition was hydrography, the other activities were also designed to serve the seafaring man. Even a small vocabulary of native words printed in the back of his *Sailing Directions* could be as essential as a chart to a sailor cast upon a foreign shore.

Unlike its predecessor, the Wilkes Expedition, the North Pacific Surveying Expedition has no magnificent set of pub-lications to show for its labors. Congress appropriated $15,000 for preparation of the reports. It was distinctly understood that they would not be printed at government expense, but presumably at that of the Smithsonian Institution. The only official productions were a series of charts. The increasing number of explorations, especially of the West, within two decades, with the resulting demands for publication of their results, had made certain congressmen very critical of govern-ment scientific publishing. This attitude was reflected by Senator Robert Ward Johnson of Arkansas, while discussing the reports of this expedition:

> I am certainly very well satisfied that we have already got a suffi-ciently large library at the expense of Congress, in regard to botany, birds, snails, reptiles, bugs, and every species of strange,

[9] William Stimpson to Commander John Rodgers, forwarded by Rodgers to the Secretary of the Navy, dated San Francisco, October 16, 1855, *ibid.*

[10] Originals and several transcriptions are among the Bureau of American Ethnology MSS, Smithsonian Institution, Washington, D. C. These were used by George Gibbs and W. H. Dall in preparation of their studies.

and, it seems to me, rather unimportant and useless, branches of natural history.[11]

Such a position meant that the scientific results of the North Pacific Surveying Expedition were published hither and yon, in about three dozen articles scattered through the *Proceedings* of the Philadelphia Academy of Natural Sciences, of the Boston Society of Natural History, of the American Academy of Arts and Sciences, and three or four other learned publications.[12] Longer works were contemplated, but if written, their fate is unknown. Were they in William Stimpson's possession and burned in the great Chicago fire? Are they still buried in an obscure file in Washington? The only published book-length report is a manuscript of Stimpson's on crustacea that turned up in the Navy Department some time after his death; it was finally printed, a half-century late, by the Smithsonian.[13]

The volume of personal adventures by Habersham was the only contemporary book to appear in English, while the nearest thing to a narrative of the expedition was written by Wilhelm Heine, artist to Commodore Perry's expedition—and published in German.[14] Hence this survey for the benefit of American commerce, which commenced at the Golden Gate, where the Pacific Railroad Surveys stopped, was permitted to sink into obscurity.

This is an opportune moment to mention the Smithsonian Institution's policy, for it was particularly important in the early decades of Alaskan exploration. The Smithsonian Institution was created by Congress in accepting and carrying out

[11] *Congressional Globe.* 35 Cong., 1 sess. Part II, 1531–32, April 8, 1858. See also the report of the Secretary of the Navy, 35 Cong., 1 sess., *Sen. Exec. Doc.* 52 (Cong. Ser. 929), XII.

[12] Listed in Max Meisel, A *Bibliography of American Natural History* . . . 1769–1865, III, 221–28.

[13] William Stimpson, *Report on the Crustacea (Brachyura and Anomura) Collected by the North Pacific Exploring Expedition, 1853–1856* (ed. by Mary J. Rathbun). (Smithsonian *Misc. Col.* XLIX, Art. III).

[14] Wilhelm Heine, *Die Expedition in die Seen von Japan unter Commando von Commodore Ringgold und Commodore John Rodgers* . . . .

the provisions of a bequest from James Smithson. His one-half-million-dollar gift was used to establish an institution for the promotion of scientific knowledge. Congress elected a board of regents which administered the funds through its permanent staff. Thus funds were available for encouragement of national science projects without appeal to Congress.

The policy adopted by the first secretary, Joseph Henry, was to do nothing that someone else would do. Thus the library was turned over to the Library of Congress. Meteorological activities were carried on until their worth was demonstrated, and the United States Signal Service took them over. Natural history and ethnology collections were made, and eventually Congress provided funds for a National Museum to be administered through the Smithsonian. Henry's policy toward collectors was similar. He would seldom buy a collection already made. Rather, he would furnish instructions, equipment, and funds for shipment to someone who wanted to make a new collection. "Thus grants of money were made, of various sums, from $5 to $250, very rarely exceeding the latter amount in any one year to any one agent."[15] The Smithsonian supplied Kane, Hayes, Hall, and many other Arctic adventurers.

Probably the earliest Smithsonian collector to enter Alaska was Robert Kennicott. He was supported primarily by the Smithsonian, with assistance from the University of Michigan, the Audubon Club of Chicago, the Chicago Academy of Sciences, and private individuals. He spent the years from 1859 to 1862 exploring the Mackenzie River of Canada and its tributaries, except that 1861 was spent mainly on the Yukon.

The principal object of the exploration was to collect materials for investigating the Zoology of the region visited. Mr. Kennicott, however, also collected specimens of plants and minerals, and gave considerable attention to the ethnology of

[15] Smithsonian Institution, *Annual Report*, 1879, 43.

the country, in observing the peculiarities of the various Indian tribes, and forming vocabularies of the languages.

Kennicott was royally received by the lonely traders of the Hudson's Bay Company. He persuaded "nearly all" of them to make meteorological observations with the equipment and logbooks supplied by the Smithsonian, and for years after that meteorological records came to the Smithsonian from all across the Canadian Arctic. Some of the traders were equally good about sending in zoological, botanical, and geological specimens.[16]

In 1863, the Smithsonian received from Kennicott forty boxes and packages, weighing three thousand pounds. This appears to have been the collection from the last half of his stay. Secretary Henry praised the ethnological collection as the finest in existence from northern America. After enumerating the classes of natural history material, Henry said he expected that Kennicott's written report would "extend very largely the admirable records presented by Sir John Richardson relative to arctic zoology."[17]

Kennicott's next assignment was as director of the Scientific Corps of the Western Union Telegraph Expedition to Alaska. One of his aides was William Healey Dall, who in the next dozen years became an outstanding authority on Alaska. They began exploration of the Bering coast and Yukon Valley. In 1866, Kennicott died suddenly, probably from a heart attack. Dall was appointed to succeed him. With the successful completion of the Atlantic cable that year, work was halted on the Alaska-Siberian telegraph line. Dall remained in Alaska for a while at his own expense, and then received an appointment with the Coast Survey that kept bringing him to Alaska for another decade.

The first United States expedition organized after the treaty

[16] Smithsonian Institution, *Annual Report*, 1862, 39–40.
[17] Smithsonian Institution, *Annual Report*, 1863, 53.

with Russia began a reconnaissance of the coast in July, 1867, three months prior to formal annexation. George Davidson was in charge of the Coast Survey party. In the group were Dr. A. Kellogg, surgeon and botanist, Theodore A. Blake, geologist, and W. G. W. Hartford, general collector. They were all known to Davidson through membership in the California Academy of Sciences.[18] Davidson wrote a valuable report, which was printed as a congressional document.[19] The portions on climate, vegetable productions, fisheries, timber, and fur-bearing animals were republished in the *U. S. Coast Pilot, Alaska*, in 1869. Davidson and Dall wrote much of this volume. The following year Dall's *Alaska and its Resources* appeared.[20]

At the same time Dall prepared a plan for a survey of the Aleutian Islands. He proposed to use a schooner of about sixty tons and a number of small boats. The schooner should be based at Unalaska, and in the space of three years, Dall planned to survey the Aleutians and the southern coast of the Bering Sea, paying particular attention to the passes through the islands. Dall proposed to save money by replacing white sailors, so far as possible, with Aleuts. He also proposed to give the schooner additional duties as a revenue cutter, but the superintendent of the Coast Survey overruled him on the ground that the duties were mutually inconsistent. Dall esti-

18 Robert E. C. Stearns, "Shells Collected by the U. S. Coast Survey Expedition to Alaska, in the year 1867," California Academy of Sciences, *Proceedings*, Vol. III (1868), 384.

19 U. S. Coast Survey, Superintendent, *Report* . . . 1867. 40 Cong., 2 sess. *House Exec. Doc.* 275 (Cong. Ser. 1344), Appendix 18, 187–329.

20 Up to 1867 the Russian authorities had conducted a magnetic and meteorological observatory on Japonski Island in Sitka harbor. It had been established in 1847, and its published records up to 1862 were available to Davidson when he compiled the first edition of the *Alaska Pilot*. Henry K. Katussowski on July 17, 1868, pointed out to the Treasury Department that there were "a couple of scientific hydrographic and magnetic observatories" which had been sustained by the Russian government, and unless provision were made for them, "irreparable losses" would result. This valuable activity was allowed to lapse. Letter to J. F. Hartley, assistant secretary of the treasury, National Archives.

Smithsonian Institution
William H. Dall

From a photograph by Clinedinst;
courtesy Smithsonian Institution
E. W. Nelson, June 20, 1901

U.S. Navy photograph
Commander Cadwallader Ringgold,
U.S.N.

A Group of Arctic Explorers
Standing, l. to r.: Robert Kennicott, Henry Ulke; seated, William Stimpson, Henry Bryant.

mated the expenses to be $45,000 for three years. H. H. McIntyre, who collaborated with him, estimated them at just under $60,000, the major discrepancy being approximately $9,000 for salaries. The estimate finally submitted was $10,000 for outfit, and $13,500 annually for three years.[21]

During 1871–73, Dall surveyed the Aleutian and Shumagin Islands. In 1874, he surveyed the coast west of Mt. Saint Elias, then entered Bering Sea and mapped the Pribilov Islands, northern Nunivak Island, and the north side of the Alaska Peninsula, adding greatly to the known detail.[22]

Dall began a survey of the Arctic coasts in 1880. Temporary stations were established at Cape Lisburne, Icy Cape, and Port Belcher. Ice prevented his reaching Point Barrow. In an effort to settle the disputed question of a flow of warm water through the Bering Strait, a hydrothermal section was made. The magnetic declinations were found to be greatly at variance with those recorded by earlier observers.[23]

In addition to his official contributions, Dall wrote a host of articles on natural history and ethnology of Alaska, the field of his special competence being the marine invertebrates. In describing the circumstances of his labors to the members of the California Academy of Sciences, he said,

> As all my work was done in the very scanty leisure afforded by a surveying party actively engaged in the field—the hours devoted to the preparation of specimens being usually stolen from sleep—the circumstances will excuse any paucity in the results.[24]

There was no paucity in Dall's literary output, for between

[21] *Survey of Alaska and the Aleutian Islands.* 41 Cong., 2 sess., *House Exec. Doc.* 255 (Cong. Ser. 1425). Compared with Dall's original in Special Agents, Alaska, File (Treasury Branch, National Archives).

[22] Hubert Howe Bancroft, *History of Alaska,* 628–29. Nourse, *American Explorations,* 599–604.

[23] U. S. Coast and Geodetic Survey, Superintendent, *Report,* 1881. 47 Cong., 1 sess., *Sen. Exec. Doc.* 49 (Cong. Ser. 1988), 45–46.

[24] William Healey Dall, "Notes on the Avi-fauna of the Aleutian Islands, from Unalaska Eastward," California Academy of Sciences, *Proceedings,* Vol. V, (1873–74), 35.

1870 and 1880 inclusive, he had published 163 articles, reviews, and notes, and a large book.[25]

Meanwhile, in 1874, the United States Signal Service had sent out a meteorological observer, Lucien McShan Turner, to St. Michael, north of the Yukon's mouth on the Bering Sea. The Signal Service had a working agreement with the Smithsonian Institution, whereby the Institution nominated men trained to serve both as weather observers and as collectors.

Turner was relieved in the summer of 1877 by Edward William Nelson, but he returned the following year and established a series of meteorological stations along the Aleutians with the aid of volunteer observers. By 1881, he was reported to have collected for the National Museum 160 species of birds,

> some of which were for the first time ascertained to occur within our limits, thirty species of fish, several species of mammals, nearly thirteen thousand specimens of insects, a good series of the land and marine shells, several thousand specimens of plants —embracing over two hundred species; and paid especial attention to collecting a complete series of implements and other articles of ethnological and archaeological character embracing over three thousand specimens, some of which were for the first time obtained. Much attention was given to the study of linguistics of the Unaleet and Malemut Orarians, Nulato, Ingalet, and Unalashkan Aleuts. The vocabularies are comprehensive, containing not only a list of words, but much of etymologic value, stories, history, and other valuable information concerning these people, of whom little was previously known.[26]

Such were the activities of this new breed of scientific observers!

Nelson, thanks to the aid of the Alaska Commercial Company's agent, was able to spend several months at a time away from his barometer and thermometers, thus widening his

---

[25] Paul Bartsch and others. *A Bibliography and Short Biographical Sketch of William Healey Dall* (Smithsonian *Misc. Col.* CIV, No. 15).

[26] Smithsonian Institution, *Annual Report*, 1881, 20–21.

collections. During his second winter, Nelson traveled by dog sledge over one thousand miles, bringing back ethnological specimens from the Kuskoquim River. The next spring he studied the breeding habits of waterfowl at the mouth of the Yukon. In 1881, he was given passage on the United States Revenue Service steamer *Corwin* to St. Lawrence Island, where he made a large collection of Eskimo remains, and to the Arctic coasts.

Nelson's collections were even larger than Turner's. They were supplemented by more than one hundred photographs and "a large amount of manuscript material . . . . The necessary expenses attending this work, outside those appertaining strictly to the meteorological work, were met by an allowance from the [Smithsonian] Institution."[27] Nelson's collections were praised in the Smithsonian *Report* for 1879 as being among the "more important" of the year. He himself was described "as being a most excellent naturalist and particularly well acquainted with the vertebrate animals of North America."[28] The United States was surely getting a bargain at the price of one sergeant's wages.

The Revenue Marine Service, like the Signal Service, encouraged its personnel to study the natural history of Alaska. Some time about 1880, its officers were instructed to make such observations when the opportunity was presented. These were made not only aboard ship and in port, but several explorations were made, notably of the Kobuk (Kowak) River, north of the Seward Peninsula. This was not done without protest at the time and energy required on top of their burdensome enough duties of navigation and patrol. Captain Michael A. Healy of the *Corwin* recommended that special observers be appointed who could bring energy and trained talents to the task.[29] This was never acted upon. Hence the reports submitted

[27] *Ibid.*, 21–22.
[28] Smithsonian Institution, *Annual Report, 1879,* 44–45.
[29] Captain Michael A. Healy in U. S. Revenue Cutter Service, . . . *Cruise of the* CORWIN . . . 1884, 20–21.

were not up to the level maintained by the Signal Service observers. Nonetheless, data from northern Alaska were scarce, and all contributions were needed.

In 1879, the U. S. Revenue Marine Service steamer *Richard Rush* penetrated to the Arctic Ocean. Captain George W. Bailey wrote a good, short account of general conditions, such as any intelligent and cultured observer might make, but he was oblivious to characteristically Arctic conditions. The only really scientific phase of the report was the section by Assistant Surgeon Robert White: "Notes on the Physical Condition of the Inhabitants of Alaska."[30]

White had offered his services to the Smithsonian Institution. As a naturalist trained in Edinburgh, he was gladly accepted and provided with the necessary equipment. His collections consisted "for the most part of embryonic or foetal seals, porpoises, &c., various fishes, and many marine invertebrates. Skins and skeletons of several species of seals were also included."[31]

The *Rush* was relieved by the *Corwin* in 1880. In addition to law enforcement, it was ordered to search for the *U.S.S. Jeannette* and two missing whalers. Swinging as far west as ice permitted, the *Corwin* sighted Herald and Wrangel Islands. Captain Calvin Leighton Hooper's report contained many observations on the Eskimos' customs, language, superstitions, and material culture; yet, like Bailey's, it was not the report of a trained observer. Hooper had also been specifically requested to investigate some dangerous shoals and check some doubtful coastlines for the United States Hydrographic Office.[32]

The following year Captain Hooper was again in command of the *Corwin* on its cruise to the Arctic Ocean. In addition to collecting hydrographic data and looking for survivors of the

[30] U. S. Revenue Cutter Service, *Alaska and its People*, 41–49.
[31] Smithsonian Institution, *Annual Report*, 1879, 45.
[32] Nourse, *American Explorations*, 430–448.

Jeannette, his instructions from the Secretary of the Treasury required "such information as may be practicable regarding the numbers, character, occupations, and general condition of the inhabitants of the adjacent coast."[33]

The scientific results of the 1881 cruise of the *Corwin* went far beyond the scope of these orders, and the reports are the most important submitted from this service. They appear in two volumes. The main volume, issued in 1884, contains a very full report of the cruise, with numerous passing observations on the history, natural history, and ethnology of the region, written by Captain Hooper. John Muir's article on glaciation in the Arctic appears here as an appendix.

The supplementary volume, issued the previous year, contains a series of scientific articles.[34] The surgeon, Irving C. Rosse, made the anthropological and medical observations; Muir did the botanizing; Edward W. Nelson summarized earlier work on ornithology and added extensive information, particularly on ranges and habitats, while Tarleton H. Bean compiled a list of fishes known to occur north of Bering Strait. Measurements of magnetic dip and variation were made at several stations, and sea temperatures were taken.

In 1882, the *Corwin* ran a line of soundings some distance to the east of Point Barrow and found the printed charts quite unreliable. Captain Michael A. Healy recommended to the Secretary of the Treasury that he be authorized to detach an

[33] *Ibid.,* 448.

[34] Hooper's volume is entitled *Cruise of the U. S. Revenue Steamer Thomas Corwin in the Arctic Ocean, 1881.* 48 Cong., 1 sess., Sen. Exec. Doc. 204. Washington, 1884.

The volume of scientific reports is entitled *Cruise of the Revenue-Steamer Corwin in Alaska and the N. W. Arctic Ocean in 1881. Notes and Memoranda: Medical and Anthropological; Botanical; Ornithological.* (2 eds.: as *Treasury Department Document No. 429;* also as *House Exec. Doc. 105,* 47 Cong., 2 sess. Washington, 1883).

The copies of each examined by the writer confuse the issue, as the titles on the covers of both are: *Arctic Cruise of the Revenue Steamer Corwin, 1881: Notes and Observations.* The Library of Congress main author entry for both is: U. S. Revenue cutter service.

officer and boat crew during the next season for a survey eastward to the Mackenzie River "and the coast thus cleared of its dangers."[35] This was not achieved until thirty years later by Ernest de Koven Leffingwell.

Interservice rivalry in exploring the interior of Arctic Alaska was another feature of the *Corwin's* cruises. In 1883, Lieutenant George M. Stoney, United States Navy, was detailed for duty on the *Corwin*. He seized the opportunity to explore Hotham Inlet and reported that a large river, the "Kowak" (now officially Kobuk) flowed into it. This had been entered by a member of Captain F. W. Beechey's expedition in 1826 and explored to the tree line by H.M.S. *Plover's* officers in 1849.[36] In the summer of 1884, Stoney and Lieutenant J. C. Cantwell of the Revenue Marine Service conducted rival parties about three hundred miles up the river. In 1885, both men were again in the field, Stoney and Cantwell proceeding up the Kobuk, while S. B. McLenegan, an engineer from the *Corwin*, explored the Noatak River, which enters Hotham Inlet to the north of the Kobuk. Stoney's party was prepared to stay the winter, and did so without any remarkable hardships or discomforts. Cantwell's reports for both 1884 and 1885 were published. He himself wrote up the narrative and ethnological notes for the 1884 report. In the same document, McLenegan did a good amateur job on the ornithology and natural history, but was admittedly inadequate on the geology and fishes.[37] The primary function of the expedition, however, was to find the headwaters of the Kobuk River: all information regarding its navigability was to be obtained, while Cantwell's orders

[35] Healy to Charles J. Folger, September 24, 1882, (Treasury Branch, National Archives).

[36] Note in *Science*, o. s. Vol. IV (1884), 539. Stoney had been making extravagant claims, or they had been made on his behalf. The editor advised Stoney to disavow them.

[37] U. S. Revenue Cutter Service, *Cruise of the Revenue Marine Steamer Corwin in the Arctic Ocean in 1884.* 50 Cong., 1 sess., *House Misc. Doc. 602* (Cong. Ser. 2583), 47–126. Note especially Cantwell's comment on his handicaps, 77.

suggested the possibility of finding river routes connecting with the Arctic Ocean or Bering Sea.

Having failed to achieve his goal in 1884, Cantwell returned to the exploration of the Kobuk in 1885. This time a trained observer was taken along: Charles H. Townsend, an assistant in the United States Fish Commission. Townsend listed the wildlife seen and the fishes caught. The botanical specimens had unfortunately been lost in transit. A full report on the fish and fisheries he reserved for another place.[38] Meanwhile a similar expedition under McLenegan explored the Noatak, which flowed into the estuary some thirty miles north of the Kobuk.

Stoney's expedition of 1885–86 consisted of five officers, one of whom fell ill and returned with the vessel; ten enlisted men; and two Eskimos with their families, who were hired at St. Michael. Two steam launches were assigned to the party and placed aboard the schooner *Viking* for transportation from Mare Island to Hotham Inlet. The expedition was liberally supplied with hand tools, boat gear, provisions, and trade goods. The scientific instruments were those required for navigation, meteorology, and rough surveying, plus two hydrometers and a dip circle. The schooner sailed from the Golden Gate on May 3, 1885, and reached Hotham Inlet on July 9.

Soundings were made in the channel, a tide gauge set up, and a survey made of the sandspit, while a meteorological log had been kept since the steam launch *Explorer* had been commissioned at Mare Island. On July 25, the party started up the river and on August 20 broke ground for their winter camp, which was built of lumber sawed in a mill they had erected. By September 8, construction was far enough along that a party was released under Ensign W. L. Howard for a reconnaissance survey up-river. On November 1, Stoney assigned

---

[38] U. S. Revenue Cutter Service, *Cruise of the Revenue Marine Steamer Corwin in the Arctic Ocean in 1885.* 49 Cong., 1 sess., *House Exec. Doc. 153* (Cong. Ser. 2400), 83–102.

subjects for study and collecting. Francis L. Nash, the surgeon, received statistics, medicine and medical statistics, ethnology, and zoology. The engineer, A. V. Zane, drew geology and mineralogy, while Howard was assigned the botany.

On December 6, the party under Nash was sent on a week's expedition up-river to collect information about the Indians. Zane was sent on a reconnaissance to St. Michael via Nulato on the Yukon, from which he returned on February 25. Stoney visited the region around Selawik Lake. With the coming of spring, more surveying expeditions were undertaken, including one to the Noatak under Ensign Howard and one toward Point Barrow under Stoney. On April 12, two parties set out. Ensign M. L. Read took a party up the Noatak, while perhaps the most venturesome undertaking of the whole expedition was entrusted to Howard. He went with natives of the vicinity over the divide until he met Eskimos from Point Barrow, whom he accompanied back to the Arctic coast.

The launches were now made ready, and the various branches of the Kobuk River were explored. Then headquarters was removed to Hotham Inlet, and work continued until August 26, when the party went aboard the *Bear* (of the Greely rescue squadron, and later famous as an Arctic revenue cutter).[39]

Stoney prepared a report of this expedition for official publication, but it was "lost" after it left the custody of the Navy Department. Interservice rivalries may be suspected. Finally, in 1899, an account was published privately in the United States Naval Institute *Proceedings.* The Naval Institute issued it as a small volume the following year. The scientific content is small. The logs of the expedition are in the National Archives. Where, one wonders, are the original reports of the longer reconnaissances?[40]

[39] Log books of the U. S. Northern Alaska Exploring Expedition, April 25, 1885, to November 8, 1886. 3 vols., MSS (War Records Branch, National Archives).

[40] Original articles: Lieutenant George M. Stoney, "Explorations in

Up to 1885, then, we find the Smithsonian Institution, the Coast and Geodetic Survey, the Signal Service, and the Revenue Marine Service, in that order, becoming interested in the scientific features of northern Alaska. The largest government undertaking was Lieutenant Ray's International Polar Year Expedition to Point Barrow, discussed earlier. The principal private survey was that of the Western Union Expedition, which was checked in mid-career. A decade passed in which nothing particularly new was inaugurated. Materials collected by Lucien Turner, Edward W. Nelson, and John Murdoch were studied, and the results published by the Bureau of American Ethnology and the Signal Service. Lucien Turner was reassigned by the Signal Service to Ungava Bay, on the shore of Hudson Strait, and under the same working agreement with the Smithsonian Institution, he collected materials on ethnology and natural history.

The next significant scientific undertaking in Alaska was destined to surpass the others. In 1895, Congress appropriated $5,000 for the investigation of coal and gold resources by the United States Geological Survey, and that summer a party examined the Pacific coastal belt. Next year three men were sent to study the Yukon placer districts. In 1897, no funds were available, but reports of gold on the Klondike brought an appropriation of $20,000 in 1898, on which four parties were sent out. By 1904, the appropriation was $80,000.[41]

In 1900, five expeditions converged on the Seward Peninsula area, for the Cape Nome gold strike had suddenly shifted interest from the Yukon. Three Geological Survey parties ran topographical surveys and studied the gold resources of the area, while the Coast and Geodetic Survey sent two steamers to survey the entire coast from St. Michael to Port Clarence.[42]

Alaska," in the *Proceedings*, Nos. 91 and 92, [533]–584, [799]–849. Book title: *Naval Explorations in Alaska.* . . .

[41] Alfred H. Brooks, "The Investigation of Alaska's Mineral Wealth," Amer. Geog. Soc. *Bulletin*, Vol. XXXVII (1905), 31–39.

[42] "Geographical Record," American Geographical Society, *Bulletin*, Vol. XXXII (1900), 361–62.

An ambitious program in 1901 saw "a network of surveys completed connecting the Yukon, Koyukuk, and Kobuk Rivers, the Arctic Ocean and Kotzebue Sound." One party crossed Alaska from its southern coast to the Arctic at the mouth of the Colville River, traveling by dog sled and canoe. Thence they turned westward to Point Barrow, finally finding a steamer at Cape Lisburne. "Theirs was probably the most notable exploration which has been made by the Geological Survey," wrote Alfred H. Brooks.[43]

In 1905, Brooks, at that time head of the Alaska division of the Geological Survey, remarked:

> It is difficult at the present day to conceive how little was known of Alaska previous to 1898 . . . . Many of the most important geographical features have been added to the map by the reconnaissance and exploration surveys of the years from 1898 to 1903, during which the principal mountain ranges have been outlined and the drainage areas defined.

The contoured maps produced by the Geological Survey were valuable alike to the prospector and the explorer, the railway and road engineer, and perhaps most of all to the miners who were investing heavily in water ditches. The reports and maps were published promptly in order to fill the pressing need.[44] Perhaps in no other phase of Arctic research has the presence of scientists paid off so promptly.

The dozen years that saw the beginning of the United States Geological Survey's work witnessed the work of four private expeditions that may be considered transitional. They proved that scientific work in Arctic Alaska could be accomplished with a minimum of organization and special facilities, even if dangers and difficulties still abounded. Thus the field was

[43] Alfred H. Brooks, *The Geography and Geology of Alaska* (U. S. Geological Survey, *Professional Papers No. 45*).
[44] Brooks, "The Investigation of Alaska's Mineral Wealth," Am. Geog. Soc., *Bulletin*, Vol. XXXVII (1905), 38–39.

open to men of limited resources as well as to expeditions costing tens of thousands of dollars.

The first expedition occupied the summer of 1896. The idea was conceived by Timothy Hopkins, the financial sponsor of Stanford University's marine biological laboratory at Pacific Grove, presumably in a conversation over the luncheon table with his friend, Captain J. N. Knowles, president of the Pacific Steam Whaling Company. The latter agreed to provide transportation to the Arctic for two Stanford students. President David Starr Jordon of Stanford selected Norman B. Scofield and Alvin Seale to make natural history collections. Their chief problem was to find out whether salmon streams entered the Arctic Ocean. Not only was this a scientific problem, but a phase of the economic problem of determining the natural resources of Alaska. At this time, exploration of the fisheries resources of Bering Sea was under way, exploitation was beginning, and this study would determine the northern limits of the resource.

The two collegians sailed out the Golden Gate on the bark *J. D. Peters*. Off King Island they transferred to the steamer *Jeanie*, which was carrying supplies to the whaling fleet that had wintered at Herschel Island. They were delayed until the ice broke in Bering Strait. Then stops were made at Point Hope and Icy Cape. Point Barrow was reached on August 6. While repairs were being made to the ship's hull, the budding scientists had an excellent opportunity to fish and shoot birds for their collections. On August 13, they sailed for Herschel Island, reaching it on the eighteenth. They fished and hunted and dredged around the west mouth of the Mackenzie River.

On September 5, the *Jeanie* began its fight to escape from the threatening Arctic ice. The vessel's keel was nearly stove in when huge waves dropped it onto the shallow sea bottom. At Point Barrow the vessel had to wait nine days until ice that had closed in between her and Bering Strait was carried offshore again. After this narrow escape from spending the winter in the Arctic, the vessel stopped at Cape Prince of Wales, and then sailed through the Bering Strait to the safer waters of Bering Sea. Although Seale and Scofield made a good collection of fishes, they failed to find commercial salmon streams along the Arctic coast.[45]

The year following the Stanford Expedition, E. A. McIlhenny, N. G. Buxton, and W. E. Snyder availed themselves of the same company's vessels for a winter's collecting at Point Barrow. McIlhenny was the hunter; the others prepared the specimens. Most of their collections appear to have gone to the Philadelphia Academy of Sciences, and to have been described under its auspices. The party was at Point Barrow one year and one week, reaching it August 10, 1897, and departing on August 18, 1898.[46]

Andrew J. Stone spent 1897 to 1899 in the Arctic collecting big game for the American Museum of Natural History. He crossed from the Stikine to the Mackenzie River, followed it to the Arctic Ocean, then swung west to Herschel Island. From Herschel Island he returned to Fort McPherson and continued eastward one thousand miles to a point past Cape Lyon. Retracing his steps to the Mackenzie, he crossed the Rocky Mountains to the Yukon, following it west to St. Michael. Including side trips, he covered about 3,330 miles by sledge in 1898–99 alone.

Stone made anthropometric measurements of natives, both Eskimo and Indian. From his own observations and information given him by hunters and officers of the Hudson's Bay Company, he obtained data on the range and ecology of the wood bison, musk ox, caribou, and several species of bighorn

---

[45] Alvin Seale, *Quest for the Golden Cloak*, 102–11. Norman Bishop Scofield. "List of Fishes in the Waters of Arctic Alaska," in David Starr Jordan and Chas. Gilbert, "The Fishes of Bering Sea," Chapter XVIII of David Starr Jordan, (ed.) *The Fur Seals and Fur-Seal Islands of the North Pacific Ocean*, Part 3, 493–509.
[46] Alfred M. Bailey, *Birds of Arctic Alaska*, 38.

sheep, at the same time collecting many specimens. He gained geographical information for the correction of "gross errors in the current maps of the region bordering the Arctic coast between the mouth of the Mackenzie and Cape Lyon."[47]

The fourth expedition was known officially as the Anglo-American Polar Expedition, or more commonly as the Mikkelsen–Leffingwell Expedition. Einar Mikkelsen and Ernest de Koven Leffingwell had become friends on the Baldwin–Ziegler Expedition. They attempted to solve a warmly debated geographical problem: the possible existence of large land areas in the Beaufort Sea north of Alaska. The *Jeannette* and the *Fram* had shown that no large land masses lay north of Siberia. Rollin A. Harris, of the Coast and Geodetic Survey, had advanced arguments based on his tide studies to show that the behavior of the Arctic tides could be explained by such a land mass, the location of which had been narrowed down to the Beaufort Sea.

Leffingwell's father put up about one-half the cost of the expedition, while Mikkelsen raised his share from scientific societies, individuals, book rights, and the Canadian government. Their schooner was named *Duchess of Bedford* in honor of one of the donors. A surgeon and naturalist were taken along, while Vilhjalmur Stefansson was invited to be the ethnologist of the party. He chose to come via the Mackenzie River, meeting them at or near Herschel Island.

Instead of reaching Banks Island as planned, the expedition found itself caught by winter at Flaxman Island, between Point Barrow and the Mackenzie. Rather than waste a year on the uncertain chance of being able to advance their base materially, the party chosen to explore Beaufort Sea started north on

[47] American Museum of Natural History, *The Andrew J. Stone Explorations in Arctic and sub-Arctic America*, especially 1–5. See further, Andrew J. Stone, "Some Results of a Natural History Journey to Northern British Columbia, in the Interest of the American Museum of Natural History," American Museum of Natural History, *Bulletin*, Vol. XIII (1900), 31–62.

March 3, 1907. They advanced over the ice but a few miles; finding it so rough that their sleds were badly smashed, they returned for new ones.

On a second try, the party got four miles out when a storm came up and they raced for home. On March 17, they started for a third time. Rather quickly, at 71° 43′ north latitude, they found the depth greater than 620 meters. Continuing north, they reached 72° 03′ three days later. They had now exceeded the 400-meter contour line by 40 miles, and there was no evidence that they had struck a merely local depression. They decided, after much discussion, to head southeast until they picked up the 400-meter line, and then follow it as far as they could. At 71° 12′ north, 148° 15′ west, they found the edge of the continental shelf, where within 2¼ miles the depth increased from 66 to more than 620 meters. They were unable, however, to answer the irritating question of the source of the heavy, old ice of the Beaufort Sea. After a hard struggle with open leads and ice drifting northwest, they reached shore on May 12, and Flaxman Island on May 15.[48]

There they found that their *Duchess* had had the calking pulled from her seams by the winter's ice, and she was no longer seaworthy. The crew was sent home by whaler; Mikkelsen later set out by dog sledge along the coast, finally reaching the white settlements. Leffingwell had become interested in the unknown geology of the region and stayed until 1908, when he went home for equipment, returning in 1909 and remaining at Flaxman Island until 1912. The 1909 trip was memorable as having been made from Seattle in a fifty-foot yawl.

Leffingwell returned for a final year in 1913–14. He spent a large portion of his time surveying the coast. Brooks credited him with "the first accurate chart of the north Arctic coast of Alaska." His coastal triangulations were of a high order. Inland, his work was primarily geological reconnaissance. Perhaps his most important general contribution was made in

[48] Einar Mikkelsen, *Conquering the Arctic Ice.*

the last year, when he produced a detailed and original study of the characteristic Arctic phenomenon of ground ice. Large masses had theretofore been more readily explained than small masses. He was able to show that the small masses were the result of water filling the cracks in the soil produced by freezing. Leffingwell had demonstrated once more that competent men are more important than large parties, for he frequently had no more than one Eskimo helper.[49]

Stefansson's great work on the Arctic, which began here, more properly belongs to the next decade; and his largest expedition was officially supported by the Canadian government. Hence the United States can claim only to have given him his start.

[49] Ernest de Koven Leffingwell, *The Canning River Region of Alaska* (U. S. Geological Survey, *Professional Papers*, No. 109).

XIII

Retrospect

||||||||||||||||||||||||||||||||||||||||||||||||

IT IS by no means unlikely that some of the lads who saw De Haven's tiny vessels unfurl their sails down by the Brooklyn Navy Yard in 1850 stood, gray-headed now, on the sea wall as the *Roosevelt* steamed into New York harbor, bearing Peary back from the Pole in 1909. In the span of a lifetime, what a host of brave men had sailed for the North from the harbors of either coast! To single out Kane, Hall, Schwatka, Peary, Dall, and Leffingwell, or some of the subordinates—Morton, Lockwood, Brainard, or Francis Long, is not to disparage the others. The love of fame lured many of them, and that love ordinarily took the form of an attempt to reach the most northerly point on the globe—the point where conditions of life would impose the greatest test of their valor and their manhood.

It is important to remember, even if Clements Markham was inclined to forget, that there was not one of these expeditions that did not in some measure increase the body of scientific knowledge. The leading scientific men of the nation had been called on to outline programs and select scientific observers. It is granted that science was sometimes the seasoning and not the substance of the expeditions.

Writers who have selected only the most spectacular expeditions—or those chronicled in the most easily accessible books—have missed the historical continuity of these expeditions.

The first United States explorations arose from the search for Sir John Franklin's lost expedition. Elisha Kent Kane received his experience under Edwin De Haven, Isaac Hayes his training under Kane, while William Morton sailed under both Kane and Hall. Charles Francis Hall's expeditions, like De Haven's and Kane's, arose from the search for Franklin, while the rescue of Hall's *Polaris* party gave George Washington De Long and Henry W. Howgate experience in the problems of Arctic exploration. Adolphus W. Greely was brought into the work by Howgate.

A third chain of personal associations began with Peary, who started on his trip of 1886 with the inspiration gained from reading about Kane, and so far as is known, with no first hand contact with Arctic explorers. Through Evelyn Briggs Baldwin, a portion of Peary's experience was passed on to Walter Wellman and Anthony J. Fiala. In Alaskan exploration, the historical chain was in considerable measure official, yet the name of William Healey Dall constantly reappears as the captain of a Coast and Geodetic Survey vessel and as adviser on other projects.

United States expeditions were limited almost entirely to three sectors: one covering Franz Josef and Spitsbergen, another extending from the Mackenzie River to Bering Strait, the third and most important centering on Smith Sound. One may divide the last, if he wishes, into those expeditions working north from Smith Sound, and those from Baffin Island west to King William's Land.

The continuity of effort is evident also in several other ways. In forty out of sixty years, one major expedition or another was in the field. Or, if one considers only the years when no expedition was being planned or was under way, there are but two breaks. From the time that the *Polaris* party returned in 1873 until Howgate became active in 1876, the only plans seem to have been in the back of Howgate's and De Long's minds. Again, in the year 1885, the only activity seems to have been in Alaska, for George W. Melville's suggestions never took root.

In terms of geographical accomplishment, Kane, Hayes, and Hall opened up the channels between northwestern Greenland and northern Ellesmere Island (Grinnell Land). It was left for the British naval expedition under Sir George Nares to give an all but final statement of the northern extension of the land mass. Peary gave the final proof, as he removed the last doubt of the nature of the area surrounding the Pole itself. As important as the extension of known lands, was the filling in of the detail of lands whose outlines were already known. Much of this was done for Franz Josef Land by the Wellman and Ziegler expeditions. Hall added materially to the knowledge of Baffin Island and Melville Peninsula. Additions to the map of Alaska were materially increased when the United States Geological Survey began to send parties into the field. Ernest de Koven Leffingwell may be selected as the outstanding single individual in this work.

The best contributions in the physical sciences fall into three categories. The first is the series of reports published in the Smithsonian *Contributions to Knowledge* on the observations of Kane, Hayes, and Sir Leopold Francis McClintock in meteorology, magnetism, and astronomy (the astronomical data supplying base points for mapping). The second consists of the reports from the International Polar Year expeditions of Greely and Patrick Henry Ray. The third is the single volume of data gathered by the two Ziegler expeditions and edited by John A. Fleming.

From the standpoint of later years, the anthropological reports of John Murdoch and Edward William Nelson from Alaska were outstanding. More or less peripheral, so far as these expeditions were concerned, were the volumes by Lucien M. Turner on the Eskimos of Fort Chimo and by Franz Boas on the Central Eskimos. From the standpoint of the day in which it was written, probably nothing represented such an advance as Charles Francis Hall's book describing his first two years among the Eskimos. The anthropological collections these men brought back were of approximately the same rank as their books. Peary, however, notably enriched the American Museum of Natural History with the collections he made among the Smith Sound Eskimos, although his writings on the subject are definitely of minor value.

In the biological sciences, as in anthropology, there were more explorers who made worth-while collections than wrote significant books. This is due primarily to the fact that the principal objective of the botanists and zoologists in the Arctic was to study the geographical distribution of species. Classification of the species in a collection was necessarily left in most cases to a museum expert. The expert drew information from the explorer's field notebooks, when possible, regarding the points where the animals were captured or had been observed, or where the plants had grown. All too often, the notes on a specimen were lacking.

Among the collectors of large mammals, Peary and Andrew J. Stone were outstanding. So many explorers collected birds that the choice of one or two individuals must necessarily be unfair to others. The men who spent several seasons near the nesting grounds of Alaska had an advantage over those who spent their time in areas not so rich in number and variety of birds. Hence, mention of Nelson, Turner, and McIlhenny is not to disparage many other collectors.

Turning from science, with much left unsaid, one should consider not only the general trends in exploration and the principal contributions of the explorers, but the principal changes in emphasis, additions to knowledge, and corrections in fact that have been brought out during the course of the study. It is worth while to stress again the continuity of effort of the explorers.

The North Pacific Surveying Expedition is shown to have been designed for two purposes. The first was to protect the rapidly developing and valuable whaling industry around Bering Strait. The second was to survey a route for ships between San Francisco and China, to carry the products which statesmen envisaged as crossing the continent on the railways that were being surveyed at the same time. It was the seaward extension of the railway surveys, creating a path from the United States' east coast to Canton itself. No connected statement of the expedition's scientific program or accomplishments seems to have been printed heretofore.

Manuscript materials have added a few embellishments to the stories of De Haven, Kane, and Hayes. While they have revealed the difficulties in which Hayes was involved after a successful expedition, no material changes have been made in the interpretation. Charles Francis Hall is one who grows in stature when one assembles all the available materials on his life. Such special knowledge as he acquired before undertaking his explorations was gained practically without guidance. His contributions to ethnology were remarkable, and the very fact of his obtaining Congressional support for his mission is a testimony to the effectiveness of his advocacy.

The Greely Expedition and the efforts to rescue it present peculiar difficulty in evaluation. Had its collections been brought back intact, it would have bulked far larger in the scientific literature of the Arctic. Its physical observations, although often uncorrected because of the loss of most of the instruments, have been rated the most important of any of those submitted by an International Polar Year expedition. They have the added distinction of being the most northerly. On the other hand, Octave Pavy's failure as naturalist leaves open to question the value that the natural history collections would have had at best.

At the time the expedition's remnant returned, opinion among Arctic explorers seemed favorable to Greely, although a strain of public opinion reprobated him personally for the cannibalism reputed to have taken place at Camp Clay. Peary reopened the question some fifteen years later, casting specific reflections on Greely's leadership. Peary was absolutely wrong in his criticism of Greely's failure to cross Smith Sound in midwinter; to his more valid criticism of the choice of a camp site, Greely at least offered good reason for his choice. Nevertheless, Greely failed to reconcile Lt. Kislingbury, which was one, if not the most important, factor in the low morale of the officers' mess. On at least two occasions, Greely might have shown greater leadership and perhaps have reached safety. Nonetheless, few men with actual Arctic experience are likely to condemn Greely, knowing as they do the personal friction and physical exhaustion that almost inevitably develop. The Greely Expedition was not the success, nor was Greely personally the failure, that at times has been made out.

Peary's long years of endeavor inevitably bulk large in this narrative. Re-examination of almost everything published by Peary and his companions simply confirms the high quality of his biography, written by another explorer of Greenland, William H. Hobbs. In regard to the controversy over Peary's inaccuracy in reporting the nature of the northeastern coast of Greenland, additional evidence supplied by Lauge Koch, to which Hobbs did not have access, does not change Koch's earlier conclusions, which Hobbs used. The years 1898–1902 were never described fully by Peary; his manuscripts, when opened to scholars, may furnish additional information. It is probable, however, that he was an irregular diarist, and the student's questions may have to go unanswered.

The information on Peary's scientific work and that of his companions has been brought together for the first time. It confirms Peary's concept of himself as primarily the trail breaker, whom the scientists could follow.

The controversy with Dr. Frederick Cook, in simplest terms, resolves itself into three questions: the truthfulness of Cook and Peary, the reliability of their companions' testimony, the physical possibility of the claims. There is strong, although not incontrovertible evidence that Cook not only knew he had not reached the highest peak of Mount McKinley, but deliberately set out to make a false claim. There have been rather detailed analyses of his book, proving the falsity of any number of statements. Finally, Cook's later conviction for fraud, in combination with his disputed exploring claims, destroys the credibility of his own testimony. On no count, however, has Peary been proved a falsifier.

A number of people, at various times, have examined both Cook's and Peary's Eskimo companions. The examiners have been unanimous in supporting Peary. Likewise, Peary had white companions to within a comparatively short distance of the Pole, and a Negro companion to the end of his journey. At no time has there ever been an inkling from them that Peary did not do exactly what he claimed. By the integrity of their own lives in after years, their credibility on this point is strengthened.

Finally, several groups of competent men have gone over Peary's astronomical observations and declared their satisfaction with them. Probably the most common superficial comment is that the distances made in twenty-four hours on Peary's return journey were fantastic. These comments are made without having compared other remarkable journeys made by dog sledge. With dogs in fair shape, headed for home, and traveling long hours, the journeys become reasonable.

The Baldwin–Ziegler Expedition has been almost universally ignored for the simple reason that no one of its members had any desire to chronicle it. The opportunity to use the Baldwin papers in the Library of Congress has exposed the basic cause of its failure in the conflict of nationalities.

The name of Walter Wellman is seldom recalled when Arctic explorers are mentioned, although his expeditions received almost as thorough coverage in national magazines as Peary's. Since he did not reach the Pole and Peary did, his fame has dimmed, and his importance as an innovator has been generally overlooked. In the 1920's Umberto Nobile in the *Norge* succeeded where Wellman had failed. Those interested in the progress of technology in relation to Arctic exploration cannot afford to ignore Wellman.

Unlike the Arctic expeditions previously considered, Alaskan explorations were noted for the paramount part played by government agencies. This was the United States' new treasure chest, and its contents had to be examined. Hence there is an abundance of technical literature and a scarcity of narrative accounts, quite the reverse of the case elsewhere. Much, no doubt, remains to be exploited in the National Archives, but examination of the report file of the Revenue Marine Service cruises indicates that, in that bureau at least, the best reports were published. Along the Arctic coast, little was done by private individuals until 1896. Prior to that, however, scientists from the Coast and Geodetic Survey and other agencies had demonstrated that the rigors of the Arctic could be overcome by small groups, and that valuable information could be acquired.

Mercy, glory, science called forth the intrepid band of Arctic explorers enrolled here, who for sixty years carried the flag of the United States to the northernmost reaches of the earth. Their names are gone from the headlines, their voices from the rostrum, and others stand in their place. Seldom are the stories of their wonderful adventures lifted down from the shelves. May it not yet be found that their most enduring monuments will be the irreplaceable volumes of scientific data?

Bibliography

||||||||||||||||||||||||||||||||||||||||||||||||

1. Manuscripts

Bache Correspondence, 1850–67. Library of Congress. Washington.
Baldwin Manuscripts, 1892–1928. Library of Congress. Washington.
Greely Papers. National Geographic Society Library. Washington. [Manuscripts are scattered through his pamphlet and clipping collection. These are not his private papers.]
Kane, Elisha Kent. Journal of the Brig *Advance*, Vol II. Stanford University Library. Stanford University, California.
Kennedy Papers, 1852–61. Peabody Library. Baltimore, Maryland.
Lever, Charles. Journal of . . . Captain's Clerk of the U.S.S. *Release*, on the voyage . . . to rescue Dr. Kane's Arctic Exploring Expedition . . . May 26 to Sept. 12, 1855. Library of Congress. Washington.
Maury Letter Books, 1843–56. Library of Congress, Washington.
Rhees Manuscripts. Huntington Library. San Marino, California.
Schott Manuscripts, c. 1855–67. Library of Congress. Washington.

2. Official Archives (Minor groups omitted)

International Polar Expedition to Lady Franklin Bay [Greely]. Natural Resources Branch, National Archives. Washington.
International Polar Expedition to Point Barrow [Ray]. Natural Resources Branch, National Archives.
North Pacific Surveying Expedition Logs, etc.; chart revision data. U. S. Hydrographic Office. Suitland, Maryland.
North Pacific Surveying Expedition, De Haven Expedition, Hayes

Bibliography

Expedition, *Polaris* Expedition, and *Jeannette* Expedition charts. Cartographic Branch, National Archives.

North Pacific Surveying Expedition Correspondence. War Records Branch, National Archives.

Northern Alaska Exploring Expedition Log Books. War Records Branch, National Archives.

Smithsonian Institution Archives. Washington.

U. S. Revenue Cutter Service Files, Alaska. Treasury Branch, National Archives.

3. *Government Documents*

Brooks, Alfred Hulse. *The Geography and Geology of Alaska.* U. S. Geological Survey, *Professional Papers*, No. 45. Washington, 1906.

Davis, Admiral Charles Henry (ed.). *Narrative of the North Polar Expedition. U. S. Ship* POLARIS. Washington, 1876.

Great Britain. Admiralty. *Manual of the Natural History, Geology, and Physics of Greenland . . . Prepared . . . Under the Direction of the Royal Society, and Edited by Prof. T. Rupert Jones . . . .* London, 1875.

Great Britain. *Parliamentary Papers*, Vol. XXXV, No. 107 (1850); Vol. XXXIII, No. 97 (1851).

Greely, Adolphus Washington. *Report on the Proceedings of the United States Expedition to Lady Franklin Bay, Grinnell Land.* 49 Cong., 1 sess., *House Misc. Doc.* 393 (Congressional Ser. 2427–28). Washington, 1888.

Harris, Rollin A. *Arctic Tides.* U. S. Coast and Geodetic Survey. Washington, 1911.

Healy. Michael A. *Report of the Cruise of the Revenue Marine Steamer* CORWIN *in the Arctic Ocean in the Year 1885.* 49 Cong., 1 sess., *House Exec. Doc.* 153 (Cong. Ser. 2400). Washington, 1887.

——— . . . *Cruise of the Revenue Marine Steamer* CORWIN *in the Arctic Ocean in the Year 1884.* 50 Cong., 1 sess., *House Misc. Doc.* 602 (Cong. Ser. 2583). Washington, 1889.

Hooper, Calvin Leighton. . . . *Cruise of the U. S. Revenue Steamer*

THOMAS CORWIN *in the Arctic Ocean, 1881.* 48 Cong., 1 sess., *Senate Exec. Doc. 204* (Cong. Ser. 2169). Washington, 1884.

Kumlien, Ludwig. *Contributions to the Natural History of Arctic America, Made in Connection with the Howgate Polar Expedition, 1877–8.* National Museum *Bulletin 15.* Washington, 1879.

Leffingwell, Ernest de Koven. *The Canning River Region of Northern Alaska.* United States Geological Survey, *Professional Paper 109.* Washington, 1919.

Murdoch, John. "Ethnological Results of the Point Barrow Expedition . . . 1881–1883." U. S. Bureau of American Ethnology, *Ninth Annual Report, 1887–1888.* Washington, 1892.

Nourse, Joseph Everett (ed.). *Narrative of the Second Arctic Expedition made by Charles F. Hall: His Voyage to Repulse Bay, Sledge Journeys to the Straits of Fury and Hecla and to King William's Land, and Residence among the Eskimos during the Year 1864–'69.* 45 Cong., 3 sess., *Senate Exec. Doc. 27.* (Cong. Ser. 1830). Washington, 1879.

Ray, Patrick Henry. *Report of the International Polar Expedition to Point Barrow, Alaska.* 48 Cong., 2 sess., *House Exec. Doc. 44* (Cong. Ser. 2298). Washington, 1885. [Issued also by U. S. Signal Office, Arctic Series of Publications, No. 1.]

Schley, Winfield Scott. . . . *Greely Relief Expedition of 1884.* 49 Cong., 2 sess., *House Misc. Doc. 157* (Cong. Ser. 2428). [Bound with second volume of Greely's *Report,* listed above.]

Sherman, Orray Taft. *Meteorological and Physical Observations on the East Coast of British America.* U. S. Signal Service, *Professional Papers, No. XI.* Washington, 1883. [Howgate's *Florence* Expedition, 1877–78.]

U. S. Coast and Geodetic Survey. . . . *Coast Pilot of Alaska, (first part) from Southern Boundary to Cook's Inlet. By George Davidson . . . 1869.* Washington, 1869.

———. *Pacific Coast Pilot. Coasts and Islands of Alaska. Second Series. Appendix. I. Meteorology . . . . II. Bibliography.* Washington, 1879.

U. S. Coast and Geodetic Survey, Superintendent. *Report, 1867–1904.* Washington, 1869–1904.

U. S. Congress. *Congressional Globe,* 31 to 42 Congresses. Washington, 1849–73.

Bibliography

U. S. Congress, 31. *Public Acts No. 4.* Approved May 2, 1850. Washington, 1850.

U. S. Congress. House of Representatives.

a. *House Executive Documents*
> 31 Cong., 1 sess., No. 16 (Cong. Ser. 576).
> 32 Cong., 1 sess., No. 2 (Cong. Ser. 635).
> 41 Cong., 2 sess., No. 255 (Cong. Ser. 1425).
> 47 Cong., 2 sess., No. 81 (Cong. Ser. 2110).
> 47 Cong. 2 sess., No. 108 (Cong. Ser. 2113).

b. *House Miscellaneous Documents*
> 48 Cong., 1 sess., No. 66 (Cong. Ser. 2243).

c. *House Reports*
> 44 Cong., 2 sess., No. 181 (Cong. Ser. 1770).

d. *House Bills*
> 44 Cong., 2 sess., *H. R.* 4339.

U. S. Congress. Senate.

a. *Senate Executive Documents*
> 32 Cong., 1 sess., No. 55 (Cong. Ser. 619).
> 35 Cong., 1 sess., No. 52 (Cong. Ser. 929).

b. *Senate Reports*
> 45 Cong., 2 sess., No. 94.
> 46 Cong., 2 sess., No. 528 (Cong. Ser. 1892).

U. S. Navy Department. Secretary. *Report, 1873, 1879–83, 1924.*

U. S. Revenue Cutter Service. *Alaska and its People* . . . . Washington, 1880.

U. S. Revenue Cutter Service. *Cruise of the* CORWIN *in Alaska and the N. W. Arctic Ocean in 1881. Notes and Memoranda: Medical and Anthropological; Botanical; Ornithological.* Treasury Department *Document No. 429.* (Congressional edition: 47 Cong., 2 sess., *House Exec. Doc. No. 105* [Cong. Ser. 2112]). Washington, 1883. See also Healy, Michael A., and Hooper, Calvin Leighton, above.

U. S. Statutes-at-Large
> 46 Cong., 2 sess. XXI, Ch. 72.
> 46 Cong., 3 sess. XXI, Ch. 133.

U. S. War Department. Signal Service. *Signal Service Notes, X.* Washington, 1883.

4. Principal Bibliographies

Bibliotheca Geographica. Herausgegeben von der Gesellschaft für Erdkunde zu Berlin. 19 vols. 1895–1912.

Chavanne, Josef, and others. Die Literatur über die Polarregionen der Erde. Wien, 1878.

Denmark. Marinens Bibliotek. Katalog over Literatur vedrörende Polaromraadernes og Verdenshavenes, Opdagelse og Udforskning, Hval-og Saelfanst, Personalhistorie, Tedsskrifter, Aarsskrifter og andre Periodica . . . . Köbenhavn, 1933–47.

Dutilly, Rev. Arthème. Bibliography of Bibliographies on the Arctic. Catholic University. Washington, 1945.

Grier, Mary Catherine. . . . Oceanography of the North Pacific Ocean, Bering Sea and Bering Strait: a Contribution toward a Bibliography. The University of Washington. Seattle, 1941.

Hasse, Adelaide R. Reports of Explorations Printed in the Documents of the United States Government. Government Printing Office. Washington, 1899.

Lauridsen, P. Bibliographia Groenlandica eller Fortegnelse paa Vaerker, Afhandlinger og danske Manuskripter, der handle om Grönland indtil Aaret 1880 incl. (Meddelelser om Grönland, XIII.) Köbenhavn, 1890.

Meisel, Max. A Bibliography of American Natural History. The Pioneer Century, 1769–1865. 3 vols. Brooklyn, New York, 1929.

Rhees, William Jones. "List of Publications of the Smithsonian Institution, 1846–1903." Smithsonian Institution Miscellaneous Collectins, XLIV. Washington, 1903.

U. S. Work Projects Administration, New York City. . . . Selected List of Bibliographies on the Polar Regions. 2 parts. New York City, n.d.

Wickersham, James. A Bibliography of Alaskan Literature, 1724–1924. Cordova, Alaska, 1927.

[The author was given the privilege of using the Arctic Institute of North America's Arctic Bibliography while still in card form.]

5. Primary Narratives of the Expeditions

(Articles in periodicals have been omitted. See footnotes and list of periodicals.)

Bibliography

Astrup, Eivind. *With Peary near the Pole.* London, 1898.

Bessels, Emil. *Die amerikanische Nordpol-Expedition.* Leipzig, 1879.

Brainard, David L. *The Outpost of the Lost.* Indianapolis, [c.1929].

Borup, George. *A Tenderfoot with Peary.* New York, [c. 1911].

Cook, Frederick Albert. *My Attainment of the Pole; being the Record of the Expedition that first reached the boreal Center, 1907–1909.* New York, 1913.

De Long, George Washington. *The Voyage of the* JEANNETTE. (ed. by Emma De Long.) 2 vols. London, 1883.

Fiala, Anthony. *Fighting the Polar Ice.* New York, 1906.

Gilder, William Henry. *Schwatka's Search; Sledging in the Arctic in Quest of the Franklin Records.* New York, 1881.

Godfrey, William C. *Godfrey's Narrative of the Last Grinnell Arctic Exploring Expedition, in Search of Sir John Franklin, 1853-4-5* . . . Philadelphia, 1857.

Greely, Adolphus Washington. *Three Years of Arctic Service. An Account of the Lady Franklin Bay Expedition of 1881–84* . . . New York, 1894. [First ed., 1885.]

Habersham, Alexander Wylly. *The North Pacific Surveying and Exploring Expedition, or My Last Cruise* . . . . Philadelphia, 1857; London, 1858.

Hall, Charles Francis. *Arctic Researches and Life among the Esquimaux* . . . . New York, 1865.

Hans Hendrik. *Memoirs of Hans Hendrik, the Arctic Traveller* . . . . (Translated from the Eskimo Language by Dr. Henry Rink . . . .) London, 1878.

Hayes, Isaac Israel. *An Arctic Boat Journey in the Autumn of 1854.* Boston, 1861.

———. *The Open Polar Sea: a Narrative of a Voyage of Discovery Towards the North Pole* . . . . London, 1867.

Henson, Matthew Alexander. *A Negro Explorer at the North Pole.* New York, [1912].

Kane, Elisha Kent. *Arctic Explorations: The Second Grinnell Expedition* . . . . 2 vols. Philadelphia, 1856.

———. *The United States Grinnell Expedition in Search of Sir John Franklin.* New ed. Philadelphia, 1856.

Klutschak, Heinrich W. *Als Eskimo unter den Eskimos. Eine Schilderung der Erlebnisse der Schwatka'schen Franklin-Aufsuchungs-Expedition in den Jahren 1878–80.* Wien, 1881.

Lanman, Charles (ed.). *Farthest North; or the Life and Explorations of Lieutenant James Booth Lockwood, of the Greely Arctic Expedition.* New York, 1885.

MacMillan, Donald Baxter. *How Peary Reached the Pole . . . .* Boston and New York, 1934.

Melville, George W. *In the Lena Delta.* Boston, 1885.

Mikkelsen, Ejnar. *Conquering the Arctic Ice.* London, 1909.

Newcomb, Raymond Lee (ed.). *Our Lost Explorers: the Narrative of the* JEANNETTE *Arctic Expedition.* Hartford, Conn., 1882.

Peary, Josephine Diebitsch. *My Arctic Journal; a Year among Icefields and Eskimos.* New York and Philadelphia, 1893.

Peary, Robert Edwin. *Nearest the Pole. A Narrative of the Polar Expedition . . . 1905–1906.* New York, 1907.

——. *The North Pole.* New York, 1910.

——. *Northward over the Great Ice.* 2 vols. London, 1898.

——. *Secrets of Polar Travel.* New York, 1917.

——. "Report of R. E. Peary . . . on Work Done in the Arctic in 1898–1902." American Geographical Society, *Bulletin,* Vol. XXXV (1903), 496–534.

Seale, Alvin. *The Quest for the Golden Cloak.* San Francisco, 1946.

Stefansson, Vilhjalmur. *The Friendly Arctic.* New York, 1921.

Stoney, George M. *Naval Explorations in Alaska. An Account of Two Naval Expeditions to Northern Alaska.* Annapolis, 1900. [Text identical with his "Explorations in Alaska," U. S. Naval Institute, *Proceedings,* No. 91, 533–84; No. 92, 799–849.]

[Tyson, George E.] *The Cruise of the* FLORENCE: *or, Extracts from the Journal of the Preliminary Arctic Expedition of 1877–78. Edited by Captain H. W. Howgate, U. S. A.* Washington, 1879.

Wellman, Walter. *The Aerial Age . . . . Airship Voyages over the Polar Sea.* New York, 1911.

6. Scientific Monographs and Selected Articles

Bailey, Alfred M. *Birds of Arctic Alaska.* Colorado Museum of Natural History, Popular Series, No. 8. [Denver], 1948.

Bibliography

Fleming, John Adam (ed.) *The Ziegler Polar Expedition, 1903–05, Anthony Fiala, Commander. Scientific Results . . . .* Washington, 1907.

Stimpson, William. *Report on the Crustacea (Brachyura and Anomura) Collected by the North Pacific Exploring Expedition, 1853–1856.* Smithsonian Miscellaneous Collections, XLIX, Art. III. Washington, 1907.

7. Secondary Works

American Geographical and Statistical Society. *The Polar Exploring Expedition.* New York, 1860. [Pamphlet containing letters from A. D. Bache, J. Henry, M. F. Maury, A. Guyot, and others, and the addresses delivered by I. I. Hayes and Francis Lieber before the Society's meeting of March 22, 1860, on behalf of Hayes's proposed expedition.]

American Museum of Natural History. *The Andrew J. Stone Explorations in Arctic and Sub-Arctic America.* New York, 1905.

Arctic Club of America. *The Arctic Club Manual.* New York, 1906.

Bartsch, Paul, and others. *A Bibliography and Short Biographical Sketch of William Healey Dall.* Smithsonian Miscellaneous Collections, CIV, No. 15. Washington, 1946.

Bancroft, Hubert Howe. *History of Alaska, 1730–1885.* Bancroft's Works, XXXIII. San Francisco, 1886.

Blake, Euphemia Vale. *Arctic Experiences: Containing George E. Tyson's Wonderful Drift on the Ice-floe, a History of the* Polaris *Expedition . . . .* New York, 1874.

Elder, William. *Biography of Elisha Kent Kane.* Philadelphia, 1858.

Ellsberg, Edward. *Hell on Ice.* New York, 1938.

Greely, Adolphus Washington. *Handbook of Polar Discoveries.* 3rd ed. Boston, 1907.

Heine, Wilhelm. *Die Expedition in die Seen von Japan unter Commando von Commodore Ringgold und Commodore John Rodgers, im Auftrage der Regierung der Vereinigten Staaten unternommen . . . 1853–1856 . . . .* 3 vols. Leipzig, 1858.

Hobbs, William Herbert. *Peary.* New York, 1936.

Howgate, Henry W. (ed.). *Congress and the North Pole. An Abstract of Arctic Legislation in the Congress of the United States.* Kansas City, Missouri, 1879.

——. *Polar Colonization. The Preliminary Arctic Expedition of 1877.* Washington, [1877?].
——. *Polar Colonization. Memorial to Congress; and Action of Scientific and Commercial Associations.* Washington, [1878].
Mackey, Thomas Jefferson. *The Hazen Court-Martial.* New York, 1885.
Nourse, Joseph Everett. *American Explorations in the Ice Zones.* 3d ed. Boston, [c. 1884].
Rhees, William Jones. *The Smithsonian Institution. Documents relative to its origin and history, 1835–1899.* Smithsonian Misc. Collections, XLII–XLIII. Washington, 1901. [Also in Congressional Series.]
Schley, Winfield Scott, and Soley, J. R. *The Rescue of Greely.* New York, 1886.
Stefansson, Vilhjalmur. *Ultima Thule: Further Mysteries of the Arctic.* New York, 1940.
——. *Unsolved Mysteries of the Arctic.* New York, 1939.

8. *Learned Periodicals*

Academy of Natural Sciences, Philadelphia, *Proceedings,* 1851–1911. Philadelphia.
American Association for the Advancement of Science, *Proceedings,* 1858–73. New York.
American Geographical Society, *Bulletin* [formerly the *Journal*], 1850–1915. New York.
American Museum of Natural History, *Bulletin,* 1888–1911. New York.
American Naturalist, 1867–84. Boston.
American Philosophical Society, *Proceedings,* 1869, 1897, 1940. Philadelphia.
American Society of Naval Engineers, *Journal,* 1905. Washington.
California Academy of Sciences, *Proceedings,* 1868–74. San Francisco.
Geographical Journal, 1894. London.
Meddelelser om Grönland, 1879–1950. Köbnhavn.
Monthly Weather Review, 1901–1907. Washington.
Petermanns Geographische Mitteilungen, 1855–1911. Gotha.

Bibliography

Science, 1883–1907. Cambridge and New York.
Scientific American, 1907. Washington.
U. S. Naval Institute, *Proceedings,* 1899. Annapolis.

9. Popular Magazines

American Review of Reviews, 1898, 1909. New York.
Century Magazine, 1898–99. New York.
Harper's New Monthly Magazine, 1851, 1862. New York.
Littell's Living Age, 1849–1908. Philadelphia.
McClure's Magazine, 1893–1907. New York.
Munsey's Magazine, 1902. New York.
National Geographic Magazine, 1888–1922. Washington.
North American Review, 1879, 1889, 1894, 1904. Boston.
United Service, 1879. Philadelphia.
University of Chicago Magazine, 1915. Chicago.

10. Annuals and Collected Works

International Polar Commission. *Communications.*
Smithsonian Institution. *Annual Report,* 1852–1911. Washington,
     1853–1912.
———. *Contributions to Knowledge,* II–XXIV. Washington,
     1851–1916.
———. *Miscellaneous Collections,* I–LX. Washington, 1862–1913.

11. Newspapers

New York *Herald.* 1883, 1909.

Index

||||||||||||||||||||||||||||||||||||||||||||

Index

Index

escape, 78–79; scientific observations, 79–80; appraisal, 80; rescue expeditions, 80–81
Jeannette Island, Siberian Arctic: 77
Jesup, Morris K.: 127, 147, 167
Jordon, David Starr: 203

Kane, Elisha Kent: 21–32
Kane, John K.: 28
Kane Expedition: 21–32; southern boat camp, 26–27; scientific observations, 29 f.; appraisal, 31–32
Kane Relief Expedition: 28–29
"Kellett Land": 186
Kennan, George: 80, 113
Kennedy, John Pendleton: 21, 28, 185
Kennedy Channel: 23, 24, 26
Kennicott, Robert: 190–91
King William's Land, Canada: 52, 84 f.
Klondike, Yukon Territory, Canada: 201
Klutschak, Henry: 84 f.
Kobuk River: 195; explored, 198–200
Koch, Lauge: 133, 133 n., 147 n., 213
Kola Peninsula, Russia: 6
Kumlien, Ludwig: 90 f.

Lady Franklin Bay: 23, 93, 97
Lady Franklin Bay Expedition: see Greely Expedition
Lancaster Sound, Canada: 11, 12
Lee, Hugh J.: 137–40
Leffingwell, Ernest de Koven: 160–61, 174, 180, 198, 205–207
Lena River Delta: 78, 79
Libbey, William, Jr.: 138, 140
Lincoln, Robert Todd: 99, 108, 109 n., 116–17
Lockwood, James B.: 100
Lockwood Island, Greenland: 58
Long, Francis: 112, 174, 177 f.
Long, John D., sec. of navy: 143
Long Island Historical Society: 48
Loomis, Elias: 90
Lynch, W. F., Capt. U.S.N.: 13–14
Lyon Inlet, mapped: 52

Mackenzie, Alexander: 10

Mackenzie River: 203, 204
MacMillan, Donald Baxter: 151 f., 157
Magnetism, terrestrial: 30–31, 80, 105, 193, 197
Marvin, Ross G.: 152, 152 n.
Maury, Matthew Fontaine: 18, 22
McClintock, Sir (Francis) Leopold: 42–43
McClure's Magazine: 174
McIlhenny, Edward Avery: 204, 211
McKinley, William: 143
McLenegan, Samuel B.: 198, 199
Melville, George W.: 72, 76, 108, 123, 161, 167
Melville Peninsula, Canada: 11; mapped, 51, 52
Mendenhall, Thomas Corwin: 161
Meteorology: 30, 104, 119, 153, 194
Meyer, Frederick: 56, 60
Mikkelsen, Einar: 160–61, 205–206
Mikkelsen-Leffingwell Expedition: 205–206
Moore, Charles A.: 143
Morton, William: 23, 63
Mount McKinley, Alaska: 158
Muir, John: 82, 197
Murdoch, John: 117 f., 210
Myer, Albert J.: 94, 97, 114 f.
Mylius-Erichsen, Ludvig: 133 n.

Nares Expedition: 97, 151
National Academy of Sciences: 55, 125, 161
National Geographic Society: 154, 166–67, 172
Natural history: 26–27, 40, 92–93, 104, 121, 140, 153–54, 187–88, 190–91, 193–95, 197, 204; appraisal, 211
Nelson, Edward William: 82, 115 f., 194–95, 197, 210, 211
New Siberian Islands: 78
New York Herald: 72, 84
New York Sun: 124, 126
New York Tribune: 164
Newcomb, Raymond Lee: 72, 79
Newcomb, Simon: 56
Newman Bay, Greenland: 58, 61

Index

Ross, John: 10, 18

Saint Michaels, Alaska: 115, 194, 200
Salisbury, Rollin D.: 140
Schley, Winfield Scott: 109f., 156
Schott, Charles A.: 40–41, 161
Schuchert, Charles: 141
Schwatka, Frederick: 83–88, 123
Schwatka Expedition: 83–88
Scientific instruments: 22, 29, 35–36, 46, 49, 56–57, 65, 100, 118, 136, 174, 199
Scientific publication: 40–41
Scofield, Norman B.: 203–204
Seale, Alvin: 203–204
Second Wellman Polar Expedition: see Wellman Expedition, 1898–99
Seward Peninsula, Alaska: 201
Sherman, John: 55
Sherman, Orray Taft, meteorologist: 90f.
Smith, Middleton: 117f.
Smithson, James: 190
Smithsonian Institution: 21, 22, 35, 40–41, 72, 79, 90, 92, 98, 113, 115, 189–91, 195, 201; publications, 210
Sonntag, August: 22, 27, 36, 38
Stanford University, marine biological laboratory: 203
Stefansson, Vilhjalmur: 4, 54, 205, 207
Stein, Robert: 141, 146
Stimpson, William: 186, 187, 189
Stokes, F. W.: 139n.
Stone, Andrew J.: 204, 211
Stoney, George M.: 198–200
Story, J. P.: 94
Svalbard: see Spitsbergen
Sverdrup, Otto: 144–45, 144n., 151, 156

Tagliabue, John: 35, 84
Tarr, Ralph S.: 141
Taylor, Pres. Zachary: 13–14
Teplitz Bay, Franz Josef Land: 180
"Term-day": 30–31, 98, 175
Thompson, R. W., sec. of navy: 73

Thule, Greenland: 27
Tookoolito, Hannah: 46f., 49, 51, 53, 62
Townsend, Charles H.: 199
Turner, Lucien McShan: 194, 201, 210, 211
Tyson, George E.: 57f., 91, 108

Ungava Bay, Labrador: 201
U. S. Bureau of American Ethnology: 201
U. S. Coast and Geodetic Survey: 22, 31, 35, 49, 56, 97, 115–17, 118, 119, 124, 152, 161, 174, 191, 192, 201
U. S. Coast Pilot, Alaska: 192
U. S. Congress: 14, 21, 28, 35, 55, 70, 80, 89, 93, 97, 185
United States Expedition to Lady Franklin Bay: see Greely Expedition
U. S. Geological Survey: 201, 202
U. S. Hydrographic Office: 60, 196
U. S. Naval Observatory: 22, 35
U. S. Navy Department: 56, 70, 71, 80, 81, 90, 124, 128, 143, 189
U. S. North Pacific Surveying Expedition: 185–88
U. S. Northern Alaska Exploring Expedition: 198–200, 200n.
U. S. Revenue Marine Service: 81f., 195f., 201
U. S. War Department: 90, 94, 95, 97; see also Lincoln, Robert Todd; U. S. Signal Corps; U. S. Signal Service
U. S. Signal Corps: 67, 97, 174
U. S. Signal Service: 56, 114f., 194, 201
U. S. Topographical Bureau: 35
U. S. Weather Bureau: 167

Vaniman, Melvin: 171
Vedoe, John: 180
Verhoeff, John M.: 126, 133, 136
Vessels:
    Advance (De Haven, Kane) 14f., 22f.
    Albert (German), 56

231